AN INTRODUCTION
TO THE PHILOSOPHICAL WORKS
OF F.S.C. NORTHROP

Fred Seddon

Problems in Contemporary Philosophy
Volume 27

The Edwin Mellen Press
Lewiston/Queenston/Lampeter

Library of Congress Cataloging-in-Publication Data

Seddon, Frederick.
   An introduction to the philosophical works of F.S.C. Northrop /
Fred Seddon.
       p.   cm.
   Includes bibliographical references.
   ISBN 0-7734-9051-5 (hard)
   1. Northrop, F.S.C. (Filmer Stuart Curkow), 1893-   .
B945.N64S43   1995
191--dc20   94-24830
                                                                        CIP

This is volume 27 in the continuing series
Problems in Contemporary Philosophy
Volume 27 ISBN 0-7734-9051-5
PCP Series ISBN 0-88946-325-5

A CIP catalog record for this book is available from the British Library.

The Edwin Mellen Press   The Edwin Mellen Press
         Box 450   Box 67
   Lewiston, New York   Queenston, Ontario
   USA 14092-0450   CANADA L0S 1L0

                  The Edwin Mellen Press, Ltd.
                     Lampeter, Dyfed, Wales
                  UNITED KINGDOM SA48 7DY

              Printed in the United States of America

For my parents, Fred and Mathilda

For my wife, Margaret

For my children, Ayn Rand and Beethoven

CONTENTS

ABBREVIATIONS..iv

PREFACE..v

ACKNOWLEDGEMENTS..vii

REMINISCENCE BY ADOLF GRÜNBAUM.............................viii

INTRODUCTION..1

CHAPTER 1 - Science and First Principles............................3

CHAPTER 2 - The Logic of the Sciences and the Humanities.....31

CHAPTER 3 - The Meeting of East and West.......................55

CHAPTER 4 - The Taming of Nations.....................................73

CHAPTER 5 - The Complexity of Legal and Ethical
Experience..99

CHAPTER 6: Philosophical Anthropology & Practical
Politics..115

CHAPTER 7 - Man, Nature and God.......................................143

CHAPTER 8 - And In The End..161

APPENDIX A - Grünbaum on Newton's Conception of
Relative Space and Time........................173

APPENDIX B - Northrop on Russian Communism......................193

APPENDIX C - McAllister on Northrop...................................215

Bibliography...229

Index...253

ABBREVIATIONS

SFP   *Science and First Principles*

MEW   *The Meeting of East and West*

MNG   *Man, Nature and God*

PAPP   *Philosophical Anthropology and Practical Politics*

CLEE   *The Complexity of Legal and Ethical Experience*

LSH   *The Logic of the Sciences and the Humanities*

TON   *The Taming of Nations*

PRO   *The Prolegomena to a 1985 Philosophiae Naturalis Principia Mathematica*

PREFACE

This is a personal record of a philosophical journey and it seems fitting that something be said about its genesis. In the second half of the 70s a dear man whose name I must shamefully admit to forgetting recommended that I read Robert Persig's *Zen and the Art of Motorcycle Maintenance.* Since I was at that time interested in neither Zen Buddhism nor motorcycles I ignored his recommendation. But he persisted and in an effort to induce me to read Persig's book, he loaned to me an old copy of *The Times Literary Supplement* in which Persig's book had been reviewed. I remember little of the review except its mention of Aristotle. Being (an remaining to this day) a lover of Aristotle (I eventually wrote my doctoral dissertation on him --as coincidentally did Northrop) I decided to purchase the book. Reading Persig's work changed my life in two respect--I bought my first motorcycle and I discovered vi

Filmer Stuart Cuckow Northrop. Persig's reference to Northrop occurs on pp. 123-4 of *Zen* and is to the book *The Meeting of East and West* of which more in due course. I ran to the library to get this work but as I was flipping throught the card catalogue I came across the title of another work by Northrop, viz., *The Logic of the Science and the Humanites* and being (and remaining to this day) a lover of logic (I eventually wrote my doctoral dissertation on logic) this was the book I took home that fateful day -- my first Northrop book. I have since read or acquired all of his important works; I have lectured and written articles on his thought and on Dec. 6, 1980 met himself. Although I arrived at his home unannounced, he ushered me into his study where we discussed his philosophy for five glorious hours. I have taught him to many bemused classes of students at Wheeling Jesuit College and have pondered his thoughts for years. This book is both an introduction to one of the great minds of the twentieth century and an extended thank you note.

Fred Seddon
Wheeling Jesuit College
Wheeling, WV
July, 1994

THE AUTHOR

Fred Seddon is the author of <u>Aristotle and Lukasiewicz on the Principle of Contradiction</u>, and dozens of articles and book reviews. He has been president of the West Virginia Philosophical Society since 1988 and has read parts of this book before that learned society. He is a member of the philosophy department at Wheeling Jesuit College in Wheeling, West Virginia.

ACKNOWLEDGEMENTS

I owe a debt of gratitude to Wheeling Jesuit College for two summer grants, 1991 and 1992, that supported my work on chapters four and six. I would also like to thank my wife Margaret and my children, Ayn Rand and Beethoven for "staying out of my way" during this project. Debts are also due to Joseph K. Wuenschell who read every chapter and provided grammatical as well as philosophical commentary and whose help and love has been as unstinting as my family's. I would also like to mention by name those members of PHI 415 Great Thinkers class for reading this text with me during the Spring '93 semester, viz., Margie Cooke, Dan Devine, Eddie O'Neill, Nancy Pogacich, Erica Russo, and Mary Sgroi. Finally, I wish to thank *my* former teacher, Professor Adolf Grünbaum, Andrew Mellon Professor of Philosophy at the University of Pittsburgh, for providing his kind reminiscence of *his* former teacher, Filmer Northrop.

A SHORT REMINISCENCE OF F. S. C. NORTHROP BY PROFESSOR ADOLF GRÜNBAUM

Professor Northrop was, for me, a highly stimulating teacher and someone for whom I had and continue to have great affection. As I recall when his book *The Meeting of East and West* came out, many of us who were his students were thrilled. It was deemed the most important intellectual event of its year of publication, 1946, by the *New York Times Book Review*.

He taught a course called something like "The Philosophical and Scientific Foundations of Social Institutions" and he gave that course in the Yale Law School at a time when he had transferred his office from the Philosophy Department to the Yale Law School. He had become interested in the philosophy of law.

But it coincided with what was, alas, the beginning of the precipitous decline of the Yale Philosophy Department. At the time when I was a graduate student, that department was rated number 1 in the country among all the graduate departments in philosophy. But it had a kind of death wish in virtue of several policies that were bound, it seems to me, to lead to a decline. And the decline has been very, very marked despite the fact that the department did acquire a scholar as eminent as Ruth Marcus who has just retired from there. But right now they are in a desperate situation to try to rebuild under the leadership of a new chairman.

I might mention that in 1962, just two years after I had become the Andrew W. Mellon Professor of Philosophy at the University of Pittsburgh, I was offered a full professorship by the Yale department. I was tempted somewhat by the presence there of Wilfrid Sellars and Alan Anderson. I had known Alan from my student days at Yale. And I knew Sellars as well.

But, first of all, I had made a commitment in1960 to be Mellon Professor here, and the administration expected me to be a magnet for building up a department and the Center for the Philosophy of Science. And secondly, I discerned the factors in the Yale department that spelled a bleak future for the it. Kingman Brewster was then Provost at Yale before he became its famous president and opponent of the View Nam war. He spent a day here in my office in the Cathedral [of Learning], trying to persuade me to go to Yale as a full professor. But I decided to stay here at Pitt.

Wilfrid Sellars then said "If Mohammed won't come to the mountain, the mountain will come to Mohammed." I had no trouble persuading the Pittsburgh administration to offer Sellars a University Professorship. He decided to come here, and then a number of the other Yale people came soon thereafter, which then earned me the sobriquet "The Pittsburgh Pirate." But I felt that we were transplanting the legacy of great Yale teachers like Northrop to Pittsburgh, rather than being disloyal to Yale.

I cherished Professor Northrop throughout my four years at Yale, and ever since.

Perhaps I should mention how concerned I was about him as a person. I remember his long-termed migraine headaches, which were horrible, and how he lived with all that pain all those years. You wouldn't know it unless you happened to have heard about it. I remember visiting him the day before he had neurosurgery, when his doctors finally decided to do an exploratory so that they might find the cause of those headaches. He was operated on by a Yale neurosurgeon named Dr. German, and I remember how very happy I was then to learn from him that his headaches had completely disappeared after the surgery. The surgery revealed that some kind of fluid was dripping onto his spinal cord as a result of some kind of a tear that he had incurred in his back near the spinal cord from throwing baseballs. He was an avid enthusiast of baseball--I do remember that. It was wonderful that the horrible pain was cured by cleaning out the area where his spinal cord was being irritated, which had then sent pain signals to his brain. I hope I've conveyed the measure of my gratitude to Professor Northrop as a teacher and philosopher, as well as the great affection I had for him personally.

Adolf Grünbaum
Andrew W. Mellon Professor of Philosophy
University of Pittsburgh
Pgh. PA 15260

INTRODUCTION

This work is not a biography of Filmer Northrop. I leave that pleasant task to those who knew him as a man, a living being of flesh and blood. The Northrop I will write about below is the Northrop of the texts, a Northrop accessible across a time span longer than a single human life. My procedure will be as follows: the first seven chapters will be devoted to an exposition of what I consider to be his most important books: *Science and First Principles, The Meeting of East and West, The Logic of the Sciences and the Humanities, The Taming of Nations, The Complexity of Legal and Ethical Experience, Philosophical Anthropology and Practical Politics,* and *Man, Nature, and God.* This study will close with a few words on the books *European Union and United States Foreign Policy: A Study in Sociological Jurisprudence* and *The Prolegomena to a 1985 Philosophiae Naturalis Principia Mathematica* plus a few important essays, most written after his retirement from Yale. To reduce the number of footnotes the following procedure has been adopted: number in parenthesis refer to pages in the book being discussed. For example, in chapter one, which is on SFP, "(5)" would mean page five of SFP. If I quote another work in the same chapter, its initials will precede the page number. For example "(MEW, 25)" found in any chapter except

the MEW chapter refers to page 25 of MEW.   Additional
material will be consigned to the footnotes.

CHAPTER 1

SCIENCE AND FIRST PRINCIPLES

Northrop's first book was the result of six lectures delivered on behalf of the Deems Foundation in 1929 at New York University. The work was published in 1931 and reissued by Ox Bow Press in 1979. The latter is identical with the earlier printing except for a five page preface which reflects Northrop's yearly meetings with Einstein at Princeton and concerns the need for a crucial experiment to adjudicate between the two possible solutions to the covariant chronogeometrical tensor equation of the general theory of relativity--the one being Northrop's solution as found in SFP. Since we will be discussing this theory at some length below, I need now only mention its name, the macroscopic atomic theory.

As Northrop tells us in the 1931 preface, the book attempts to provide a logical analysis of the first principles of science. Since it is philosophy's function to examine the first principles of all the sciences, one might well retitle this work, *Science and Philosophy*. The major concern in the following will be with the philosophy.

Chapter one sketches what Northrop takes to be three mutually exclusive and jointly exhaustive philosophies of science; the physical, the mathematical and the functional.

Each of these theories is associated with certain famous figures in Greek science and philosophy. The physical theory had its origin in the Greek materialists and Thales is its father. The mathematical theory owes a debt to Pythagoras and Plato. And lastly the genesis of the functional theory can be traced to Hippocrates, Empedocles, and Aristotle. We shall consider each theory in turn.

THE PHYSICAL THEORY

This theory states that ultimate reality is stuff or matter in motion. Though the Milesians quibbled over the nature of the stuff, they all agreed upon the physical theory of nature, and the importance of eternity over time. For these ancient thinkers, the stuff of which all else was composed was eternal and could neither come into or go out of existence. The composite was the temporal, and the simple or non-composite was the eternal. Northrop calls this identification of the real with the physical and the eternal "the principle of being." In order to understand Northrop's thought, it is crucial to be crystal clear about the meaning of the principle of being. What it means is simply stated. It means that the real does not change its properties. Men may go bald, cats grow old and stars supernovae, but the ultimate physical constituents never change their properties, whatever these properties may be. The unchanging nature of these (let us call them atoms, herein used philosophically rather that scientifically and referring to the ultimate physical constituents of reality) atoms is the basis of the doctrine of mechanical causation, the principle of identity, and other corollaries of which the most important for our purposes is the existence of a macroscopic atomic physical referent in addition to the traditional atoms. It is this referent, hereafter called the macroscopic atom, which is the lietmotiv of *Science and First Principles* and its application in biology, psychology, physiology, theology as well as theoretical physics represents an incredible feat of insight and integration by Northrop. We shall have more to say about the macroscopic atom later.

THE MATHEMATICAL THEORY

The mathematical theory of the first principles of science and nature agrees with the physical theory in accepting the principle of being, i.e., the real does not change it properties. This implies the principle of identity and the principle of mechanical causation. Unlike the physical theory however, it holds that ultimate reality consists in mathematical relations that can only be known by pure reason and this leads to two important consequences; (1) the introduction of the hypothetical deductive scientific methodology, and (2) a depreciation of the world as revealed to sense perception. Finally, the mathematical theory does not postulate the existence of a macroscopic atom. Since the mathematical theory does not loom large in what is to follow, it will be given short shrift. The interested reader is directed to SFP.

THE FUNCTIONAL THEORY

Lastly we have the functional theory of nature and its knowledge. Intimately concerned with biological phenomenon, proponents of this theory were early on fascinated with the organism and its problematic, especially that of organization. Given the discovery of a prototypical evolutionary theory by Empedocles, the functional theory does away with the principle of being and hence the principle of identity. These are replaced by the principles of becoming and teleology. Who knows, this theory asks rhetorically, what evolutionary processes will develop on the morrow? Reality is conceived to be a constant process, the *telos* or end of which must be observed in order to be known. The epistemological consequences of this are that reality is contained in the world of sense perception and reason is limited to the function of an abstractor of concepts and theories from the welter of sensory data. All knowledge not only begins in sense experience but also arises out of this confrontation. Matter and form (the fundamental terms in the physical and mathematical theories respectively) are now demoted, so to speak, from the ontologically independent status of substance to the ontologically dependent status of mere attributes. Since attributes cannot act upon one another, an efficient cause, (composed of matter and form) is necessitated to reduce the potential to the actual. As can now be appreciated, we have scientific justification for the four causes (αἰτία) of Aristotle. But even these efficient causes are ultimately abstractions from the one dynamic individual substance which is nature as a whole.

Before leaving this exposition of the three basic kinds of philosophies of science and in order to give the reader an appreciation of the scientific reasoning that Northrop finds at the basis of these theories, it may be profitable to consider how Aristotle (according to Northrop) came to reject the physical and mathematical for the functional view. (Nothing will be lost if the reader skips the next three paragraphs until the need for them is felt.) Northrop believes such a reconstruction of Aristotle's thought is necessary in order to allay suspicions that philosophers merely set down their bizarre opinions in total disregard of the scientific milieu. In fact, as Northrop points out, most of the greatest philosophers in the history of the West were scientists as well as philosophers. Let us turn to Aristotle's reasons for rejecting both the mathematical and the physical theories of nature.

Northrop finds two sources for Aristotle's rejections of the two earlier philosophies of science one biological, the other mathematical. The former appears in the text under consideration, the latter in MEW p. 263. But it will be convenient to consider them both now, beginning with the former.

The biological reasons for Aristotle's rejection of the atomic theory have to do with the so called problem of the organization and generation of human life. If reality is nothing but atomic matter whirling in the void, how can we account for the obvious "clumping" that occurs all around us, especially and most dramatically those clumps we call living beings? Obviously some formal principle is necessary, but how to account for it? We could simply posit disembodied forms whose job is to organize matter. But a disembodied form, in and of itself, cannot organize chaotic matter. How could it? Only matter can affect the space-time pathways of matter. Aristotle's solution was to regard both matter and form as attributes of a substance, rather than substances themselves. They are causes, but only in a passive sense. The active cause of organization he baptized the agent or efficient cause. The agent, which is always already an amalgam of matter and form, obviously has the matter to affect other matter, so we don't have to invoke the miraculous every time birth occurs and in addition it can impart form (as organization) because it has form as well as matter also. Although form and matter are equivalent in the sense of passive causes (i.e., neither can act on the other), they are epistemologically equiprimordial. This means that neither can be used to explain the other. But this entails that form (in the sense of generation) is also irreducible and Northrop says that this forced Aristotle to replace the principle of being (the real does not change its properties) with the principle of becoming (the real does change its properties). But without some form of conservation principle like the principle of being, mechanical causation must be replaced with teleological causation. We don't know how things are going to turn out till we get to the future and see how they turned out. With the notion of teleology we now have in place the four causes of Aristotle and see how they all were, in some sense, necessitated by his biological studies.

Let us now turn to the mathematical considerations. The reader doubtless knows that, for the Greeks, mathematics held the esteemed place we currently grant to theoretical physics. What this means is simply that to run afoul of mathematics was no small matter--in fact, it was the death knell for any such theory. The temporary death of Democritian atomism at the hands of Plato (who probably was repeating the ideas of Pythagoras) was due to the discovery of the method of exhaustion (similar to the methods used in modern day calculus) which requires that one be able to find a magnitude smaller than any given magnitude. In other words, the method of exhaustion requires that there are no smallest magnitudes. But atoms are, by definition, the smallest magnitudes possible. Therefore, either atomism goes or (this method of) mathematics goes. Plato chose to junk simple atomism and replace it with triangular atomism which he thought could solve the rather different problem of irrational numbers. Rather than linger over Plato's irrational atomic triangles, let cut to the chase. Aristotle concluded that any view which asserted the existence of "atomic bodies must needs come into conflict with the mathematical sciences."[1] It really doesn't matter whether your atoms are round units or triangular units, both make the method of exhaustion impossible. Hence Aristotle had good scientific reasons for rejecting both the physical and the mathematical theories of nature and man.

Northrop summarizes the three theories outlined above as follows:

> To assert that the real is being and is physical is to assert the physical theory of nature; that the real is being and is rational, the mathematical; that the real is becoming, the functional theory.
> The physical theory involves the following corollaries: (1) the principle of identity, (2) the priority of eternity over temporality, (3) the principle of mechanical causa-

---

[1] Cf. De Caelo, 306a27 cited in MEW 268.

tion, (4) the doctrine that all non-spatial relations are effects of atomic motion, and (5) the existence of a referent
in addition to the microscopic particles.

The mathematical theory implies (1) the principle of
identity, (2) the principle of mechanical causation, (3) the
doctrine that only relations are causes, (4) the thesis that
the method of hypothesis is the fundamental scientific
method, and (5) the epistemological principle that the
real world is suggested by, but not contained in, the
world of sensation.

The functional theory involves (1) the principle of
teleology, (2) the primacy of the method of abstraction,
(3) the epistemological principle that the real world is
contained in the world of sensation, (4) the doctrine that
matter and form are mere attributes of a process, or
"event" or dynamic type of substance, and (5) the thesis
that there is only one real individual in nature which is
the "event", or process, or dynamic substance termed
nature as a whole. (24-5)

We have not examined all of the above theories in detail. That
pleasant task is left as an exercise for the reader. Most are not
controversial, but item (5) under the physical theory would be
were it better known. The referent Northrop speaks of is the
macroscopic atom alluded to above, and if the interpretation
offered in this chapter is correct, it is the lynch pin of SFP and
one of Northrop's most important metaphysical concepts.   To
appreciate this we have to accomplish two tasks: (1) we have to
put more flesh on the bones of this theory and then, (2) look at
the number of problems it solves.

Taking the latter first--Northrop believes that the macroscopic atomic theory solves the following seven problems in the
disciplines indicated: (1) in theoretical physics it provides a
referent for motion (and atomicity) that has been needed since
Einstein jettisoned the Newtonian concept of absolute space; (2)
in thermodynamics, it provides a new interpretation of the sec-

ond law (in the sense of a primary interpretation that founds the more commonplace statistical meaning) and thus provides an explanation for not only the disorganizing aspects of nature but also for its obvious organizing aspects such as found in living entities; (3) it solves the problem of organization and generation in biology; (4) it provides ultimate physical support to the genetics of evolution; (5) it is a co-explainer to the rational, imaginative and logical character of man; (6) it co-explains the possibility of human experience and epistemology; and (7) it provides the foundations for a robust two-god theology, thereby healing the rift that has grown between science, and theology since the beginning of the current scientific revolution.

One thing is clear, the macroscopic theory is no mere curiosity propounded to solve a motion problem in relativity physics. It is rather a central notion in Northrop's philosophy and a first principle of his metaphysics. What is the nature of this free creation of the mind of F. S. C. Northrop?

In order of discovery, the macroscopic atom suggested itself to Northrop during the writing of his Ph. D. dissertation on purely biological problems, but, in SFP, it makes its first appearance in a discussion of the theory of relativity, the subject matter and title of chapter two.

In teaching the macroscopic theory to classes that are almost invariable in their lack of a student who knows calculus, let alone theoretical physics, I have them imagine a huge beach ball filled with BBs. The BBs are the microscopic atoms (remember we are using atoms in a philosophical sense to refer to the latest, smallest thing in physics whether it be electron, quark or what have you) and the beach ball is the macroscopic atom. They seem to have much less difficulty with this notion that with, say, Aristotle's hylemorphism. With that picture before us, let us note some of the properties of this big atom. [I will talk briefly of ten: it is simple, primary, co-creator, eternal, conscious, physical, non-omnipotent, rational, spherical, transcendent/immanent.] Since it is atomic, it is simple in the sense of having no parts, therefore we don't have to worry about it breaking up. It is primary and cannot be explained with reference to any other being rather all compound beings are to be explained, in part, by reference to the macroscopic atom. It is conscious and everything within it forms the content of its consciousness. (Northrop is a panpsychist of which more in due course.) Without this all-embracing physical atom, all would be flux, therefore it is the co-creator[2] (with the microscopic atoms) of all complex things. Here creation means rearrangement. Northrop does not countenance and regards as meaningless the notion of creation ex nihilio. Obviously it is physical as are all the primary existents in any physical theory of nature and man. The reason Northrop regards it as non-omnipotent is due to the energy of the microscopic atoms. Were the macroscopic atom all powerful, it would congest everything into a motionless lump. But there is motion, therefore omnipotence is ruled out. Its rationality follows from the fact that Northrop identifies rationality with form, and it has a form, as does all matter, therefore it is rational. In fact it is the most rational thing that exists since it contains all forms within it and no forms exist without it. It is transcendent in the sense that nothing exists outside of it and immanent in the sense that it has (or is) an inner field.

Of the ten attributes listed above, we shall concentrate on three, the physical, the rational or formal and the psychical for more extensive elaboration. The reader is, of course, encouraged to explore the others in any detail that is congenial.

Every atom in Northrop's system is physical, formal and psychical. For Northrop, to be physical means either of two

---

2 See chapter six for more on co-creation.

mutually exclusive things; to be a thing that moves or to be a referent for the things that move.   The macroscopic atom is physical in the latter sense, i.e., it is a referent for the motion of the little atoms contained within it.   That the little atoms need a referent for motion became clear to the West with Parmenides. (SFP, 8)   He proved that if you had nothing but matter, you could not have motion, in fact, you could not even have *two* atoms, to say nothing of an infinite number (Democritus) or a very large finite number (Northrop and others).   Let us consider the motion problem first.   In order to move, matter has to have some *place* to move to.   If there were nothing but matter, there would be no place for the matter to move to and hence no motion.   So the early atomists came up with the notion of the void (or space) to provide a*where to* for the moving atoms to go.   The void has had a long run in the history of science and philosophy, and no good atomist would be caught dead without his void.   Newton's absolute space is his analog to the ancient void.   But Einstein, when he abandoned the notion of absolute space, removed the referent and place of motion from the scientific scene.   Northrop met with Einstein in Berlin in June of 1927 and the latter admitted that some kind of referent had to be found and "that the covariant chronogeo-metrical tensor of his (1916) equation permits two alternative solutions -- one the generally accepted one. . . in which the Hubble constant in the red shift from distant stars is inter-preted as a constant expansion of the distance between all stellar objects, with the one dimensional time-flow a constant." (p. x) The other solution is Northrop's macroscopic atomic the-ory in which the Hubble red shift is interpreted "as a slowing up of the one-dimensional time flow." (p. x)[3]   The philosophical

---

[3] Whitehead developed a third solution to the covariant chronogeometical tensor but its depends on his own idiosyncratic theory of relativity and has not found any

problem with the ordinary, generally accepted interpretation of relativity theory is that it fails to provide a referent for motion and hence, if it were the whole truth, motion would be impossible. But there is motion, therefore we need a referent for that motion.

At least as intrinsically interesting an argument is Parmenides' claim that in order to have more than one atom, the void (or a cognate cousin) must be presupposed. The argument is rather simple. (8)[4] Physical manyness requires something non-physical to enable a separation between the atoms to occur and permit numerical differentiation. With no space between the atoms they would be one, not many. Here we see that space not only provides the necessary referent for motion but also for the notion of manyness. Without the referent, no motion and no manyness. A physical theory of nature demands both matter *and* space if one is to have *many* things in *motion*. So much for the physicality of the atoms.

All of Northrop's atoms are also formal. This position follows from his rejection of the mathematical theory of nature which allows forms to exist apart from any and all matter. But the physical theory of nature permits no such separation of matter and form. All form is embodied and all matter has formal properties. In a sense this is not an argument but a restatement of the physical theory itself. But Northrop does have an argument. If formal causes are necessary to explain nature and man, "it must change the direction of motion of physical particles. Before such a task, however, a disembodied form is

---

acceptance in the scientific community thus far. Northrop's theory is couched in the Einsteinian theory. Interestingly Whitehead admits on p. 390 of Process and Reality that Northrop's macroscopic atomic theory is the only alternative, besides his own, to the popular one.

[4] Cf. Kant's statement at A263/B319 of the Critique of Pure Reason that "Difference of spatial position at one and the same time is still an adequate ground for the numerical difference of the object, . . ."

useless only an external physical force will suffice." (19)   To ask a form to change the path of even a single particle is like asking an equation to power the Concorde across the Atlantic. If forms are to function as causes they must be embodied forms.   In this Northrop is surely following Aristotle's principle of hylemorphism; no form without matter and vice versa.

But Northrop's most controversial position with respect to his atoms is the claim that they are conscious.   Not that the doctrine of panpsychism is without a stable of famous names[5] in the Western tradition and Northrop was certainly influenced by Whitehead[6] in this matter.   Nevertheless, most thinkers shy away from panpsychism for a variety of reasons none of which we shall examine here.   Suffice it to cite Wittgenstein who in the *Philosophical Investigations* (§ 390) finds the whole idea of *kein Interesse*.   Northrop did find the idea interesting and a look at his argument follows.

As we shall see in the next chapter, Northrop endorses a global bifurcation in epistemology, a distinction between two ways of knowing the world which for our present purposes may be denoted by reason and sense.   This ancient   (it goes back to at least Parmenides) distinction enables us to know the relation between the psychical on the one hand and the physical, formal aspect of the atoms on the other.   In addition to reason, we are beings who sense the world and ourselves.   Now when we sense ourselves we sense ourselves to be conscious. Hence our atoms must be conscious also.   But the word "also" is misleading here.   It is not the case that we *and* our atoms are

------

5 The Encyclopaedia of Philosophy lists over three dozen philosophers who have endorsed panpsychism in some form. The Wittgenstein citation is also from the same article.

6 Whitehead's Science and the Modern World is referenced in the bibliography to chapter six of SFP.

conscious. The relation between ourselves as we experience ourselves and ourselves as we know ourselves via current philosophical and scientific theory is the relation of identity. There are not two beings here, us and our atoms. There is just ourselves and we are atomic in nature. We know our atoms by being conscious of ourselves. Put syllogistically we have: whatever we immediately sense ourselves to be our atoms are and we immediately sense ourselves to be conscious, therefore, our atoms are conscious. Northrop concludes "Man . . . is conscious; . . . because the ultimate atomic entities of which everything is constituted have psychical . . . properties." (253)

But why doesn't this argument commit the fallacy of division? This fallacy results from the assumption that properties pertaining to the whole (in this case, man) are also properties of the parts (the atoms) that constitute the whole. This is sometimes true as, e.g., in the case of spatially extended things that are constituted of spatially extended things. Sometimes it is false as, e.g., in the case of a 4,000 pound car that is not made of 4,000 pound parts.

The fallacy of division can occur only when we are dealing with emergent qualities or properties. There are some thinkers who deny absolute emergence and insist that *all* qualities are in principle predictable. Others hold that certain qualities are emergent and in principle unpredictable.[7] If one treats an *emergent* quality of a whole as if it also pertained to the parts, then one commits the fallacy of division. On the other hand, if one can move from qualities pertaining to the whole to qualities pertaining to the part then one is dealing with non-emergent qualities.

---

[7] For a fuller discussion of this issue cf. Arthur Pap's An Introduction to the Philosophy of Science, Glencoe, The Free Press, 1962, 364-72.

That Northrop regards consciousness as a non-emergent property becomes evident when he writes that ". . . no mere increase in physical relata will give one an experienced blue." If nothing existed but the many physical-formal microscopic atoms and the one physical-formal macroscopic atom-- Bergmann's truncated world -- then neither seen colors, heard sounds, felt pleasure and pains, in short all the secondary and tertiary qualities (in the sense meant by Galileo, not Locke) would not exist. But they do exist. Therefore, we need another factor to account for these. This factor is consciousness, and it is a metaphysical primary since it is non-emergent.[8] Any factor (in the physical theory of nature and man) can only "get here" in either of two ways; it is an eternal part of the universe or it emerged from a mixing of the non-emergent eternal parts. Since "no mere increase in physical relata will give one an experienced blue" consciousness cannot be an emergent property of those things possessing it. But if consciousness is non-emergent, it must be eternal.

But what proof does Northrop proffer for the crucial premise that "no mere increase in physical relata will give one an experienced blue"? Within the space of two pages (251 and 252) he repeats this premise four times in slightly different words. On p. 251 he writes, "For no possible combination of colourless atoms or fields can ever give rise to a blue." On 252, in addition to the proposition given above we also have "For no mere combination of colourless atoms and fields can give a perceived blue" and ". . . no amount of combination or deduction can ever derive them [experienced colours and sounds] from only the physical and formal properties of the atomic entities

---

8 As a point of clarification, had Northrop accepted the functional theory of nature and man, emergent properties would then be metaphysical primaries. The price one pays for that is lack of predictive power due to the impossibility of conservation laws or mathematical invarients.

which we have found it necessary to accept." Since repetition is not proof, it reminds one of those passages in the works of Beethoven when, rather than modulate from one key to another in the usual ways, he bangs repeatedly on a chord or phrase in the new key and by mere force of genius moves us into a new musical space. But we do not grant such similar modulatory techniques to the philosopher. So we are left asking for a demonstration for the premise in question.

Perhaps equally pressing a question is one that always occurs immediately upon hearing a panpsychist argument, viz., what does the panpsychist mean by consciousness? The answer to the second provides insight into how Northrop answers the first. By consciousness he means "bare indeterminate experienced quality." Hegel was, of course, right when he said that all definitions are useless until one understands all that is packed into the predicate side of the judgment. What Northrop means by consciousness is less than enlightening until one understands what he means by "bare", "indeterminate", etc. By an experienced quality, Northrop means one that is immediately given, i.e., "one that is not known by reason" and *cannot* be known by theoretical means. One has to be conscious in order to know what consciousness is. "And by experienced quality in its bareness and indeterminateness we mean immediately given quality . . . abstracted from that which makes one of its instances or parts different from one another." (256) Northrop then borrows from W. E. Johnson the word "determinable" and writes that "experienced quality in its bareness and indeterminateness" is "the determinable of all determinables". (257)[9] Johnson originally used the word to indicate the relationship between, say, *red* and *color*[10] and names the

---

[9] W. E. Johnson, Logic, 3 vols., New York, Dover, 1964, vol. 1, 174.

former the determinate and the latter the determinable. For Northrop the determinate nature of any quality can be accounted for by the physical and formal properties of the quality under consideration. He writes that "the *determinate* character of the color of this page is as completely conditioned by the physical and formal properties of the system of atoms and fields of the macroscopic theory, as is the page's chemical constitution." (256) Since the determinate nature is determined by the physical and formal nature of the atoms, the only thing left as a contribution of the psychical aspect of the atoms is the indeterminate, the incommunicable (by theoretical means) "feel" of red, cold, tangy etc.

Now that we have some idea of what Northrop means by consciousness, let us return to the first question listed above, i.e., how does he prove that consciousness is non-emergent? Or as we quoted above, how does he prove that "no mere increase in physical relata will give one an experienced blue"?

There is no proof in the text per se. One could anachronistically abstract from his essay on Whitehead Northrop's brief history of modern philosophy's attempt to deduce consciousness from matter. This essay appeared in a collection edited by Schilpp as part of the Library of Living Philosophers series on pages 165-209. But such a history (from Hobbes and Galileo to Kant) seems to place too much reliance on a materialism three centuries old. Just because Hobbes was unable to produce a conscious rabbit out of a material hat does not impact modern attempts at the same conjuring trick. Not only that, from Northrop's perspective the enterprise was doomed to failure because "no mere increase in physical relata will give one an experienced blue." But isn't this circular? It does seem clear that Northrop is using the failure of the materialist thinkers of the past to account for consciousness to place the

---

10 Pace Johnson, I use the American spelling.

burden of proof on those materialists who claim that consciousness is an emergent property. But who has the burden of
proof here? I know of no general argument to establish who
has the burden in any given case. [In Anglo-American legal
theory it is a cliché that the burden of proof lies with the pros-
ecution, i.e., with those asserting guilt, usually the state. The
state is making a positive claim and the burden is on them to
prove beyond a reasonable doubt that the accused is guilty of
the crime. Some states do require that for certain kinds of de-
fenses, e.g., insanity, the burden shifts away from the prosecu-
tion to the defense attorney since the latter is now making a
positive assertion, viz., the accused was incompetent at the
time of the commission of the criminal act.[11] But this is hardly
a general argument. And all countries are not in agreement
with Britain and the United States on this doctrine.

Let's beat about in the neighboring bushes. It might pay
dividends to contrast an emergent with a non-emergent item
within Northrop's system.

We shall use life as the example of an emergent property
and, naturally, consciousness as a non-emergent property. This
approach has the additional bonus of allowing us to refer, albeit
briefly, to chapter four of SFP wherein Northrop develops his
notion of life.

The key thinker in this chapter is Lavoisier. Since the
physical theory of nature and man does not take, as does
Aristotle's functional theory, the facts of generation and organization as primaries, life must be defined in terms of the physical and formal properties of the atoms. Some of the most stir-
ring pages in SFP are those in which Northrop recounts the intellectual discoveries of the young Frenchman. For our pur-

---

[11] Debts to the "Criminal Law" article in the 14th edition of the <u>Encyclopaedia Britannica</u>.

poses we must skip down to the conclusion of his researches and to the definition of life he gives, viz., that the "living thing is a physico-chemical system involving a temporary dynamic equilibrium between internal and external physico-chemical materials." Life emerges whenever the equilibrium is attained and death occurs whenever the equilibrium is destroyed. A living thing is a clump of atoms in a temporary balance with the rest of nature, including of course the congesting influence of the big atom. Life is non-eternal and hence emergent (subject to generation and corruption).

Now what about consciousness? In order for consciousness to be an emergent property it would have to be physical or formal in its very nature. It would have to be like life, definable in terms of the physical and formal properties of the atoms. But here a problem occurs. If Northrop is correct in his description of the psychical as indeterminant, any attempt to get an emergent consciousness would mean getting the indeterminant from the determinant. Physics and chemistry, in their formal hypothetical-deductiveness, would have to produce something in the theorems of the system that was not in the premises. But this would violate the canons of logic and we should think long before we do that. [Not that science does not often violate the rules of strict logic. For example, when scientists reason from a theory to some experimental consequences and then, after running the experiment(s) any given number of times pronounce the theory confirmed, they are, of course, committing the fallacy of affirming the consequent.[1 2] Nevertheless, caution is called for and every violation has its price. In the case of the fallacy mentioned above, the price is the loss of the kind of certainty that strict deduction guarantees. It should be obvious how much hangs on Northrop's

---

[12] For Northrop's treatment of this topic the reader is directed to LSH, 146-8.

equating consciousness with the indeterminate and one would like to have some arguments to support such a definition. Fortunately we have three in the text and it is to these that we now turn.

Argument 1 for the indeterminate nature of conscious-ness has been touched upon already and we need do no more here than to indicate its name and reiterate a brief description of it. I call the argument the "remainder argument" and it can be found on p. 255 where Northrop tells us that in order to dis-cover the precise nature of the psychical and its contribution to observed nature, "we have but to determine what the remain-der [hence the name] in observed nature is, which the physical and the formal does not produce. . ." This remainder exhibits itself in the so-called secondary and tertiary qualities.[13] But Northrop is careful to point out that the fact that the normal percipient will experience white and black rather than red and green when reading these pages is completely determined by the physical and formal properties of the page, the percipient, the light source etc.   What the physical and formal properties of the atoms do not condition is the indeterminate "feel" that white and black conveys to all sighted persons who attend to this page.   Hence that indeterminate quality must be the con-tribution of consciousness.

The second argument I call the "analysis argument" and it can be found on p. 257 of SFP.   In observed nature we find oxygen, hydrogen and water.   "Their observed attributes have this peculiar character: the observed properties of one cannot be determined by an examination of the observed properties of

---

[13] Northrop uses the term "secondary quality" in the Galilean rather than the Lockean sense. Remember that for Galileo but not for Locke, secondary qualities were subjective in the sense that if one would remove the subject there would be no color, sound, smell etc.

the other."[14]   But the precise opposite is true of these items considered as part of atomic theory, for from the "combination of atoms of oxygen with atoms of hydrogen in proper proportion it follows necessarily that the product will be the atomic system which is water." Under analysis, we find that water, as it is known by reason, reduces to a common denominator and is commensurable, whereas water as it is known by sensation does not reduce to a common denominator and therefore is not commensurable.   Northrop concludes that sensation introduces "an element of bare quality which must be experienced to be known, and which is so indeterminant that no deductions can be made from it."

The third and final argument is a rather curious one and may be termed the "uniquely known argument."   Try as I might I have been unable to improve by précis the longish two paragraph quotation that follows:

> Some may wonder why the physicist has not discovered the psychical character of the atomic entities. But the reason is clear. Since the psychical is bare *experienced* quality it can only be known immediately. Thus the psychical character of an atom can be known only by being the atom in question. But the physicist, as physicist, only considers the atom in the relation of otherness to the knowing subject. Hence, his failure to find its psychical character is necessary.
>
> Two objective determinations of the precise character of the psychical have been given. Both agree in defining it as bare indeterminate experi-

---

14 An even more dramatic example of observed incommeasurablity vs. scientific commeasurability is given by Jacob Bronowski on p. 321 of his The Ascent of Man where he writes about how remarkable it is that "a white fizzy metal like sodium, and a yellowish poisonous gas like chlorine, should finish up by making a stable structure, common salt."

enced quality. We noted that if the atoms possess this property, it can only be known as a subjective fact when the object which it qualifies and the knowing subject are identical. These considerations enable us to deduce a consequence of our theory of the nature of the psychical, and to put it to another test. Because the barely psychical can only be known in itself, aside from its presence in objective observed nature when the knower and the entity or entities which the psychical qualifies are identical, and because man is all the atoms which the psychical qualifies in one of their many particularizations, it follows that the only system in which the barely psychical should exhibit itself to man in its own purity, unmixed with the physical and the formal, is himself. Hence, if our theory is true it follows that man will find a quality of being in himself which he finds immediately in no other system which he knows. Does our theory meet this test? The answer is affirmative. Man finds something in himself which he discovers immediately in no other creature or object. It is consciousness. Moreover, when one cuts off or abstracts from all physical and formal effects upon oneself, and turns back into the pure experience of one's own being, what does one find but the very definition of the psychical which we have given. Nothing remains but bare indeterminate experience. (258)

Now that we have finished the exposition of the tripartite nature of the atoms of Northrop's system, there remains some theological and epistemological cashing in. I use the phrase "cashing in" because Northrop adds nothing new to the basic metaphysical schema we have adumbrated in order to detail his theories of God and knowledge. His theology is in that sense much like Aristotle's -- a consequence of his speculations on matter and motion. Let us turn first to his theology and finally to some epistemological considerations.

In contrast to the Jewish, Christian and Islamic traditions, there are for Northrop two Gods, not one.[15] The first God he identifies with the macroscopic atom, thereby joining that small group of Western thinkers for whom God has a body.[16] In addition to the physical, formal and psychical character of the macroscopic atom [= God], this atom is also primary, a co-creator, eternal, rational, simple, spherical, transcendent and immanent. The latter two attributes may seem to be contradictory, but the atom is transcendent in the sense that nothing is outside it and immanent in the sense that the congestion that it induces upon the microscopic atoms is brought about by its inner field. Hence its immanence.

Northrop's theology is unlikely to satisfy many. After all, he admits that we are merely adding a name and not another meaning to the macroscopic atom when we call it God. "It is to be emphasized that names do not give meaning to things. Like any assignment of a symbol, the attribution of the term, *divine*, to the macroscopic atom is a mere convention. Not one attribute of this atom is changed by this act." (279)

Finally, Northrop reveals one other consequence of his metaphysics of tri-charactered atoms, viz., "it appears that there is more than one god."[17] (281) This second god Northrop identifies as "the order of nature as a whole." (282) Here again Northrop employs the same theological methodology. He simply lists the characteristics of this "order of nature" and

---

[15] Of course, in the case of the Catholics, there are three persons in one God, but there is still only one God. The question of the Eastern tradition will be discussed in chapter three.

[16] Spinoza comes to mind.

[17] Why the use of lower case here to spell 'god' after pages of "God" is open to speculation. Perhaps the influence of thousands of years of monotheism is the answer.

finds that these characteristics are those the Greeks thought indicative of divinity. It is a conscious, rational, eternal individual and Northrop states that any entity exhibiting such properties "may be termed a divine being."

Does one pray to these Gods? Not hardly. At least not in the usual sense. "The Greek notion that rationality, which is the mark of divinity, is located in inorganic nature, and that man converts his instinctively irrational nature into a truly religious rational one, by learning to define his terms, and by studying mathematics and astronomy . . ." (232) is as close as Northrop gets to the ordinary notion of prayer--which is none too close. The notion of the "God of the philosophers" is a familiar one. Northrop has provided us with the "prayer of the philosophers"--the one that Socrates led on a daily basis in the marketplace. So much for Northrop's theology; at least within the context of SFP.

What consequences does Northrop's metaphysics have for his epistemology? It gets its due in the final pages of SFP because the problem of knowledge is "the most difficult of all scientific problems." (283) Although we shall have more to say about Northrop's epistemology in the next chapter, there are some issues that need to be discussed within the context of the problematic of SFP, viz., that of the relationship between science and first principles, specifically epistemological first principles. Let us begin by asking what the problem is.[18]

The problem has to do with the kinetic atomic theories of Galilei,[19] Newton, Dalton etc. According to Northrop, a purely

---

[18] To anticipate somewhat, one can see here in germ the methodology of his philosophy of science (understood broadly) that Northrop will expose in LSH, viz., the problem comes first. The problem; not natural history data collection, not induction, not deduction etc.

kinetic atomic theory can give rise to order or disorder and there seems to be "no relations or connections in nature that are necessary."[20] (284) What is here today may be gone tomorrow. Hume, as is well known, cashed this theory into its logical consequences. "[I]f there are no necessary connections there can be no causality, and without causality, no scientific laws." (Ibid.) Putting Northrop's reply in the simplest form we have the following modus tollens. If there are no necessary connections then no science. But there is science, therefore there are necessary connections. But this conclusion indicates that something must be wrong with the traditional theory of kinetic atomic motion. And the theory is wrong either in whole or in part. Not willing to abandon science, Northrop re-examines the premises upon which the argument rests. In fact, SFP is such a re-examination.

Since the many atoms of the traditional atomic theory give rise to the problem of knowledge which is the problem of necessary connections, and since we don't want to jettison science, Northrop suggests we add something to the traditional theory to solve the problem.[21] Now this sounds a bit ad hoc, until we realized that the entity Northrop has in mind to add to the older theory is none other than the macroscopic atom itself.[22] "The necessary relatedness in nature which must be

---

[19] In all of Northrop's books he uses this spelling insead of "Galileo."

[20] There seems to be a tension if not a downright contradiction between this sentence from 284 and one on 244 which draws a different concludion about Newton's system, viz., that Newton took his theory to be a theory about "one necessary purely mechanical cast-iron universe."

[21] Chapter one also gives additional reasons for rejecting the only possible competitors to the physical theory of nature, viz., the mathematical and the functional theories.

[22] The reader must remember that at this place (p. 288) in the book, Northrop has already used the problem of organization in biology, the problem of motion and change in physics, the problems in thermodynamics and evolution as grounds

present if science, . . . is to exist, has its basis in this atom."
(288)

What is the argument that leads to this conclusion. What
is the argument that the macroscopic atom makes scientific
knowledge possible. It is a reprise of the argument from the
first chapter, an argument that was made by the Greeks when
they faced the problems of atomicity and motion.

To make it contemporary we must recall that "when
Galilei discovered time to be important, it was natural to regard
it as a primary concept also." Hence the notion of absolute time
that we find, for example, in Newton. Problem was, since time
was defined in terms of motion and motion was defined in
terms of time, we found ourselves arguing in a circle. But
what is more important for our immediate purpose, in addition
to the *petitio* just mentioned, is Hume's analysis of causality.
"Once time is taken as a primary concept in terms of which all
else is defined, in short once everything is regarded as a purely
temporal system of relations, no necessary connections can exist and Hume's conclusion is inevitable."

Enter Einstein. Time is no longer a primary, it is relative
to absolute light propagation. That's the good news, so to
speak. The bad news is that what relativity did for time it also
did for space, leaving matter and motion without the referent
the Greeks demonstrated to be necessary. Not only do we
need a referent (a non-moving something) to provide the referent for motion, we also need it to provide a referent for
manyness. How can there be *many* little atoms if that's all
there is--little atoms. What makes one atom to be other than
and distinct from another atom? ". . . one atom can be distinguished from another only in terms of its unique relation to

---

for the introduciton of the macroscopic atom--these considerations considerably
reduce the feeling of ad hocness in a reader who has patiently plowed through the
text from p. 1 to p. 288.

some common referent." (9) These considerations led Northrop to the introduction of the macroscopic atom (the common referent) to do the job absolute space used to do before it was so unceremoniously dethroned by Einstein.   In other words, the traditional kinematic atomic theory is not false, but merely incomplete.

In order to differentiate his from the traditional theory, Northrop has dubbed it the macroscopic atomic theory.   The basic entities of the system are the one macroscopic atom and the many little atoms, the latter being responsible for the temporary relatedness we find in nature while the former is responsible for the necessary connections and constancy's that exhibit themselves, especially in the general macroscopic characteristics of nature, thereby providing the necessary connectedness we find in mathematics, logic etc. (288)   We now have a physical basis for the necessary connectedness science requires.

Note that since his is a species of the physical theory of nature detailed above, all *formal* properties are either relations between *physical* relata or aspects of those relata.   More consistently Aristotelian than Aristotle, there is for Northrop, no μορφή (form) without ὕλη (matter). Therefore, although the macroscopic atom is an unmoved mover, it is, pace Aristotle, an unmoved mover with a body.

If the above is correct, Northrop has provided us with "a new theory of the first principles of science, [with] the fertility to account for their [i.e., stuff and change] existence, our capacity to know them, and the scientific methods which are involved in the processes of knowledge." (289)   It is to these methods or logics that he now turns in LSH.

CHAPTER 2

THE LOGIC OF THE SCIENCES AND THE HUMANITIES

Although LSH sports a copyright date of 1947 and hence is a year younger than MEW, I will consider it out of chronological order because it contains the most explicit statement of Northrop's epistemology in his own jargon and makes the presentation of MEW as well as his subsequent books easier, assuming, of course, that one has expended the effort required to master the new language.

LSH contains twenty-four chapters, most of which are reprinted from "diverse professional journals in the fields of the natural sciences, the social sciences, both factual and normative, philosophy and the humanities" (vii) bearing publication dates between 1935 and 1946.[23] As the title indicates, the book construes logic in the broadest sense, a sense in which it means "scientific method" and its cognates. Among the disciplines examined against the backdrop of Northrop's epistemology are the physical sciences, biology,[24] poetry, quantum mechanics, classical economics, sociology, religion, politics etc. The first seven chapters are foundational and epistemological.

---

23 Chapters 1-4 and 6-7 and 19 are original with LSH.

24 Northrop's dissertation was on The Problem of Organization in Biology. See bibliography.

Of these, chapter five is Northrop's tour de force, with seven almost equally important. These two will be the focus of this chapter.

A brief review of the first four is necessary, however, in order to set up these two chapters. Chapter One, "The Initiation of Inquiry" puts into bold relief the importance of correct beginnings, and is also an examination of four authorities on the proper scientific method: Bacon, Descartes, Cohen and Dewey. Despite the obvious disagreements between these thinkers, Northrop finds that they all agree that we must reject traditional beliefs. The very notion of a problem (or anomaly as it will later be called by Kuhn and others) presupposes that something is wrong with the traditional solutions and that taking them for granted constitutes a *petitio*. "The point is that inquiry does not start unless there is a problem. And the presence of a problem means that the traditional beliefs are in question." (16)   And although Dewey has the right answer concerning what to do after one has realized or confronted the problematic situation, viz., begin with the problem, he moves too quickly into the "proposing hypotheses phase" of scientific method to appreciate the difference between the recognition of a problem and its analysis.   Hence Northrop's reason for spending chapter two on   "The Analysis of the Problem."[25]

---

[25] I have constructed the following chart as an aid to understanding Northrop's three stage theory of scientific inquiry.

Stage 1. The Problem Stage (Chs. 1 & 2)
    a. Recognition (Ch. 1)
    b. Analysis (Ch. 2)

Stage 2. The Natural History Stage (Ch. 3)
    a. Observation
    b. Description
    c. Classification

Stage 3. The Hypothetical Deductive Stage (Chs. 4 & 6)
    a. Intuitional

Ultimately Northrop will develop a three stage theory of scientific inquiry.

Stage one is concerned with problem recognition and analysis. The analysis of a problem may reveal formal logical problems, here Hilbert on Euclid comes to mind or factual problems, the discovery of a new planet or a new virus or value problems, whether communism or capitalism is the system we ought to champion?   Value problems themselves are amenable to further analysis into descriptive and evaluative--a description of how communism works is not the same as a recommendation of a consummation devoutly to be wished. Consequently, Northrop distinguishes between "factual social theories" and "normative social theories."   Since MEW is a book length application of the latter distinction, the reader is referred to the next chapter for details on the execution of such a methodology.

Stage two, the natural history stage, appears once the analysis of the problem has opened a space for factual research.   This involves not one but three separate though related methods: the method of observation, the method of description, and the method of classification.   This stage ends "when the facts designated by the analysis of the problem in the first stage are immediately apprehended by observation, expressed in terms of concepts with carefully controlled denotative meanings by description, and systematized by classification." (35)   Only while using the observational method does one escape what later thinkers[26] were to call the "theory-ladenness" of terms since there are no terms to be theory laden.

---

b. Postulational

26 Feyerabend, Hanson, Kuhn and Toulmin are names that leap to mind on this issue. Interested readers may consult Carl R. Kordig's "The Theory-Ladenness of Observation" in the March 1971 number of The Review of Metaphysics for a critical discussion of these authors and bibliographical references.

Northrop literally means pure observation of pure fact. When one begins to describe this pure fact, one gets "described fact" rather than "pure fact." And described fact involves concepts and propositions, i.e., theory.

But, and here is a crucial but, the type of theory that is possible in the natural history stage of inquiry is not to be confused with the type that arises in the hypothetically deductively formulated stage of inquiry. This difference has been characterized in various ways by numerous thinkers. Since Northrop characterizes this difference in terms of his possible concepts, I will say a brief word about his chapter four, "The Stage of Deductively Formulated Theory" and then proceed to chapter five.

The third stage of scientific inquiry, that of deductively formulated theory, follows upon the description and classification of the facts. It now makes sense to proceed to hypotheses. If it is the case that the problem encountered can be solved by collecting, describing and classifying the relevant facts,[27] the third stage is unnecessary. If however, the problem proves recalcitrant, not only must an appeal to unobservable entities be made, but a *new* kind of concept must be employed to deal with such unobservables. But what are the various kinds of concepts? It is to this question that Northrop turns in chapter five.

The complete title of chapter five is reminiscent of those long winded titles popular in the eighteenth century. It reads, "The Possible Concepts by Intuition and Concepts by Postulation as a Basic Terminology for Comparative Philosophy."[28] These two names, intuition and postulation, in-

---

[27] One example of this is Aristotle's Historia Animalium.

[28] The chapter was originally a talk presented at the East-West Philosopher's Conference at the University of Hawaii in 1939 and first printed as Chapter VIII

dicate differences due to source. The source of the meaning of the concept is the source of its difference for Northrop. This can be seen from the definitions of these two type of concepts. "A concept by intuition is one which denotes, and the complete meaning of which is given by, something which is immediately apprehended." (82)   Northrop gives blue in "the sense of the sensed color" as an example of a concept by intuition.

The other kind of concepts are concepts by postulation. "A concept by postulation is one the meaning of which in whole or in part is designated by the postulates of the deductive theory in which it occurs." (83)   Blue "in the sense of the number of a wave length in electromagnetic theory is a concept by postulation." (Ibid.)   These are the two broadest genuses of concepts for Northrop. Let us now turn to a detailed examination of, first, the concepts by postulation and second, the concepts by intuition.

There are four species of concepts by postulation: intellection, imagination, perception and a fourth to be discussed below as a bridge to the concepts by intuition. Concepts by perception are the easiest to understand and we shall begin with them. Recall the definition of the concepts by postulation- - "A concept by postulation is one the meaning of which in whole or in part is designated by the postulates of the deductive theory in which it occurs." The reason for the phrase "in whole or in part" becomes clear upon a careful perusal of the definition of the concepts by perception: concepts which designate "factors which are in part sensed and in part imagined." (94)   A table or a chair may suffice as an example of a concept by perception. Not only do we *not* perceive the entire chair in any given perception, (think of the revealing-concealing de-

in Philosophy--East and West, edited by Charles A. Moore, Princeton University Press, 1944, 168-190.

scription of perception given by Merleau-Ponty) we never perceive it unperceived.   We are forced to imagine what it is like
when not perceived.   And yet we common-sensically believe
that the chair persists when we are not looking at it.   It persists, we also believe,   when no one, not just ourselves,   is
looking at it.   When we are not looking (you may substitute the
sense modality of your choice here) at it we, at least in our pre-
scientific stage, imagine it to be exactly as it is when we are
looking at it.   We are, at this stage, naive or direct realists.

Note another consequence of Northrop's definition of concepts by perception--we do not observe chairs in the sense of
pure and immediate apprehension.   Three dimensional spatio-
temporally persisting even when unobserved chairs are *not*
observed.[29]   If one recalls the definition of   concepts by
intuition one can appreciate why this must be so.   The
"complete meaning" is given in immediate apprehension--no
additional content has to be imagined.   (In fact, such an
addition moves one over into concepts by postulation.)   This is
obviously not the case with tables, chairs, other people etc.

The second species under concepts by postulation are the
concepts by imagination.   These are concepts "designating factors which can be imagined but cannot be sensed" even in part.
Northrop instances the ether concept of classical physics and
the Bohr atom, with its imaginable electrons orbiting like

---

[29] Note the style here. It may be termed the "adjective pile-up" style and I use
it in conscious imitation of Northrop. In order to get clear in philosophy, one
often has to resort to a mode of writing that at first may sound obfuscating. I can
only confess that I got use to it and now am shocked when someone objects to this
rhetorical device. But think of the qualifying adjectives necessary to clearly
convey in what sense Aristotle, Anselm, Kant and G. E. Moore are all realists. As
an example of Northrop's adjective pileup consider the following true sentence.
"We observed concept by intuition blue but we do not observe concept by
postulation that is a concept by intellection blue." Such extreme measures are
necessary to unpack the seemingly false "We observe and we do not observe blue."

planets a sun-like nucleus. These examples also relate to a distinct phase in scientific theory construction. Some problems can be resolved by resorting to entities and relations that, while they cannot be perceived, can be imagined. But there are problems that cannot be solved even by the seemingly liberal "constraints" of Walt Disney's imagination. Such a situation leads to the highest and most uncommon-sensical of the concepts by postulation, viz., the concepts by intellection, defined by Northrop as "designating factors which can be neither imagined nor sensed." The space-time continuum of Einstein's relativity theory, Plato's atomic ratios and Jeffersonian rights are examples of these rarified concepts.

Finally, Northrop discusses a fourth class of concepts by postulation, which, like the schemata of Kant, have a foot, so to speak, in both the epistemic worlds of postulation as well as intuition. These hybrids he calls "Logical Concepts by Intuition" and defines them as concepts "designating factors, the content of which is given through the senses or by mere abstraction from the totality of sense awareness, and whose logical universality and immortality are given by postulation." Aristotle's "unmoved mover", Whitehead's "eternal objects" and Santayana's "essences" are examples of the last category of concepts by postulation. I shall not linger on them because they are hardly mentioned in the remainder of his corpus.[30] Nevertheless they do "provide a natural transition" to the other generic type of concept, viz., the concepts by intuition.

Northrop claims that we "must start with the all-embracing immediacy from which any theory . . . takes it inception." (95) While atomists (either in the sense data or the naive realist object sense) probably would disagree, I will not take up the

---

[30] They do play, however, an important role in the intuitional type of hypothetical deductive system. See ch. 6 of LSH, pp. 105ff.

cudgels against them here.[31] Suffice it to say that Northrop describes this immediacy as a field or continuum which is differentiated.   It is differentiated to the senses, either inner or
outer, not to the intellect.   To underscore this fact, Northrop
refers to it as aesthetic.   This adjective is necessary to insure
that one understands "that it is the qualitatively ineffable,
emotionally moving continuum of colors, sounds and feelings
which the artist presents in its immediacy, not the logically defined continuum of mathematical physics which is a concept by
postulation." (95-6)   Since the continuum is aesthetic, differentiated and a continuum, what better name for it than the
differentiated aesthetic continuum.   Since the differentiated
aesthetic continuum is everything that we immediately apprehend, all other concepts by intuition can be derived from it by
a process of abstraction.   Northrop means by "abstraction" a
consideration or focus on factors of the differentiated aesthetic
continuum apart from the "immediately apprehended context."
For example, one can focus on a particular pain, or a particular
red, ignoring the sounds, smells or any other aspect of the
context in which the pain or the red occurs.   The pain or the
red is still, nevertheless, a concept by intuition.   Abstraction in
Northrop's sense is not to be confused with the postulation of
entities, properties or relations not given by immediate awareness.   As we let the context fade into the background of our
sensory focus, we are still immediately aware of some content
and all immediate awareness is to be referenced by using concepts by intuition.

Thus far we have two such concepts: the differentiated
aesthetic continuum itself and the differentiations--the pain or
the red and other radical empirical items.   If one recalls that

---

[31] The interested reader may consult appendix C for a defence of Northrop
against the naive realism of Joseph McAllister.

the latter concepts are got by abstraction, one might ask if, instead of focusing on the differentiations within the differentiated aesthetic continuum, could one abstract from them and focus on the continuum? Northrop answers yes to this query and calls the result the undifferentiated aesthetic continuum.

The undifferentiated aesthetic continuum is the most difficult of the concepts by intuition for Western minds to grasp. Northrop attributes this to the influence of Berkeley and Hume, both of whom emphasize the differentiations and regard the field or the continuum as a mere aggregation of the secondary and tertiary qualities. On the other hand, the Eastern mind has little difficulty with the undifferentiated aesthetic continuum as we will see in the next chapter when we discuss the philosophy, religion and culture of the Orient.

Northrop also distinguishes two classes of the differentiations--those given through the external senses and hence called concepts by sensation and those given through introspection and, naturally enough called concepts by introspection. "Wants" as that concept appears in the Austrian theory of economics and "images of phantasy" are examples of the latter type.

For completeness, mention must be made of a fourth type of concept by intuition. This is obtained by focusing on one differentiation and considering it inseparable from the undifferentiated aesthetic continuum. Northrop calls this a field concept by inspection. It plays no role in his subsequent works and will be ignored.

The following classifications, originally provided by Northrop on pp. 94-5 and 99 of the concepts by postulation and the concepts by intuition respectively, may be useful to summarize the above.

CONCEPTS BY POSTULATION

I Concepts by Intellection = Concepts by postulation designating   factors which can be neither imagined nor sensed.

    (a) Monistic. e.g., The space-time continuum of Einstein's field physics.

    (b) Pluralistic. e.g., Plato's atomic ratios.

II   Concepts by Imagination = Concepts by postulation designating factors which can be imagined but cannot be sensed.

    (a) Monistic. e.g., The ether concept of classical pre-relativistic field physics.

    (b) Pluralistic. e.g., The atoms and molecules of classical particle physics.

III Concept by Perception = Concepts by postulation designating factors which are in part sensed and in part imagined.

    (a) Monistic. e.g., The public space of daily life.

    (b) Pluralistic. e.g., Other persons, tables, chairs, and the spherical moon with its back side which we do not see as well as its presented side which we do see.

IV Logical Concepts by Intuition = Concepts by postulation designating factors, the content of which is given through the senses or by mere abstraction from the totality of sense awareness, and whose logical universality and immortality are given by postulation.

    (a) Monistic. e.g., The "Unmoved Mover" in Aristotle's metaphysics.

    (b) Pluralistic. e.g., Whitehead's "eternal objects," Santayana's "essences" or Aristotle's "ideas."

CONCEPTS BY INTUITION

I The Concept of the Differentiated Aesthetic Continuum = The totality of the immediately apprehended with nothing abstracted away.

II The Concept of the Indeterminate or Undifferentiated Aesthetic Continuum = The immediately apprehended continuum apart from all differentiations.

III The Concepts of the Differentiations = Concept by Inspection = Atomic Concepts by Inspection = The specific inspected qualities or differentiations considered apart from the continuum.
    (a) Concepts by Sensation = III given through the senses.
    (b) Concepts by Introspection = III given introspectively.

IV Field Concepts by Inspection = any instance of III considered as inseparable from II.

According to Northrop, these two types of concepts exhaust the available concepts (i.e., providing terms with meanings) from which any scientific or philosophical theory can be constructed and therefore provides a means to do comparative philosophy, analyze and solve the problem of world peace, tame nations, provide a philosophical anthropology, explain why economists from Smith to Marx were incapable of provide a dynamics to supplement their statics, and to ground art and religion as well as legal and ethical theory. All of these are promissory notes, of course, to be cashed in the remainder of this book.

To anticipate somewhat consider comparative philosophy. Positivism, according to Northrop is the "thesis that there are only concepts by intuition." (99) Any "metaphysical" theories, on the other hand, maintain "that there are also concepts by postulation." (99) Oriental religion, philosophy and science have almost exclusively relied on concepts by intuition (one exception being the Chinese legal realists for which see CLEE). Austrian economics employs only concepts by intuition whereas Smith and Marx used concepts by postulation. "Soul" is a legitimate concept by intuition but has had no success (in

terms of predictive power) as a concept by postulation. Both
Berkeley and Newton agree that "red" is a concept by intuition,
but Newton also uses it as a concept by postulation, a use most
strenuously denied by the Bishop. One last example. To solve
the problem about whether the tree falling in the forest makes
a sound when no one is in the forest to hear it, simply specify if
"sound is being used in its concept by postulation or its concept
by intuition sense". It makes a sound in the former sense but
not in the latter.

   These two types of concepts give rise to two distinct
types of deductively formulated theory. If the scientist identifies the primitive entities and relations with directly sensed
entities and relations he produces one kind of theory--called
by Northrop the "abstractive deductively formulated theory".
(107) But if he employs concepts by postulation (other than
the logical concept by postulation) as a means for articulating
his basic propositions, another and different kind of system is
produced--a "hypothetically inferred deductively formulated
theory". (109) Whitehead's philosophy of nature is an instance
of the first and Einstein's theory for the second. One of the
more interesting consequences of the differences between the
two types of theories is how the axioms of each system are
empirically verified. For the abstractive deductively formulated theory they are "directly verified empirically" and the
theorems are believed to be true because of deduction. For the
hypothetically inferred deductively formulated theory the axioms are only indirectly verified empirically via the consequences of the deduced theorems. The existence of the method
of direct empirical verification for the abstractive deductively
formulated theory gives the lie to pragmatism (as the whole
truth of scientific method) "which locates not merely all verification but even all meaning in the future consequences of one's
hypothesis, . . ." (107) While this may be accurate for, say,

modern theoretical physics, it is obviously not so for Whitehead's philosophy of nature, Austrian economics etc.

Put schematically, the logic of the Austrian economists' procedure is modus ponens; A is the case and if A then B, therefore B. The physicists' procedure is if A, then B and B is the case, therefore A. The physicist commits the fallacy of affirming the consequent. This isn't, however, as disastrous in physics as in logic. What it means is that while the theory is confirmed when B is observed, the uniqueness of A is not thereby established. Other theories may account for B. But this does not damn A. It merely means that unlike Austrian economics, we can never be certain of the axioms that occur in hypothetically inferred deductively formulated theories.[32] But isn't this too much of a downside? Wouldn't we be better off scrapping hypothetically inferred deductively formulated theories with their lack of certainty for the comfortable assurance provided by abstractive deductively formulated theories? The short answer is no and there are two reasons for this reply. (1) we move to hypothetically inferred deductively formulated theories when the problem cannot be solved by "an appeal to directly observable data alone." (115) (2) All abstractive deductively formulated theories lack predictive power. Why this is so has to do with the type of concepts that such theories employ. Concepts by intuition, as David Hume was the first to point out, "exhibit no necessary connections." (Ibid.) Therefore there is no way to connect one's present intuitions to tomorrow's intuitions. The best Hume could do was proffer animal hope that the future would be like the past. "Little can be deduced from a mere subjective psychological hope." (115) What one would like to have is a relation such as logical implication.

---

[32] For the religious and moral consequences of this fact, see "Some Realism about Altruism" in MNG.

If entities or relations in the present logically imply entities or relations in the future, then we can predict that future and more effectively plan long range. Positing entities with eternal natures or relations involving conservation laws solves this problem, but such entities or relations are concepts by postulation--hence the move to hypothetically inferred deductively formulated theory.

To make this more concrete, consider the difference between Humean causality (the kind used in Austrian economics) and Newtonian causality. Only the latter gives rise to predictive consequences. The former is a mere subjective hope that the future will be like the past, a hope based on psychological habit. Causality of the Newtonian kind is equivalent to logical implication.

But even this is not enough. The mere presence of concepts by postulation is only a necessary condition for predictive power. Just because we know, by postulation, the nature of the entities and relations involved in any particular science one further ingredient is necessary before predictive power is realized, viz., conservation laws. "The total quantitative volume of them [factors defining the system at any given time] must neither increase nor decrease with time." It takes little wit to appreciate that human wants (a key concept in economics) do not obey such laws, whereas conservation laws are ubiquitous in physics, chemistry etc.

There remains one crucial notion that must be discussed before the entire Northropean epistemology is exposed. And it has to do with a question that every bifurcationist epistemology, not only Northrop's, has to face. Thinkers as diverse as Plato, Augustine, Democritus, Kant, Einstein must ask and answer the question "What is the relationship between the two types of concepts?" Plato uses the word μέθεξις (participation) or μίμησις (imitation) to characterize this relationship. Kant uses schemata; Reichenbach, co-ordinate definition. For

Northrop the name is epistemic correlation. What is named by this name? As far as a definition is concerned, Northrop provides the following: "an epistemic correlation is a relation joining an unobserved component of anything designated by a concept by postulation to its directly inspected component denoted by a concept by intuition." (119) To recur to an earlier example, sensed blue is related to theoretic blue by an epistemic correlation. Note what this relation is *not*. It is not the relation of "causality" or "identity". Concept by postulation blue does not *cause* concept by intuition blue. Concept by intuition blue is a multi-valued relation as Northrop, following Whitehead's analysis, reports in SFP. One relata of concept by intuition blue is the angstrom number currently associated with concept by postulation blue.[33] To assume that only one of the relata of a relation could cause that relation is as silly as assuming that the female (or the male) member of a marriage causes of the marriage.

Nor is the proper relation between postulation and intuition "identity",[34] as can easily been seen using "blue". Concept by postulation blue is not identical with concept by intuition blue, but is just one among many relata that go to form this complex secondary quality.

Or consider the following:

---

[33] For those familiar with the notation of symbolic logic the following example may help. Since concept by intuition blue is a multivalued relation we may symbolize it as follows: Babcd... where B = blue; a = light; b = intervening medium; c = percipient d = concept by postulation blue, i.e., the angstrom number etc. In English it is easy to confuse the two "blues" but no one could confuse "Babcdef..." (i.e., concept by intuition blue) with "Bd" (i.e., concept by postulation blue). Cf. next paragraph in the text.

[34] The only exception to this statement is when the object being known and the subject doing the knowing are identical. In other words, the concept by intuition "me" is identical to the concepts by postulation "me". I'm not sure I fully understand this.

It often happens, early in a play, that one is unable
to determine whether the directly inspected data
which one notes backstage are *merely* two-dimensional images of bookends painted on a curtain or
the correlates of the bookends of *real* three-dimensional books located on a shelf. Hence, one is confronted with the problem concerning whether the
visual image which one inspects is to be epistemically correlated with *merely* a two-dimensional
surface on a two-dimensional curtain or with one
two-dimensional surface of a three-dimensional
book. As the play develops one of the characters
goes backstage and pulls out the book. The images
associated with the latter act are compatible only
with one of the two possible hypotheses concerning
the epistemic correlate of the original data. Thus
one interpretation is eliminated, the hypothesis of
real three-dimensional books is established. (121-2.
Emphasis mine [35])

Neither identity nor causality is the proper relation between
the book and my visual image. (As for the relation of "appearance", see chapter three below.)

Note that the problem is What is the epistemic correlate
of one's directly inspected visual image? The problem is not
what is really real. Unlike (certain interpretations of) Plato and
Plotinus, there is in Northrop no propensity to degrade or
downgrade the world as it is known via concepts by intuition.
To experience the visual image in the theater is as epistemically valuable as knowing postulationally that it is, say, a curtain or a bookcase filled with books. The two sources of all our

---

[35] I don't know why Northrop uses "merely" to modify certain and "real" to
modify books. Both are equally valid epistemic correlates for the visual image in
question and both are equally real within a certain context of knowledge. The
"merely" and the "real" only seem appropriate after the wrong hypothesis has
been eliminated.

knowledge give information that is both complementary and supplementary. Without concepts by intuition we could never know the world in its particularity without concepts by postulation we could never know the world in its universality and necessity. We shall see more of the complementary nature of Northrop's epistemology when we examine MEW.

The procedure in the theater case described above is obviously "inductive"--we start with a concept by intuition experience and "guess" the nature of its epistemic correlate. But epistemic correlations are also needed if one is engaged in the converse procedure. Northrop instances Einstein's problem of "finding the empirically given epistemic correlates" of the ten variables of his metric tensor. Einstein already had the postulated factors that are known by concepts by postulation, but he needed to determine the operationally empirical epistemic correlates of these variables. (122)

To give one last example, section 22 of Einstein's 1916 GTR paper can be read as the elaboration of three of the most famous epistemic correlations in the history of science, viz., the behavior of rods and clocks in the static gravitational field, the bending of light rays and the motion of the perihelion of Mercury. Einstein specified what must obtain experimentally in order to confirm his theory.[36] So much for epistemic correlations.

We now have enough information to give a name to Northrop's epistemology. He calls it "logical realism in epis-

---

[36] The full title of chapter seven is "Epistemic correlations and operational definitions" and the reader interested in the similiarities and differences between the two from Northrop's point of view is advised to read the chapter for details. Suffice it to say that "operational meanings are not the basic meanings of the concepts constituting the deductively formulated theory" but are derived from "the basic concepts of mathematics and mathematical logic and from the" imagination of the most speculative metaphysical imaginations. (123)

temic correlation with radical empiricism." In other words, reason (in the form of concepts by postulation) epistemically correlated with the senses (in the form of concepts by intuition).

Chapters eight to twenty-four represent applications of
Northrop's epistemology to the logic of various sciences and
humanities. All of these chapters (except 19) were printed
elsewhere before inclusion in LSH. Obviously even a cursory
examination of all of them is out of the question here and I
have decided to restrict myself to two chapters X and XIII on
the body/mind problem and classical economic science respectively. Those more interested in quantum physics, biology,
poetry, sociology, world peace, religion and logic are directed to
LSH itself.

Northrop's solution to the mind-body problem depends
on his bifurcationist epistemology. He claims that each word,
"body" and "mind", has been used in two different senses and
little or no attention has been paid to this ambiguity. Concept
by intuition body does not get its meaning in the same way as
concept by postulation body. The same can be said of mind.
We have, in effect, four concepts, not two. And of the four, we
will discover only three of them are legitimate. Let's explore
this in more detail.

If we are talking about body in "terms of neurological
and other physiological concepts, which in turn are defined in
terms of chemical and physical concepts" (194) then we are
dealing with body as known through concepts by postulation.
On the other hand, if we are talking about the body given in
immediate, ineffable experience, then we are talking about the
body as known through concepts by intuition. The joining of
these two realms of knowledge via epistemic correlations gives
the body as completely known. This knowledge arrives on
parallel tracks, but it is a parallelism "not between body and
mind [the mistake the traditional parallelists made] but between the person as immediately apprehended as an associa-

tion and continuous sequence of sensuous aesthetic qualities denoted by concepts by intuition and the person as theoretically conceived as a neurological physiochemical system designated by concepts by postulation." (194-5)

These same considerations apply to "mind". If we mean "mind" in the sense of what is immediately given to consciousness then it is a concept by intuition and in that regard, not one whit different from body in its concept by intuition meaning. They are both immediately given, ineffable etc. What we have here is a "continuum of diverse factors presented with immediacy." "One feels a pain as one apprehends the yellow patch in the sky now. The realm given by concepts by intuition denotes one continuous world, not two diverse worlds, even when one concept by intuition bears the tag 'mental' and the other concept by intuition bears the tag 'physical'." (195)

But there is a second meaning to the word "mind", the one that goes back to Descartes and Locke and caused the problem we are attending to right now. "Mind" as a mental substance, inhabiting a different world from the world of science (or extension) and qualified by a list of predicates exclusive of the scientist's notion of body. The problem with this notion of "mind" is that it is "so empty and ambiguous that nothing of any definiteness can be deduced from it." (196) Yet the very meaning of such a concept, a concept by postulation, is to be found in its deductive consequences. Hence it has been discarded by most scientists and philosophers. Such treatment Northrop applauds.

Once it has been realized that it was concept by postulation mind that was causing the problem, getting rid of it is certainly one solution. But we must remember we have not eliminated concept by intuition mind. Its importance for, say, medicine is obvious. It enables you to tell the doctor "where it hurts." Then the doctor can apply concept by postulation knowledge of your body to, hopefully, make it stop hurting.

Now we can appreciate Northrop's conclusion that the "ultimate dualism is not between "body" and "mind," but between the immediately apprehended component of the person denoted by concepts by intuition and the theoretic component designated by verified scientific theory that is stated completely in terms of concepts by postulation. The complete person in his unity is these two aesthetic and theoretic components joined by the two-termed relation of epistemic correlation." (199)   Finally, let us turn to Austrian economics.

This essay on Austrian economics has a story behind it which Northrop relates in his *Prolegomena to a 1985 Philosophiae Naturalis Principia Mathematica*. In the early 1940's Joseph Schumpeter was conducting a graduate seminar in the department of economics at Yale University in which he was giving evidence of a purported theoretical economic dynamics. [This would make economics a predictive science.]   Northrop was asked to give a paper and in that paper he defended the view of Lionel Robbins that economic science has only a statics and not a dynamics and therefore had little or no predictive power.   So impressed was Schumpeter with Northrop's paper that he graciously requested Northrop to allow him to submit it to the Harvard Quarterly Economic Review where it was printed in November of 1941 and later in LSH.   Few scholars are so generous in the face of the death of their own theories. What was in that paper?

First it is necessary to be clear concerning what Northrop is NOT asserting vis-a-vis economic science. He is not claiming that they have no natural history data--obviously they do. Plenty of data!   Nor is he claiming, and this is the more important of the two claims, that they lack a deductively formulated theory.   What Northrop denies is that they can move via logical implication of deductive consequences, rather than "speculative extrapolation of the empirical curves of past economic events," to a description of a future state.   To prove this Northrop focuses on "(1) the basic concepts and postulates of economics, and (2) its empirical method of verification." (237)

The fundamental concept of all modern economics is "value."[37] It "reflects the want of some individual for some object or service. This means that the subject matter of economics is not the physical object or behavior itself but the desire of the individual for the object." (238) This means that an economic good is a relation (not an object or service) between the introspective desire of the valuer and the object or service desired. "Wants" is the primary concept and "preference" the fundamental relation in economics. This leads to the first postulate: "the foundation of the theory of value is the assumption that the different things that the individual wants to do have a different order." (239) The second postulate is "there are more than one factor of production." And thirdly, "we are not certain of future scarcities."[38] This last postulate seals, by itself, the fate of future predictions but Northrop thinks that concentration on the first postulate will yield more epistemological fruit and we shall follow his lead here.

That wants are the irreducible starting point of economics dooms in advance all those who would struggle to find in the object, some quality (labor was the most often proposed candidate from Smith to Marx) that makes it valuable. Wants are neither concept by postulation common sense objects (or services) nor immediately inspected concept by intuition sense data. Wants are concepts by intuition data given introspec-

---

[37] In order to distinguish economic value from ethical and political value Northrop uses valuation for the former. I will, however, use value throughout the remaider of this chapter.

[38] Northrop takes the three quotations from Lionel Robbins' An Essay on the Nature and Significance of Economic Science from 1935. A more recent effort, Man, Economy and the State, 1962, by the Austrian economist Murray Rothbard, contains the same postulates on its first five pages.

tively. But then the problem shifts. We no longer are looking for an economic dynamics but a criterion for public validity instead. How do we know economics is true for all individuals since we cannot introspect their introspected wants? According to Northrop, this is accomplished by ignoring what each individual wants on the species level and moving to the generic levels of wants, i.e., wants apart from any content. From this we get a universal truth, individuals have wants that they order according to a preference hierarchy.

But back to dynamics. The first requirement of any dynamics is the definition of "the state of the system at a given time, not merely with respect to its *generic* but also its *specific* properties. (244, Emphasis mine.) We have seen that economics fails this test. But even were this not true, even if economics could define the state of the system at a given time, since it lacks conservation laws (wants *do* increase and decrease over time) there is no way to establish the relation of necessary connection between present and future states. We may generalize this point by saying that any science that has a dynamics necessarily has specific (and not just generic) conservation laws of some kind. Since economic wants do not obey conservation laws, it is in principle impossible for economics to have a dynamics. This will remain true as long as the basic concepts are concept by intuition wants that remain in constant flux. Hume demonstrated that as long as we remain on the radical empirical level, mechanical causation, in the sense used by Newton, is a chimera.

To summarize: If, for a dynamics, one needs to know the specific properties of the fundamental entities of the system and that these entities or their properties obey conservation laws, economics fails on both counts.

There is one further consequence of Northrop analysis of economics that I want to mention, and that is its method of verifying its basic concepts and postulates. Since in physics the basic concepts and postulates refer to that which is in principle unobservable, verification takes place indirectly through the deduction of consequences and via epistemic correlations that specify experimental data that can then be checked by observation. But in economics, the postulates are radical empirical concept by intuition introspective wants and preferences that are self-evidently recognized to be true by anyone who cares to introspect for themselves. Thus the concepts and postulates are verified directly, not indirectly. As Northrop writes, "Physics tests its deductive theory indirectly by empirically checking its theorems; economics, directly by empirically confirming its postulates." (247)

Finally, consider the following epistemological consequence. We can take the last quoted sentence and, by generalizing over the nouns in physics and in economics, produce the notion that sciences whose basic concepts and postulates are concepts by postulation verify their deductive theory indirectly by empirically checking its theorems; sciences whose basic concepts and postulates are concepts by intuition verify those concepts and postulates directly. Thus we now have, at least along one dimension, an exact understanding of the differences between said sciences.

To summarize. According to Northrop, scientific inquiry takes place in three stages; the problem stage, the natural history stage and the hypothetical deductive stage. Each of these stages has several methods, distinct and irreducible to the others.

We are now ready for a book length application of Northrop's three stage theory of scientific inquiry, viz., to the book MEW.

CHAPTER 3

THE MEETING OF EAST AND WEST

Now that we have Northrop's epistemological terminology in place, the remainder of his work can be understood against that backdrop. MEW is an inquiry into world cultures as a propaedeutic to any future world understanding. Such world understanding is a necessary prelude to a just peace among nations. (We shall return to this theme of a just peace in chapter five.) With an unquenchable faith in the power of ideas, Northrop believes that in order to understand any given culture, one must needs understand their underlying philosophy and that is his project in MEW.

A succinct statement of that project is given by Northrop on p. 31-2 of LSH and is reproduced below. Note also how this statement conforms to the three stages of scientific inquiry as detailed in LSH.

[MEW] is concerned with the most pressing problem of value of our day--the problem, namely, of resolving the normative ideological conflicts which threaten the peace of the world. The first chapter, recording the first stage of inquiry, indicates how an analysis of this normative problem guides one to the specific factual information which must be determined before further effective discussion of the

problem can occur. . . . Chapters II to XI of MEW,
representing the second stage of inquiry, then
record the determination of these relevant facts by
methods which are as inductive and Baconian as the
subject matter will permit . . . . Chapter XII, the
third stage of inquiry, in MEW, because of the more
precise, purely factual information which the
Baconian second stage of the inquiry provided, then
succeeds in cornering the initial problem of value in
a specific and empirically answerable question of
fact, . . .The important thing to notice about the
analysis of the problem of value in MEW is that as
the analysis guided one to the relevant factual information necessary to clearly under-stand the
problem, the initial question, which appeared first
as a question of value to which scientific methods
did not seem to apply, became transformed over, as
the statement of the basic difficulty become more
evident and precise, into a specific question of fact
which scientific methods and scientific evidence
could and did answer.

Although chapter one of MEW gives the initial statement
of the problem, its most perspicuous formulation can be found
at the beginning of chapter twelve and falls into four major
parts:

(1) the relating of the East and the West; (2) the
similar merging of the Latin and Anglo-Saxon cultures; (3) the mutual reinforcement of democratic
and communistic values; and (4) the reconciliation
of the true and valuable portions of the Western
medieval and modern worlds. (436)

Northrop then goes on to state that running through these four
problems like a single thread in a gigantic tapestry is the general problem of "harmonizing the sciences and the humanities."
(436) Chapters two through eleven are concerned with revealing the basic philosophical assumptions that underlie these

problems. These philosophical assumptions lead to differences that are of two types: "those which differ because they refer to different factors [hereafter DF] in the nature of things, and those which conflict because they are affirming contradictory things of the same factor; [hereafter SF]." (437) These two factors are the aesthetic and theoretic factors, referred to by concepts by intuition and concepts by postulation respectively. The first difference that Northrop writes of in the passage quoted above can serve as an example of a DF problem. It has to do with the clash between those Eastern thinkers who find the aesthetic factor and hence reality as known by concepts by intuition to be paramount, and those (typically and predominantly the Western thinkers) who find the theoretical factor and hence reality as known by concepts by postulation to be of supreme importance.

The second difference that causes problems occurs between those who make contradictory assertions about the same factor [SF], usually the theoretic factor. Newton and Einstein can be instanced here since each make incompatible claims about absolute (or concept by postulation) space and time.[39]

Problem (1), is a DF problem, as has already been stated. All DF problems can be resolved by "removing the notion of each people that *nothing but* its theory is correct, thereby permitting each party to add to its own traditional ideals the equally perfect values of the other culture." (437) At the risk of trivializing the problem, consider an argument between Berkeley and Newton about whether a tree falling in an uninhabited forest make a sound. Berkeley says no; Newton yes. The difficulty is insuperable as long as either man thinks that sound is *nothing but* what his theory says it is. Once they real-

---

[39] For details see my essay "Grünbaum on Newton's Conception of Relative Space and Time" in the Appendix.

ize that sound has a concept by intuition as well as a concept by postulation meaning it turns out that they are both correct. There is no concept by intuition sound as long as no one is there to hear it (Berkeley) but there is a concept by postulation sound (Newton) even if the forest is empty of all hearers.

To appreciate how this solves problem (1) simply substitute "East" for "Berkeley" and "West" for "Newton" and you get a quick idea of how Northrop plans to reconcile the difficulties between East and West.[40] There is no *intrinsic* conflict between, say, the meditational experience of the Tao and the theoretic knowledge of the Euclidean geometry or Gibbs' statistical mechanics or Newtonian physics. These are simply more sophisticated versions of the non-conflictual relationship between Berkeley's and Newton's "sound" or between Van Gogh's green and electromagnetic green.

The solution to problem (1) also contains *part* of the solution to problem (2), the merging of the Latin and Anglo cultures. Taking Mexico as an example and referring back to his examination of that particular Latin-American culture in chapter 2, he reminds us of its "highly developed appreciation of the aesthetic and its religion of the emotions"-- all concept by intuition factors. We have already seen in our examination of problem (1) that these factors are compatible with the concept by postulation factors of the North. What makes the Latin-American problem more complex is the existence of two further problems, numbered (3) and (4) by Northrop. Due to the influence of communism and Catholicism, we must find a way to reconcile what is valuable in those factors with the valuable portions of democracy and modern Protestantism if reconciliation is to be possible. Since these problems are sepa-

---

[40] Despite my best efforts there is no way to read this sentence without a feeling of trivialization. The only remedy is a close perusal of Northrop entire text, especially chapters nine through eleven wherein Northrop reveals his deep understanding of Eastern philosophy, religion and culture.

rately numbered we shall follow Northrop and consider them sequentially.

Problem (3) concerns the "mutual reinforcement of democratic and communistic values." Northrop deals with this issue in pp. 465-471 of chapter XII. These (Northrop's) pages represent a distillation of chapters III and IV on British and American democracy and chapter VI on Russian Communism and the interested reader is referred to them for a more detailed elaboration on the shorten version that follows.

The locus of the first reinforcement of democratic and communistic values that Northrop discusses is in economics. As we saw in the preceding chapter, the Jevonian and Austrian economic theories are based, in their concepts and postulates, on concepts by intuition. The Communistic theory of economic value is based on concepts by postulation, especially abstract labor as the essence of all goods and services. Since these economic theories refer to different factors, the problem is a DF one, and hence should be reconcilable in the same way that problem (1) was. But, *pace* Northrop's optimism, no one has been able to develop a Marxian dynamics to complement the statics of the Austrians. In fact, as Northrop himself pointed out in his essay on Austrian economics in LSH, *no* concept by postulation economic science has been able to develop a dynamics. In this respect, Northrop's "solution" to the economic differences between democracy and communism seem more like a promissory note than his solutions to, say, problem (1) where both the concepts by intuition Eastern ideals and the concepts by postulation Western ideals already exist and have informed their respective cultures for thousands of years. Nevertheless, Northrop's strategy is identical with the one used to solve problem (1), since there is no *a priori* conflict between concepts by intuition and concepts by postulation.[41]

But economics is not the be all and end all of the theory of man and nature. Before democracy and communism can successfully reinforce each other, the "unjustified portions of . . . Marxian philosophy must be dropped" specifically, the Hegelian and Marxian notion that "the negation of any theory or thesis gives one and only one antithesis, and one and only one attendant synthesis." (467)   Whether in science or philosophy, this part of the dialectic seems false in the light of the following case histories. Take mathematics. Rejecting the parallel postulate in Euclid does not necessitate that the non-Euclidean geometry that one generates will allow none or many parallels to be drawn to a given line. In fact, an infinite number of geometries can be obtained from the negation of that famous postulate, depending on what it is replaced with. In Roman Catholicism, the partial negation of Augustine in the 13th century does not necessitate the philosophy of St. Thomas. You really need the inventive genius of Thomas and his free creations of the human mind to get what Thomas produced. Thomism is not a necessary and inevitable consequence of the dialectical negation of Augustine.

Although not mentioned in chapter XII, one must also reject any vestige of naive realism to the extent that it infests the thought of Marx via the influence of Feuerbach.[42] Northrop demonstrates that naive realism is self-contradictory on p. 66 of PAPP as follows:

---

[41] With the collapse of Communism, at least in Eastern Europe, and the clamoring of the people for a market economy, this "problem" may cease to be a problem.

[42] For more on the naive realism of Feuerbach and its influence on Russian Communism, see PAPP, p. 66 and my essay "Northrop on Russian Communism" in Studies in Soviet Thought, 32 (1986) 133-154.

The mark of such an epistemology is that it attempts to define the purportedly public substances in terms of directly sensed or introspected properties. But all sensed or imagined items of knowledge are imageful and all images are relative, not merely to the observer's frame of reference and to the percipient, but even . . . to different senses organs and moments of perception of the same percipient. The naive realist means, however, by his public substances something that exists with its determinate imageful properties independently of its relation to the observer. Clearly, therefore, it is self-contradictory to define an object existing independently of its relation to the observer in terms of sensed or introspected imageful properties all of which are relative to the perceiver.

This is a SF problem. Naive realism is incompatible with logical realism (or scientific realism) and since the latter is confirmed and the former not, the former must go.

As for (4), "the reconciliation of the true and valuable portions of the Western medieval and modern worlds", this is also predominately a SF problem. The method of solving SF type problems has been noted above; find the contradiction and eliminate it.

When Northrop talks about medieval philosophy and theology, he usually has St. Thomas Aquinas in mind. What are the "true and valuable portions" of St. Thomas, and what has to go--that is the question.[43]

First, "Aristotle's conception of nature as a hierarchic system governed by final causes" (282); second, the negative attitude toward democracy as expressed (and quoted by

---

[43] Most of what follows can be found in chapter VII of MEW, "Roman Catholic Culture and Greek Science."

Northrop on 282) by Pope Leo XIII in his Encyclical, *Immortale Dei*, of 1885 which denounces the notion that all men are "equal in this life. . .[and] that each is so far master of himself as in no way to come under the authority of another . . ." This hierarchic political notion follows from the Catholic hierarchic notion of nature.   Both Aristotle's conception of nature and the Pope's conception of politics based on a false natural science must go.

To see what are the merits of the medieval Catholic theology one has only to contrast it with modern Protestantism. The soul/body dichotomy and the widening gap between religion and science, ethics and science, art and science, all leading to moral and spiritual relativism are some of the demerits of modern Protestantism, which does not suffer from a want of knowledge, but rather a hodge-podge of disparate knowledges lacking the "saving, organizing interconnections between the different portions of human knowledge." (288)   In a word, integration.   We need a modern Aquinas to integrate contemporary science, religion, ethics, art, politics etc.   The tool of such an integration is philosophy, pursued according to the method of its Greek founders, [i.e.,] natural science made articulate with respect to its basic assumptions on the theoretical side. Conversely, natural science is, with respect to philosophy, the anchor to windward which prevents philosophy from degenerating into idle, futile speculation, and which through philosophy prevents humanism from degenerating into moral relativism and sophistry.   (288) I would suggest, and this book is dedicated to the proposition, that Northrop is an integrator in the tradition of St. Thomas.

Having now indicated the direction of Northrop's proposed solutions to the four basic problems of MEW, I want to direct the reader's attention to the paragraph from 436 in which Northrop outlined the problems and to the fifth problem which he did not number but I enclosed in square brackets.

His reason for not giving a separate number to the problem of "harmonizing the sciences and the humanities" is that it runs through the other four. Since it is more general, its solution is more difficult but involves one of Northrop's greatest insights, viz., epistemic correlations.   It is also the solution to the Galilean, Cartesian modern problem--the nature of appearance. (440-454)

With the rise of modern science came the reintroduction of the notion that the sensed world is not the same as the intellected world.   We can see this in "Galilei's statement that sensed heat does not belong to the object and Newton's emphasis upon the difference between sensed space and time and mathematical space and time. . ." (439) But no sooner does one make such a bifurcation then one is confronted with question "How is the world of sense related to the world of reason?" The answer given was that the world of sense is a *mere* appearance of the <u>real</u> world known by science.   The scientists were especially fond of this explanation--after all, it gave them a corner on the reality market and kicked the poet and his ilk right where Plato had kicked him two millennia earlier.

The observer was responsible for the appearance, since without the observer, no appearance.   Remove the observer and all sensed qualities "would be abolished and annihilated" taught Galileo. (440)

Let us take a closer look at "appearance" relation. Appearance was understood to be a three term relation "in which the material object in the 'true, real and mathematical' space and time of the theoretic component is one term, the observer is a second term, and the apparent sensed qualities in the apparent relative sensed space and time of the aesthetic component are a third term." (440)

The question as to the nature of this "observer" naturally arose and Northrop reviews various answers.   For example, Hobbes, in strict materialist fashion, thought that the observer could be nothing but material atoms, but such an answer broke down when it was noted that according to Newton's laws, such an observer would only "undergo certain accelerations" and not give rise to a world of secondary qualities. This seemed to necessitate a type of substance that could give rise to the very qualities we all experience. Enter Locke's "mental substance" theory. On one level this solved the problem, especially if, like Locke, one did not look too deeply into a solution that, in retrospect, seems suspiciously ad hoc. On another level, it gave rise to "all the problems of modern philosophy and psychology." (441) I shall not rehearse those difficulties here. Suffice it to say that no one was able to provide a satisfactory solution to the "appearance" question, specifically, the problem of how a material atom(s) was able to jump across (theoretic) space and bang into an unbangable-into purely spiritual mind and give rise to, say, a color, proved insuperable.

This gives one pause to reconsider the so-called "solution". As we saw in chapter two during our examination of the soul/body problem, there is no reason to retain the idea of a mental substance in its concept by postulation meaning. Without a mental substance there is nothing to which a body could appear, and so we can jettison the "appearance" relation.

Northrop suggests we replace the defunct "appearance" relation with his notion of "epistemic correlation" consider as a two term relation capable of integrating and uniting the aesthetic concept by intuition aspect of *any given thing* with its theoretic concept by postulation aspect. The two-termedness of the epistemic correlation reflects the fact that we have two ways of knowing the world, sense and reason, as well as our philosophical need to integrate these two ways. Without this integration, we either get particular knowledge in all its sensuousness, but little or no predictive power and no universality; or we get the power and universality of syntactical equations of the real without any of the warmth of felt qualities. Why

philosophers in the tradition felt that they had to choose between nominalism and realism vis-a-vis their fundamental
concepts for under-standing the world beggars the imagination
and is, according to Northrop, one of great "errors of traditional
science and of traditional philosophy." Since philosophy is a
domain in which reason is predominant, and reason finds the
universality and abstractness of concepts congenial, the sensed
world was usually deprecated and those who did not join in
this deprecation, who saw the tremendous value in art, the
emotions etc., were known as irrationalists and often denied
the status of philosophers, and certainly of scientists. It also
led to the identification of the sensed world with the principle
of evil. (Identified by Plato as the "indeterminate dyad" and
by Aristotle as "prime matter.") But the dispute between the
particular and the universal, between rationalism and empiricism, between sense and reason is wrong and unnecessary.
The aesthetic aspect of the world is just as important and certainly as fundamental and irreducible as the theoretic. But one
can never realize this as long as one regards the sensed world
as a "mere" appearance of the "real" world. Northrop's insight
is to realize and take advantage of the two fundamental ways
we have of knowing "the world" and to connect them by epistemic correlations. Using Northrop's jargon we can summarize
the above by saying that the concept by intuition "blue" is not a
mere appearance of concept by postulation "blue". Rather the
former is one way and the latter is another way of knowing,
what in some sense, is the same item. The latter is not the
cause of the former, nor is it identical with it, nor is it an appearance of it. Rather they are correlatives; complementary
ways of knowing and hence both good. (See Figures I and II on
next page.)

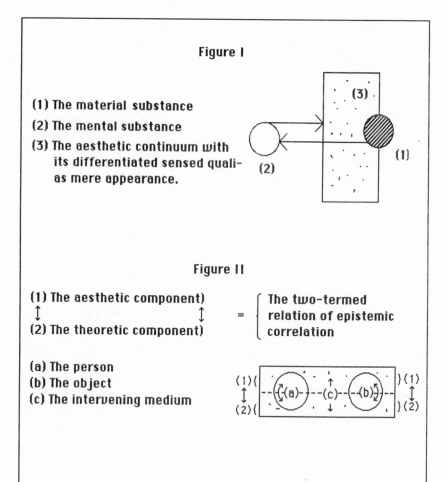

Figure I

(1) The material substance
(2) The mental substance
(3) The aesthetic continuum with
   its differentiated sensed quali-
   as mere appearance.

Figure II

(1) The aesthetic component)
(2) The theoretic component)

= { The two-termed
    relation of epistemic
    correlation

(a) The person
(b) The object
(c) The intervening medium

Reprinted from MEW p. 453

> Therefore, we may conclude that any complete thing whatever must be regarded as made up of (a) the ineffable, emotional, aesthetic materials of the equally ineffable and emotional aesthetic continuum common to oneself and all things, and (b) the unseen theoretic component which can be adequately designated only by thought and postulationally prescribed theory checked through its deductive consequences. (450)

Two complications must now be indicated, but the reader who desires a more elementary introduction may skip or skim this and the following two paragraphs. The first complication has to do with the fact that not all epistemic correlations are one-one. A one-one correlation exists, for example, in the relation between the points and lines of a map and the cities and the roads of a particular geographic area. Were this the case of the aesthetic and the theoretic, there would be an identity of form between them. But this is rarely the case. "It is this which permits sensed nature to differ from experimentally verified mathematically defined, theoretically conceived nature." (451)

The second complication arises from a fact noticed by Whitehead, viz., that "'Sensed objects ingress into nature in many-termed relations.'" (452) Red is not an intrinsic quality or property of the rose, but a multi-valued function of the observer's rod and cones, the intervening medium, the object itself etc. "These considerations force us to conclude that the relation of a sensed quality to the, in part, theoretically designated object which it is seen apparently to qualify, is not a two-termed relation of intrinsic predication, but a many-termed relation." (452)

Now this fact has typically been supposed to require the positing of a mental substance to function as one of the relata and for whom the color is a mere appearance. But this is incorrect. For the color of the rose is a function "of the observer's bodily sense organs" as well as other factors. We can change the color we see by altering our rods and cones, wearing sunglasses or getting drunk. The relativity is a relativity to our bodies, not to some ghost locked up inside us.

Putting this in terms of the concepts of this chapter, Northrop writes that the relativity of the color of the rose "is the result of a naturalistic relation between the rose which is an aesthetically immediate-theoretically designated object, the intervening medium which is an aesthetically immediate-theoretically designated object, and the observer who in turn is an aesthetically immediate-theoretically designated object."[44] (453) Using the adjectival expression "aesthetically immediate-theoretically designated object" before all of the relata [the rose, the intervening medium and the observer] serves to bring home the important difference between Northrop's theory and the dualist approaches of Descartes and Locke. Both the observer and the object observed are in the same aesthetic-theoretically designated world of discourse, and the problems of interaction between a soul and body, between ghosts and ghasts[45] cease to exist. Knowledge then becomes a purely naturalistic affair reminiscent of Aristotle's dictum at the beginning of the ΠΕΡΙ ΨΥΧΗΣ that the study of the soul is part of natural philosophy.

A final question remains. How does replacing the three termed relation "appearance" with the two termed relation

---

44 I assume Northrop would include the light source, either as part of the aesthetically immediate-theoretically designated intervening medium, or on its own.

45 Northrop's coinage to designate the material equivalent of a ghost. Since a ghost is a soul without a body, a ghast is a body without a soul. There are neither ghost nor ghasts in Northrop's system.

"epistemic correlation" solve the problem concerning the relationship between the sciences and the humanities? First of all, what is the problem? It is a breakdown in communication. "At best scientists and humanists find it difficult to communicate with one another. At worst, bitterness occurs."[46] For a generalist and integrationist like Northrop, a breakdown in communication between disciplines devoted to giving one the ability to know oneself and the world is a major disaster, akin to a breakdown in the central nervous system of an animal. Successful communication requires that someone (probably philosophers) "specify the more elementary common denominator factors which are necessary to relate the *specific contents* of successively generalized theories of naturalistic scientific knowledge in Western culture to the *specific contents* of its various humanistic intrinsic [non-instrumental] values." In order to make Northrop's answer as concrete as possible, let us look at his own example science and its relationship to the art of music.

In 4.014 of the *Tractatus* Wittgenstein writes,

A gramophone record, the musical idea, the written notes, and the sound waves, all stand to one another in the same internal relation of depicting that holds between language and the world.
They are all constructed according to a common logical pattern.

---

[46] F. S. C. Northrop, "The Relation between Naturalistic Scientific Knowledge and Humanistic Intrinsic Values in Western Culture", from Contemporary American Philosophers, 2nd series, ed. J. E. Smith, (London, Allen and Unwin, 1970), 107. The next quotation is from the same page. Northrop wrote on this problem throughout his entire life. The first major article, "The Functions and Future of Poetry" appeared in Furioso (VOL. 1, #4, 1941) and was subsequently reprinted as chapter ix of LSH; the problem was also discussed in the current chapter of MEW and the article just quoted. In the text I will followed the latter.

Without suggesting that Northrop would buy into Wittgenstein's picture theory of meaning, the thought expressed here is one of "formal similarity." The scientific laws of acoustics known since the time of Democritus and Theaetetus and given mathematical expression in Book VII of Euclid are confirmed today not only in the physics laboratory but also in the concert hall. "For were the composer's, conductor's and all the player's scores not formally similar, in the mathematical logician's many-entity-termed relationally analytic sense of similar relations, the result would be auditory anarchy . . . instead of . . . Western classical music. . ."[47] It is surely no accident the Pythagoras was credited with both mathematical and musical innovations. And it is the Pythagorean or Diatonic scale, with its Euclid Book VII natural number ratios, that is the invariant standard by which all Western music is judged to be beautiful.[48]

Similar ratios must also be built into the performers instruments so that they may properly function when the conductor arithmetically beats out the tempo. Northrop concludes that "the similar relationally analytic ratios not only literally measure intrinsic or ideal beauty, but also, by way of the score and instruments, measure operationally defined instrumental beauty."[49] From this Northrop concludes that one can confirm the acoustical theories of Democritus in two ways--"in any laboratory course on the physics of sound, but also by anyone who

---

[47] Ibid. 128.

[48] Exception must be made for post-Bach keyboard instruments that have been well tempered to accord with Book V, definition 5 of Euclid. The key ratio for the well tempered scale the twelfth root of 2 over 1, i.e., $^{12}\sqrt{2}/1$.

[49] See Northrop's "The Relationally Analytic and the Impressionistically Concrete Components of Western Music" in <u>Journal of Research in Music Education</u>, Vol. 19, #4, 1971, 401.

goes to a symphony and fully understands and concretely experiences what is occurring there."[50]

The heard sound is epistemically correlated with the theoretical sound, the latter is not a mere appearance of the former. Art is as equally and fundamentally valuable a way of knowing the world as science. Since epistemology is one of the most difficult disciplines that man must master, it is silly to reject any viable method of gaining knowledge simply because, by some a priori criterion, they are unlike some preferred method(s).

Much of Northrop's theory is difficult, both to acquire and retain. In order to ease the task somewhat it may be helpful to concretize the theory in the figure of a man who most dramatically embodies it. To pick "one man in the Western history who more than any other came nearer to the full richness of the truth, the choice would fall . . . on the great Florentine, Leonardo da Vinci. For with him . . . aesthetic and . . . scientific knowledge are indissolubly wedded because the foundations of immediate experience and rational knowledge are one and the same." (SFP, 292)

---

[50] Ibid. 401-2.

CHAPTER 4

THE TAMING OF NATIONS

As he did in MEW and true to the epistemology detailed in LSH, Northrop begins TON with a statement of the problem to be solved, viz., how can we achieve a successful international policy? How is it possible for nation's to collaborate? This assumes that it is desirable for nations to engage in collaboration, an assumption that Northrop argues for in chapter two. He believes that in this atomic age, our only choice is collaboration or suicide.[51] But is collaboration possible? ". . . can there be a science of international relations?" (2)

Northrop's affirmative reply to the last question is couched in terms of a chemistry analogy.

> No one would suppose that he had created a science of chemistry if he approached the subject from the stand point of the properties of merely one of the chemical elements. An objective, sympathetic description and understanding of all the different kinds of chemical material in the universe is obviously necessary for chemical science. (2-3)

---

51 The alternatives he discusses and dismisses in chapter two are power politics and isolationism.

Likewise with international relations. Before any theory of foreign policy for any nation can be proffered, the character of at least all major nations must be determined. Fortunately, there are the three sciences of cultural sociology, cultural anthropology and the philosophy of culture that can, when used properly, provide the method for determining the character of any nation.

Once the character of any nation is determined, Northrop then applies Ehrlich's suggestions for the creation of effective positive law, i.e., base the latter on the very character of that particular political unit.[52]   This character Ehrlich calls the living law.

> Positive law is effective law only when it corresponds to the underlying living law. By positive law Ehrlich meant the legal constitutions and statutes that are introduced and the legal institutions which apply and enforce these constitutional principles and constitutionally legislated statutes. By the living law, he meant the underlying community habits and embodied norms of the majority of the people to which the positive law is applied, quite apart from the positive law itself. (265)

Northrop concludes that for effective international policy for any nation three tasks must be accomplished: first, the living law of each national and cultural group must be specified. Second, the relationships between each national and cultural group must also be determined. In some cases the living law of one nation may be compatible with the living law of another.

---

[52]   One can imagine the complexities of the living law when the "unit" is the whole world.

But in other cases this may not be so. Finally, the third task is to create a foreign policy as well as an international positive law "in the light of these international living law findings."

But perhaps it might be objected that a foreign policy of isolationism backed by overpowering defensive military might is the answer. We'll simply mind our own business. Northrop's chapter two, with its title "Pearl Harbor, Hiroshima and Korea", is designed to answer this query.   He quotes Senator Arthur H. Vanderberg who wrote that Dec. 7, 1941 "ended isolationism for any realist." (11)

Hiroshima taught us that even defensive power politics can be literal dynamite in an atomic age. A more peaceful means of settling disputes needs to be found.

Between Hiroshima and Korea, the United Nations was born in San Francisco. Northrop has some interesting things to say about the U. N., of which more in due course. Within the context of our current chapter, he is concerned to focus on some of the positive accomplishments of the U. N. in its response to the very real challenge in Korea.[53]

First, the legally constituted world community demonstrated in a way which any prospective aggressor will not forget that the legally self-organized world community does not propose, after the manner of the League of Nations before the aggression of Japan in Manchuria and Mussolini in Abyssinia, to be an institution of mere peace-affirming oratory and dead-letter words. Secondly, Northrop believes that the U. N. action in Korea makes it evident to aggressor nations that we will not have another Munich and to the war such conferences inevitably lead. When brigands talk peace but act war, defensive power is the proper answer. Northrop concludes that the U. N.

---

53   The similarities with the Gulf "War" are many and it may not be amiss for the reader to draw the obvious conclusions about what Northrop would have thought of the handling of Iraq by the U. N. For the weaknesses of the U. N., see below.

and the United States can be proud of Korea. Hindsight reveals that, despite having the third largest military budget in the world, North Korea still has to be content with the adjective "North" as part of it name. Northrop summarizes his findings as follows:

> Pearl Harbor demonstrates the political and finan-
> cial folly of neutrality and its isolationism and of
> both defensive and offensive power politics as a
> basis for the foreign policy of the United States or
> any other nation. It reminds us that there are
> Asian imperialists. Hiroshima tells us that we are
> in an atomic age, and thereby makes the establish-
> ment of an effective, legally constituted world
> community a child of necessity. Korea . . . tells us,
> for all its shortcomings [that the U. N. is] something
> more than verbal oratory obscuring a dead letter
> and has in all probability already prevented a third
> world war. (24-5)

But if Korea represents a prideful event for the U. N. and the United States, Northrop does not think the same can be said for India and its response.

India was a signatory to the United Nations charter in 1945. That document clearly indicates the methods of peaceful resolution that the U. N. may employ against any aggressor, viz., "law backed by police power." Note that this is not the method of Mahatma Gandhi in which non-attachment and me-diation are employed and recourse to force of any kind is for-bidden.[54] Yet Prime Minister Nehru could not have been more

---

54 Those who love paradoxes of self reference would no doubt point out that Gandhi was very "attached" to this method and would not compromise his position through "mediation". To quote Northrop "For all its intuitive, open-hearted toleration and its 'middle way,' Gandhiji's and the traditional Asian's moral way to peace is not neutral. It takes a side; the intuitive Asian side." (60)

explicit when he told the Congress of the United States that whenever "'freedom is endangered, or justice threatened, or where aggression takes place, we cannot be and shall not be neutral.'" (29) Less than a year later, when North Korea aggressed upon the South, not only did Nehru announce India's neutrality, but, as the many quotations which Northrop intercalates throughout chapter three indicate, he accused "the majority of the United Nations and especially the United States" of warmongering and warmaking. (30) Of the three reasons given by Nehru for this shameful about-face, the most pertinent for our purposes is Gandhi's philosophy of non-violence. As pointed out above, this is not the way to peace adopted by the signatories of the United Nations charter. And they are not compatible methods, at least in the sense that if one eschews violence even against force wielding aggressor nations, then one cannot logically endorse or employ violence when the going gets tough. Perhaps Nehru had a change of heart, if not of head. Recalling the overwhelming influence that Gandhi had on him, it is quite conceivable that Nehru felt that a return to the methods of non-violence was appropriate. [Northrop is reluctant to give the Prime Minister this out, especially since Nehru is not above sending in the police to quell riots in his own country. More on this in due course.] It would seem that an examination of the spiritual principles of Gandhi are called for.

For Gandhi, the "Hindu's *Bhagavadgita* is 'the book par excellence for the knowledge of the Truth'". Actually, the situation is a little more complicated. Not only was Gandhi influenced by Christian and Muslim religious works, but his reading of the *Gita* is a selective one, as anyone familiar with the text can appreciate. Gone are the incitements to war, the prescriptions for a rigid caste society and the appeal to legal codes as a means for settling disputes. Given these redactions, Gandhi's Hinduism is equivalent to Buddhism. Here we have a purely Asian Hinduism with the ancient Aryan elements dropped.[55]   The Laws of Manu are one of these elements. "Of him who is always ready to strike, the whole world stand in awe; let him therefore make all creatures subject to himself even by the employment of force." (90)   This is precisely what Gandhi rejected.

According to him, the fundamental teaching of the *Gita* is to teach us how to "act without desire for the fruit" of one's acts.   To live without attachment to any determinate thing.   The only "attachment" is to "the intuitively felt, all-embracing immediacy in its timelessness and formlessness which is Brahman", i.e., to what Northrop has termed the undifferentiated aesthetic continuum.

In practice, when disputes arise, one avoids, as far as possible, the appeal to determinate legal codes and "pursues the Buddhist-Gita 'middle way' between the determinate theses of the disputants, by fostering the all-embracing intuitively felt formlessness common to all men and things." (57)

But is this effective for world law?   One doubts it, especially if one looks not at Nehru's Gandhian words when he states that India must remain neutral vis-a-vis Korea, but at his actions within the borders of his own India.   Time and again New Delhi has had to send in the army, e.g., in "Hyderabad, Kashmir and the other princely states and Pakistan." (60)   Far from the method of Gandhi being effective for the world, it has had very limited success even in India itself.   After gaining its freedom from the British, "[m]assacres of Hindus, Sikhs and Muslims broke out almost everywhere.   Tens upon tens of thousands were butchered in cold blood.   Constitutional pro-

---

55 These elements were the result of the Aryan invasion that occurred around 1500 B. C. Northrop also reminds us of the two other major additions to ancient purely Asian Indian culture, the Muslim invasion of 1192 A. D. and the British invasion of 1757.

cesses backed by police power were required to bring the situation back into a semblance of order." (87)

Two conclusions force themselves upon Northrop. First, Nehru and India cannot be exonerated in their position of neutrality toward Korea and antipathy toward the United Nations and the United States concerning Korea. Second, Gandhi's Buddhist-Gita method of peaceful mediation cannot supplant the United Nations law backed by police power method. Nevertheless, one must always remember it forms a part of the living law of not only India, but of Asia in general.

> The mentality of Asia proper rises out of Hinduism, Buddhism, Taoismand Confucianism. This Far Eastern mentality embraces India (except for her remaining Muslim minority), Tibet, Burma, Thailand, Ceylon, Bali, Indo-China, China, Korea and Japan. The four Far Eastern religions and philosophies proved the basis of . . . 'the solidarity between Asians.' This solidarity is to be distinguished from the solidarity of Islam as well as from the influence of Western nationalism whether the latter be exerted by the free democracies or by Marxist Soviet Communism. (68)

Now for a brief glance at Islam. Northrop devotes chapters five and eight to Islam. [The latter bears the rather prophetic title "The Resurgence of Islam" and anyone reading the text today, after the 1991 Gulf War, has to remind themselves that this book was copyrighted in 1952.]

Islam is closer to the West than either of India's two systems we have examined thus far. Both Aryan Hinduism and non-Aryan Hinduism required much of the sympathetic researcher, the gap is so great. In Northrop's technical terminology we can state that the gap arises from the fact the Far East places a greater (almost exclusive) emphasis on concepts by intuition, especially the undifferentiated aesthetic continuum whereas the West has chosen to focus, thanks to the Greeks, on concepts by postulation, especially those by intellection for its understanding of nature, man and God.

But Islam shares many of our cultural sources, specifically "the religion of the Old and New Testaments the science and philosophy of the Greeks." (69)   Islam adds to these "the revelation of God through Mohammed as recorded in the Quran," which they regard as the fulfillment of a movement begun with Moses and carried forward by Jesus.

What does Islam have in common with the Hebrew-Christian tradition?   First, all of nature, man included, is "the creation of an omniscient and omnipotent personal God who is immortal and *determinate* in character. . . . Second, each individual person has a determinate immortal soul, different from that of any other person." (70)   This leads to the conception of moral man as one who lives by, and if necessary dies for, a set of determinate principles.   Add this to the Greek discovery that an individual man or event is "an instance of technically formulated universal laws" and one produces the Western conception of justice before which all men are equal.[56]

RUSSIAN COMMUNISM

Northrop believes that a consistent philosophy, i.e., his, has the virtue of identifying and integrating the basic insights of the classical West with the intuitively given, all embracing vastness of the East.   But he warns, there is "one difficulty in

---

[56] This paragraph should not be construed in such a way so as to conceal the fact that there are many differences between Islam and the Hebrew-Christian tradition. Northrop himself mentions in chapter 6 of TON two of the most important points of divergence; viz., the Islamic emphasis on the necessary unity of church and state as well as the close connection between the military and the religious aspects of life.

the way. This is Russian Communism." (226) It is to an examination of this system of ideas that we now turn.

Although Northrop devotes all of chapter twelve to an analysis of communism, this is not the first nor the last time he will do so. The first occasion was in 1946 in MEW. His last investigation occurred in 1960 in PAPP. Sheer numbers tell us why. Communism is in whole or in part the ruling belief system of nearly two-thirds of the world's population. No plan for world law can hope to succeed that does not take communism into account. Our exposition will incorporate materials from all three of these chapter length studies.[57]

The fountainhead for the philosophy of communism is, of course, Karl Marx. To understand Marx we must understand the three chief ideological influences on him, viz., German philosophy, French Socialism and English political economy. From the first, the figure of Hegel is paramount since it was through the lenses of the Hegelian dialectic that Marx viewed the other two. As Lenin wrote in his Teaching of Karl Marx: "Marx and Engels regarded Hegelian dialectics . . . as the greatest achievement of classical German philosophy." (MEW, 223) This enabled Marx to regard those democratic rights respecting cultures influenced by Locke and Hume, not as the final telos of Western political development, but as the antithesis of the thesis known as medieval aristocracy and in need of real revolution in order to achieve the ultimate synthesis in communism. Mention must also be made of Luther. "When Luther struck his blow for the German people, he shifted man's conception of nature and the relation of himself to nature as known through the universal laws of deductively formulated scientific theory to nature as given inductively." (246) That

---

57 What follows is a much shorter version of my paper "Northrop on Russian Communism" that appeared in Studies in Soviet Thought, 32, (1986) 133-154. See appendix B for the longer version.

meant the virtual elimination of concepts by postulation (and a
fortiori concepts by intellection) as an instrument for understanding man and their replacement with radical empirical
concepts by intuition, effectively restricting the intent of Jesus
and the New Testament to the interpretation of each individual
German reader rather than to a corps of scholastically trained
experts.   Henceforth man would be known as nothing more
than a "mere citizen of the German Volk" Marx continued this
fractionating process by replacing the nation with the small
class of oppressed factory workers.   "Thereby moral man was
corrupted from being a citizen of the universe, under determinate laws the same for all men [including Jews], into being
the leader of the members of a small class in society guided by
a restricted and arbitrary concern with nothing but material
clothes, shoes, technological tools and other purely material
values." (207)

Northrop also mentions Feuerbach, from whom Marx took
and modified both naive realism and materialism.   From Smith
and Ricardo he took and modified the labor theory of value.
Although this is of the utmost importance for Marx's purpose,
we needn't linger over it, since it represents a point of similarity rather than difference between Marx and the free democ-
racies who rely on Smith, Ricardo et al.   To appreciate why
Northrop sees communism as an obstacle to world peace, it is
necessary to focus on the *differences*   between it and capitalism, not the similarities.   An especially important difference
is the communistic theory of the state.

Marx accepts the Hegelian distinction between "society"
and the "state."   Society, defined as "the organic system of
individuals determined by the production relations in the dialectical process of history" has always existed, whereas the
state, defined as "a more restricted social organization within
society, arising out of the dialectical conflict of class interests
by mean of which those who control the means of production

oppress those who do not , . . . " (MEW, 234) has not, at least in its modern, oppressive and increasingly alienated form. Since the capitalists will not hand over the reins of the state willingly, revolution is dialectically logically required. This will bring the proletariat, or more correctly the Party vanguard into power and constitutes the first stage of the revolution eventuating in a stateless and classless society. But why is the first stage necessary at all--why not simply move to the stateless condition--what need have we of the dictatorship of the Party vanguard and the state control which is its necessary manifestation? If Marx had been simply a power political thinker, seizure of the apparatus of power would have been sufficient and the revolution would have been a one-step procedure. But Marx knew that positive law and all the guns in the state's arsenal are not enough to insure acceptance of the living law. As soon as the habits and beliefs of the masses are brought into line with Marxian theory, (and this is one of the most important functions of the Communist state) the second stage will appear and the state will automatically wither away.

It hardly needs to be mentioned that this is not the Jeffersonian conception of a limited state charged with the protection of individual rights of life, property etc. This forebodes an encounter between communism and democracy.

Lenin tells us that "Democracy is of great importance for the working class in its struggle for freedom against the capitalists. But democracy is by no means a boundary that must be not overstepped it is only one of the stages in the process of development from feudalism to capitalism, and from capitalism to communism." (MEW, 293-4) This is democracy as a mere means to an end, a mere dialectical moment on the inevitable road to the revolution.

Democracy has a post-revolutionary sense, but again it represents an evanescent state at best which will wither away to give place to pure communism. Note that neither pre- nor post-revolutionary democracy is what the West means by democracy. So when the words "democracy" and "democratic reform" are bandied about at high-level conference tables, our politicians are in never-never land if they think they have gained a victory when the Communists agree to democratic re- forms, democratic processes   etc. for a pre-revolutionary coun- try, since democracy means a withering away of democracy in a post-revolutionary Communist state.

Nor is the constitution of 1936 evidence of a move away from the Marxian toward the Lockean concept of democracy. Northrop cites two articles from the Russian Constitution to show this, Articles 131 and 141.   Article 131 concludes as fol- lows: "Persons making attacks upon public socialist property shall be regarded as enemies of the people."   According to Beatrice Webb this means that "No criticism of the living phi- losophy of the Communist party is permitted in the Soviet Union . . . There is a[n] absolute prohibition within the USSR of any propaganda advocating the return of the Communist party to capitalist profit-making, or even to any independent think- ing on the fundamental social issues about possible new ways of organizing men in society, new forms of social activity, and new development of the socially established code of conduct." (MEW, 242)   So much for freedom of speech.   Northrop is also concerned about the meaning of Article 141 as it affects "guar- anteed freedoms."   "Candidates for elections shall be nominated by electoral districts.   The right to nominate candidates   shall be ensured to public organizations trade unions co-operatives organizations of youth cultural societies."   Stalin himself ex- pands this to mean: "In the Soviet Union, in the land where the dictatorship of the proletariat is in force, no important political or organizational problem is ever decided by our soviets (the elected legislative bodies) and other mass organizations, with- out directives from our Party.   In this sense, we may say that the dictatorship of the proletariat is substantially the dictatorship of the Party, as the force which effectively guides the proletariat." (MEW, 243)   Since political power rests with the Party and not with the people, membership becomes a necessity--yet as the Webbs have written, the party is very selective in its recruitment (2 1/2 million members from a nation of 192 million in 1946), the main criterion being acceptance of the creed of Karl Marx.   That creed " . . . will have nothing to do the with supernatural.   It admits nothing to be true which cannot be demonstrated by the 'scientific method' of observation, experimentation, ratiocination and verification."   (MEW, 244) Northrop notes sardonically that Marxism itself does not pass such a test.

   But what of this claim to be scientific in their philosophy. With SFP behind us, we are especially cognizant of the ambiguity in the word "science." Northrop reminds us of the bifurcation of science from morality by Kant and the primacy given to the latter by Fichte.   Henceforth, ". . . instead of the theory of man and nature discovered by a factually controlled scientific study determining man's beliefs and evolving historical, cultural institutions, the process of history itself became the determining factor, . . ." (Ibid.) Couple this with the Hegelian presupposition that nature obeys the logic of dialectic and the claim that the communists ". . . are realistic, scientific empiricists looking objectively at the historical process and merely reporting what is happening to it as a whole is a sheer pose. . ." (MEW, 246)   The magnitude of the pose is eloquently revealed by the fact that science and dialectic are incompatible, as an examination of the scientific theories and the nature they expose indicates.   Northrop opines that in none of the major theories of nature since Newton does the nature revealed by those theories exhibit the dialectic.   If this be the case, then we can demonstrate by reference to nature that at least one point of the communistic   philosophical theory is unequivocally false.[58] Nor is nature revealed to be revolutionary--rather biological nature appears to be evolutionary. In addition, ". . . the advent of a new species does not involve the wiping out of the preceding species by a logic of negation after the manner in which the proletariat is supposed to wipe out the bourgeoisie." (MEW, 250-1) More important for the purposes of world law, the dialectic does not even apply, in toto, to the reconstruction of cultural institutions when a new philosophy replaces an older one, e.g., when Thomas Aquinas moved the Catholic Church from Augustine and Plato to Aristotle. If Northrop is correct, one is confronted with the following alternative: science or dialectic.[59]   Science excludes dialectic and revolution, whereas dialectic excludes, or at least ignores, the results of Newton, Gibbs, Maxwell et al. Had science been the determining factor, the logic of identity would have replaced the logic of dialectic and an evolutionary approach to world communism would have replaced the revolutionary method. That some contemporary Marxists are advocating at least the evolutionary theory of development places them in the pro-science wing of modern day Marxism.

TON's specific contribution to the analysis of communism comes in the emphasis it gives to the role of force as a political tool. This is not news (nor was it news in 1952, TON's copyright date). The communists have never attempted to conceal its importance to them.   In the final paragraph of 'The

---

[58] For a recent examination of the scientific brief against communism, the interested reader is referred to Loren R. Graham's masterful Science, Philosophy and Human Behavior in the Soviet Union, Columbia University Press, 1987. See also my review of said book in Studies in Soviet Thought, Vol 40, 1991.

[59] Lysenko comes to mind. For an exhaustive study of that case as illustrative of Northrop's point see Graham, op cit.

Programme of the Communist International' we read: "The Communists disdain to conceal their views and aims. They openly declare that their aims can be attained only by the forcible overthrow of all the existing social conditions." (228) Stalin has seconded this notion in both *Dialectical and Historical Materialism* and in a series of lectures given to the student of the Sverdlov University in 1924 and entitled *Foundations of Leninism*. He talks of "ruthlessly suppress(ing) the counter-revolutionary activity of the ecclesiastical organizations . . . " and he quotes Marx approvingly when he advises men to "fight it out . . . and to expand the scope of the Russian revolution to the international arena" and "smash social-chauvinism and social-pacifism." (233, 241, 247) Force is needed in order to give to the revolutionary the opportunity to "crush, to smash to bits, to wipe off the face of the earth the bourgeois state machinery . . ." (253) Echoing the sentiments of Lenin, Stalin advises the victorious proletariat of one country to send "its military forces against the exploiting classes and their states." (Ibid.)

The implications of such a policy in international affairs is obvious ". . . A General Staff which insists that recourse to force is a moral necessity for the salvation of its own people will [have no] moral scruples about the use of force against foreigners." (Ibid.) Protection against such a nation guided by such an ideology is, ". . . an alternative ideology backed with the police power necessary to protect its adherents." (254)

As far as effective international law goes, Korovin, one of Russia's authorities on the subject of international law has written that such a law among nations ". . .presupposes some common evaluation, unity of conviction--legal, ethical and political. . ."[60] Any beginning student knows that this condition is not met by the two major powers and should not be surprised when Korovin concludes that ". . . an intercourse on the basis of intellectual unity . . . between countries of bourgeois and socialist cultures, cannot exist as a rule, and hence the rules of international law covering this intercourse become pointless." (255) But if any beginner can know this it takes a more informed student of Soviet Communism to realize that international law is impossible even between Russia and other communists nations since Article 14 of the Constitution ". . . lists those matters reserved to the Soviet Union and hence not within the jurisdiction of the 'sovereign autonomous republics'." (256) Almost every single state function is listed and one can only conclude that the ultimate end of Soviet Communism is not peace through international law, but rather unity under Soviet domestic law. This is the not a very optimistic conclusion.

In PAPP, Northrop makes several predictions (always a dangerous practice for a philosopher) concerning the Soviet Union and some recommendations for the West in the face of these prognostications. Here space permits a simple listing.

(1) No popular revolt of the masses in the near future. Popular revolts presuppose a difference between the overt and covert philosophy of the people and their leaders. There is no evidence of any systematic educational popular movement away from Hegel, Feuerbach and Marx to, say, Locke, Hume and Jevons. To suppose the Russian people are going to reject Communism for Capitalism and express this rejection in a coup d'état is to engage in the "most fanciful day-dreaming."

---

[60] 254. The Korovin quotation is from an article entitled "Soviet Concept of the State, Internatinal Law and Sovereignty" in The American Journal of International Law 43, 1949, 36.

(2) No real peace.   Northrop provides both empirical and theoretical arguments for this claim.   On the empirical side, he points to the fact that every time the Soviet leaders sue for peace or demand a summit conference, their demands are accompanied by a threat of war at some place in the world.   (In 1991, for example, the Soviets have demanded billions in aid or they will explode.) Moreover, the Soviets refuse to discuss any topic other than the political battleground of the moment and of their choosing.

On the theoretical side, Northrop points to their education system that still teaches "the two basic Hegelian-Feuerbachian materialistic premises of their thinking, but also the third and fourth level, more opportunistic procedural derivative applications which give the instrumental rules for applying the premises to particular circumstances of the moment." (PAPP, 272-3)   These tactics run the gamut from conciliatory warmongering, from appeal to verifiable international law, to lies and threats--all designed with one purpose in mind--world domination by the dictatorship of the proletariat.   We are inextricably led to

(3) No end to the Cold War.[61] Here the reasons Northrop marshals are nearly identical with (2) above and we can profitably skip to the final forecast, i.e.,

(4)   Trade alone will not do it.   To assume that the West should shrug off their skepticism and engage in profit-making business as usual with the Soviets presupposes the following counter-factuals: (a) the Russians believe in the virtues of the profit-making system (b) they want peaceful co-existence and

---

[61] I originally wrote these lines in 1986. With the fall of the Berlin Wall and the "collapse" of Marxism in Eastern Europe, I was tempted to remove (3) but decided to let it stand. Historians will decide if and when the Cold War ended. Besides, if Northrop erred here, we should know that as well as when he was prescient.

(c) they have rejected Hegel, Feuerbach, Marx, Lenin et al. for Locke, Bentham and Ludwig Von Mises.

So what? What impact should the above have on U. S. foreign policy. First, one must answer the following questions if disaster is to be avoided in dealing with any foreign politician.

> (1) To what political party in his own nation does he belong? (2) What are the elementary concepts and propositions which specify the goal-value political aims of this party? (3) To what extent is this set of philosophical beliefs taught universally throughout the educational system or inculcated emotively and covertly in religious or political ceremonies or by the public press? What percentage of the people in his nation vote for his party? (5) Most important of all, what was the educational and cultural living law philosophy of the people of his nation and its plural religious communities antecedent to his advent to political office? (PAPP 274)

These questions have relatively easy answers for a philosophical monolith like the Soviet Union, and they cause Northrop to conclude with advice both pessimistic and realistic. First, we must get our philosophical house in order and decide the goal-values for which our massive weapons are the "necessary defense." For Northrop, these include at minimum (1) training in aesthetic sensibility to enable the student and politician to distinguish between the concept by intuition radical empirical data and (2) the concept by postulation meaning he infers from (1). (3) Awareness of the neurophysiological nature of man and the directly inspected ideas that constitute their epistemic correlates.[62] (4) Training in mathematics and

---

[62] I shall have more to say about the neurophysiological nature of man and their epistemic correlates in chapter 6.

symbolic logic as well as (5) mathematical physics and (6) the
concept by postulation meaning of the Jefferson principle.[63]

Second, we must, in effect, circle the wagons and be constantly on guard against a nation whose fundamental premises
not only permit but encourage aggression in the achievement
of their purposes.[64]

Thus far, we have looked at Asia, with special emphasis
on India, Islam, and Marxist Communism.

The fourth major concern in TON is with Western civilization, by which Northrop means not only the United States,
which he will   examine in the last chapter of TON, but also
Australia, Canada, Ibero-America, and New Zealand.   The classical spiritual values of the West are two in number: (1) Greco-
Roman science and philosophy with their unique concept of
law, and (2) Hebrew-Christian religion.   (186) Beginning with
the Hebrew component, Northrop, after admitting that many
aspects of society as depicted in the Old Testament are identical
with the Asian, notes there are marked difference between
them, especially in the area of settling disputes.   As noted
above, the Asian prefers to avoid the law, believing that it
leads to a litigious society and ill feeling between citizens, and
rely as much as possible on meditational techniques.

The Old Testament[65], on the contrary, is a hymn to the
law.   Far from fearing disputatiousness, it teaches that the "law
transforms men into moral beings."   (188) After two pages of

---

63   The Jefferson principle will also be treated in chapter 6.

64   I have allowed this section on philosophical predictions to stand despite, or
more correctly, because of the flux in what used to be the Soviet Union. By the
time you read these lines Heraclitus may have become Parmenides again,
nevertheless, the above remains what Northrop wrote and that is what I have
dedicated myself to transmitting.

65   NB. TORAH, or the first five books of the Bible, means "written law." Cf. The
Essential Talmud by Adin Steinslatz, (Basic Books, 1976),4.

quotations from the Old Testament, Northrop turns to the New with the observation that it "continues in the same vein." (188)

But there is a radical difference between the concept of law in the two Testaments. Northrop sees this difference in Jesus' words that he came to break up the joint family.[66] This revolutionary difference Northrop attributes to the influence of the Stoic Romans who had created a whole new conception of law based on the discovery of concept by postulation science and philosophy by the Greeks. "The spiritual foundations of Western civilization are the product of this synthesis in Christianized Rome of Judaism and Greek scientific natural philosophy." (189) It was the Stoics who defined man as universal man, thus going beyond the parochial distinction between, say, Greek and barbarian. This conception enabled the West to "achieve political unity over social groups and geographical areas extending far beyond the Hebrew or Asian joint families or tribes, a political union, moreover, the moral communal roots of which have nothing to do with family, tribe, status or inductively given station." (189) The Pax Romana is the first instance of this unity on a grand scale; the second, the political unity achieved in Spain, the Middle East and India under Islamic law.

This conception of "man and nature was called the λόγος (logos)" and this not only defined man and nature, it also provided "the criterion of the divine as the first verse of the Fourth Gospel tells us."[67] (193) In the beginning was the Word (logos).

---

[66] Luke, 12:53 "They will be divided, father against son and son against father; mother against daughter and daughter against the mother; mother-in-law against her daughter-in-law and daughter-in-law against mother-in-law.

[67] John 1:1 - "In the beginning was the Word." See chapter 8 for a radical new translation and interpretation of this famous sentence.

Not only did this conception of logos gives rise to the "Stoic Roman Western legal science with its technical formulation," it also gave rise to the invention of the concept of the "just war" which is an integral part of the notion of international law as embodied in the United Nations.

"Truly an event of momentous importance occurred on the surface of this earth when Greek mathematical scientists, using logical and mathematical construction and deduction as well as observations and experimentation, found a new way of knowing and thinking about man and nature." (195)

The last political unit to be considered is the United States. But here it is necessary to interrupt the flow of the story to note a very specific detail of Northrop's attitude to the U. N. Actually, it concerns the veto now reserved for members of the Security Council. What is it about this exclusive veto that concerns Northrop?

First, let us consider the context. Northrop is reproaching Nehru for India's neutrality vis-a-vis Korea and is making the point that "legal institutions are doomed to failure if the leaders of the living law majority do not rally to the support of not merely the law-making body's decision but also to the law-making body's policeman." (268) He also points out the error of those who would condemn the Soviet Union for using their veto against the police action. The reason for this is simple the United States, as well as the Soviet Union, reserves the right to a veto and would have hardly entered the U. N. without reserving such a right. "But if such a right is legally justified for the these powers, it is certainly equally legally justified for the Government of India." (268) Likewise for any other nation.

Those who perceive this exclusive Security Council veto as a problem have suggested either (1) its mere removal, or (2) that a majority vote of the General Assembly should be permitted to override the veto of the Security Council. Both are wrong.

(1) is by far the worse council. "No nation will ever accept, nor should it ever accept, any positive legal decision by
any legal body that violates its own indigenous living law
norms." (269) The veto is one means, albeit a poor one, to
protect one's own living law. But, it will be objected, since few
nations have the same living law, there is no possibility of a
United Nations based on a single, unique living law of its members. Not only is there no single underlying living law, but, as
TON and MEW have shown, the various living laws are diverse
and, in some cases, contradictory. So it would seem a veto is
essential.

Yet Northrop points out, one cannot have effective law
where the veto exists. Taking an example from criminal law,
Northrop states that the law against murder would be useless if
the murderer reserved the right to veto the enforcement of
that law in his own case. So it would seem a veto is counter-
productive.

How can this impossible predicament be resolved? How
can we get effective international law? By employing Ehrlich's
criterion of effective law. Effective positive law must be based
on living law. And although there exists no single living law
the same for all nations, there does exist what Northrop calls
"living law pluralism." Who would deny that Islam is different
from Catholicism, which is different from Taoism or
Jeffersonian republicanism? We must construct international
law on that basis. Instead of pleasant sounding nouns like
democracy, peace, justice which are devoid of content, any international law must base itself on the fact of living law pluralism and guarantee same. Such a charter would "guarantee to
each ideology and nation of the world protection of its particular norms in its own living law geographical area." (271) [The
United Nations forces can throw Iraq out of Kuwait but it cannot throw Saddam Hussain out of office.] Therefore it would
not need a veto. In addition to the *absolute* respect for the

living law customs of every member nation and in order to make such a guarantee efficacious, "any member nation would have to specify its own "ideology and living law norms." (272) In other words, the only concession made by each member nation to the world organization is *that part of their life which is international in character*." (272)   These two requirements obviate the need for a veto and hence remove that particular horn of the above dilemma.   From the point of view of the U. N., the only wars would be civil.   (Remember, the primary function of the U. N. is to avoid world or international wars.)   If North Korea or Iraq tried to aggressively invade a neighbor, the entire world community would respond as a unit backing up the U. N. decision to use police force to stop the aggression.   Nehru types could not have recourse to (a specially selected portion of their)   local living law customs to remain neutral.   The *only* crime, from a U. N. point of view, would be external aggression by one member nation against another member nation, and the only response would be the appropriate retaliation.

To make Northrop's point clearer consider that the only principle of the U. N. would be the principle of living law pluralism--hence the only type of wrongdoing would be that which violates living law pluralism.   "The basis for the police action, for example, against the North Koreans, is not the fact that we do not hold an ideology identical with theirs but that they have violated the principle of living law pluralism by aggressively interfering with the right of the South Koreans to build their social institutions on whatever ideology they choose or circumstances have led them to." (273)   To participate in the U. N. police force therefore does not compel, say, India, to adopt the ideology of the U. S. or of the North Koreans.   They only have to agree on the principle of living law pluralism--and one would know that they did by observing   that they are members of the U. N.

To conclude this digression. Northrop would call for the following reforms of the United Nations charter. (1) Eliminate the *exclusive* veto by eliminating all vetoes. (2) Establish that the sole function of the U. N. is the protection of living law pluralism. So much for Northrop's position on the United Nations.

THE UNITED STATES

The final chapter of TON, "From Philadelphia to Cosmopolis" deals with the United States and its spiritual foundations. To discover those foundations, one must follow Northrop to the city mentioned in the chapter's title.

On May 10, 1775, the Second Continental Congress met in that famous American city to draft a resolution to defend their impending revolution. To defend it in the name, not of might, but of right the natural rights of all men to life, liberty, property and the pursuit of happiness. The foundation of these rights is to be found "in the equal status of all men before 'the Laws of Nature and of Nature's God.'" (318) Not cultural and social "isms," but nature "is man's spiritual tutor." But this learning from nature is not that of naive concept by intuition observation, but rather, as Northrop instances by reference to the surveyor Peter Jefferson, the observations that arise from concept by postulation theory-laden "geometrical and optical laws and principles." (319) Peter sent son Thomas to William and Mary College, where, under the influence of Dr. William Small, a man whom Jefferson credits with fixing the "destiny of my life," he learned the mathematical universalism of Isaac Newton, which necessitated giving a new content to the concept "nature." That content and its impact on the philosophical foundations of America came from Bacon, Newton and Locke, Jefferson's personal "trinity of the three greatest men the world had ever produced." (319) This trinity provided "the theoretically constructed constitutional law entered into by a

contract modeled on the universal laws of Newton's natural science and grounded in man's equality before such laws of nature that Jefferson, Adams, Franklin and their fellow authors of
the Declaration of Independence and the Constitution of the
United States found the spiritual source of the equality and
freedom of their countrymen under law." This provides the
standard by which the good and the just are to be determined.

The contrast between universally known law and tribal
man-to-man feelings comes out in Northrop's quotation of
Emerson who said "Let us have a little algebra instead of this
trite rhetoric,--universal signs, instead of these village symbols,--and we shall both be gainers." Or "Our action should rest
mathematically on our substance [since] all things work exactly
according to their quality and according to their quantity."
(322)

And as for those who see Americans as overly concerned
with the latest gadgets, Northrop writes (as if in anticipation of
Michael Novak) "What other people term gadgets become,
when truly understood, the expression of this spontaneous divine creativity." Northrop knows that technology is rooted in
the discovery of concept by postulation laws of nature and that
these discoveries "presuppose the freely inquiring human spirit
nurtured, fed and stimulated by the universal spirit of nature."
(327)

To recapitulate and summarize, Northrop sees the chance
for peace in the world to depend on the taming of nations and
that such a taming requires us to understand the philosophical
and cultural principles upon which the various nations are
based. He explores way to permit compatibilities to flourish
and contradictions to be resolved. In particular he spends a
good deal of time on four cultural groups viz., the Asian, with
emphasis on India, Islam, and Russian Communism; and the
West, with emphasis on the United States. In the course of
these explorations he examines the limited but vital role the

United Nations can be expected to play in the pursuit of world peace. He concludes by saying that in the move to a cosmopolis of tomorrow, neither "power politics nor eclecticism but spiritual naturalistically grounded universalism is the scientific, realistic and only practical way to relate ourselves to other peoples and nations." (336)

CHAPTER 5

THE COMPLEXITY OF LEGAL AND ETHICAL EXPERIENCE

In 1959, 1960 and 1962, Northrop published three books that are essentially collections of essays written between the years of 1944 and 1961. We will consider, in the next three chapters, these works in order of their publication dates. Our concern in this chapter is with CLEE. With the exception of chapters i, xxi, and xxii, all of CLEE's essays are reprints.

Chapter one is a short, introductory essay in which Northrop distinguishes law from other major disciplines, viz., the natural and social sciences, religion and personal morality, literature and the fine arts, medicine and psychology. Law is characterized by the fact that it is the locus of the meeting of the "is" with the "ought." (Such an opening tips Northrop's hand--he certainly believes the relationship between the two is an intimate one, of which more in due course.)[68] Secondly, law is the meeting place of public and private experience and Northrop instances the "finalizing of a will and the legal transfer of a wood lot"--and I would mention marriage where one can also witness the interface of the most intense emotions with the legal apparatus of the state.

---

[68] See also chapter 7 of PAPP and my exposition in chapter 6 below.

Law is also founded on experience, but that alone hardly serves to differentiate it from the disciplines mentioned above. The crucial question is How is law derived from experience? In other words, what facts of experience constitute the necessary and sufficient conditions for law.

Since legal experience is complex (hence the title), a method sophisticated enough to handle the complexities is needed.   Northrop, contrary to the Scandinavian and American non-cognitivists, believes that the method of law is scientific method.   (Recall in chapter three how the problems summarized in chapter twelve of MEW which superficially seemed to be purely ethical or cultural turned into questions of natural science.) Lest this seem question begging, the powerful instrument of philosophical analysis must be called into play, as it always must in cases of disagreement over first principles. And that is precisely what legal positivism, pragmatic legal realism, intuitive ethical jurisprudence, anthropological or sociological jurisprudence,[69] and naturalistic jurisprudence are struggling over--first principles.   But surely, it will be objected, there are many members of the legal profession who claim that they have no legal philosophy and as a result look with lofty disdain if not plain disgust at the efforts of a philosopher to clarify their domain.   But in law, "as in others things, we shall find that the only difference between a person "without a philosophy" and someone with a philosophy is that the latter knows what his philosophy is, and is therefore, more able to make clear and justify the premises that are implicit in his statements of the facts of his experience and his judgments about those facts." (6)

---

[69] That the science of sociological jurisprudence was important to Northrop can be inferred from the subtitle of his 1954 work European Union and United States Foreign Policy: A Study in Sociological Jurisprudence.

Lest this sound like special pleading by a philosopher, it is necessary to point out that Northrop also wants experience to "speak for itself." But men, especially sophisticated lawyers, judges and even law professors are hardly blank tablets--all of their statements will be "theory laden" to such an extent that their descriptions will be in terms of the very theories they espouse. To solve this paradox, Northrop states that he intends to employ "the more inductive and natural history approach [see LSH, ch. III for details] to legal and political problems . . ." to see if a clue can be discovered to "an adequate theory of legal experience and of legal method. . ." (7) Since "old theories of law mirror the day before yesterday's legal experiences" we had better begin with a statement of the problems of "legal philosophy in the contemporary world." Hence the title of the book's second chapter.

But before we examine that chapter let us place Northrop's own definition of law on the table.

> Law is an ordering of human beings with respect to one another and to nature. A law is good if it orders these humans beings with respect to one another and nature in the light of a true, and as far as possible complete, knowledge of what men and nature are. A law is bad not because it is naughty but because in its ordering of men with respect to nature it puts them together in relation to nature is a way that is contrary to what true scientific knowledge reveals both men and nature to be. (11)

What facts of human experience give rise to the need for such an ordering of human beings? The answer is disputes between men--both rational and irrational--living together in society. Men have been disputing with one another long before Hammurabi, but what is distinctive about our own age are three facts that make the contemporary scene unique: "(1) the release of atomic energy; (2) the shift of the political focus of the world from Western Europe towards Asia; and (3) the inescapably ideological[70] character of both domestic and international social problems." (p. 8)

What is the relevance of (1)?   Since part of what law means is an "ordering of human beings with respect to . . . nature", a knowledge of nature is necessary.   The release of atomic energy was made possible by Einstein's theory of relativity which revealed to modern man a new conception of nature, in the concept by postulation sense.   Northrop asks us to compare the conception of nature in the nineteenth-century with our own.   In the nineteenth century, the science that was most relevant to legal theory was thermodynamics.   It told us that man, in order to survive, must locate, obtain and convert energy from reserves that were believe to be limited to small pools whose release was costly and difficult.   But thanks to Einstein, we have found ways to release dangerously large amounts of energy and now our problem is one of control.   The problem of the atomic age is the reverse of the thermodynamic age.

This has repercussions for natural law theory also.   In addition to the philosophical one of demonstrating, *pace* Hume, its relevance, the content of the law has to be dramatically changed to bring it in line with contemporary developments in the natural sciences.   After all, it is the task of the natural scientists to study nature.   The natural philosophy and physics of Aristotle and St. Thomas simply will not do.

(2) is especially relevant in order for any international law to be successful.   "A jurisprudence which faces the legal needs of the contemporary world must derive its method and

---

70 This term is often used in a pejorative sense. Northorp usage is neutral and means "philosophical."

its theory from a study of Oriental as well as Occidental law." (15)

In (3), Northrop uses the term "ideology" to mean the "key basic concepts of any culture, without which the living law underlying the codified law of that culture is not understood, . . ." (16)   In other words, "ideology" means "philosophy," and should not be understood in the negative and critical senses that have accumulated about this word since Marx.

Ideology applies to both domestic and international social problems.   As an example of the former he cites the case of Brown v. Board of Education wherein nine men on the Supreme Court gave voice to a radically different ideology than that possessed by the majority of people living in the south.   As an example of the latter, one need but mention the fact that nations have differing and, in some cases, contradictory ideologies. When nations have different basic principles, they have difficulty talking to one another and may prefer to fight it out.   This latter course is particularly dangerous when the fighting nations have nuclear arsenals at their disposal.

Given (1), (2) and (3), Northrop concludes that the "traditional theories, methods and courses in jurisprudence" are in the main, failures. (18)   What is needed is an ethical and legal theory that can serve to adjudicate the domestic and international problems of our time.   But is there "any method valid for all by means of which a theory specifying determinate goal values can be shown to be true or false.   The problem, at bottom, is whether personal ethical or social normative statements are cognitive or merely emotive and hortatory." (19) If the former is the case, then the scientific method which provides such a measure of truth and falsity must also be made explicit.

In chapter three, Northrop introduces a tripartite distinction that he will employ throughout the remainder of the book, viz., the distinction between the positive law, the living law and the natural law.

How does Northrop use these terms? Positive law is law as it appears in "the cases and propositions in law books. . ." (63)   For the legal positivist,   the meaning for words like "legally just" are radical empirical concepts by intuition meanings given immediately in experience.

Living law means what "anthropologists call 'the pattern of a culture'" or "the mores of society." (25)   Here the meanings of legal terms derive from the "common qualitative normative principles for ordering their social relations."   (26)

Finally there is natural law.   Although Northrop has many interesting and provocative things to say about both positive and living law and the relationships that obtain between them, I want to concentrate upon his discussion of natural law.[71]

One of the motives for the appeal to natural law is that it provides an escape from the relativity of positive and living law maxims.   It is, therefore, ironic that natural law jurisprudence should find itself subject to a relativity that it thought it could escape by an appeal to nature.   It is, perhaps, doubly ironic that the man who points to this disturbing relativity, would himself be a natural law theorist.   Hence an essay (ch. xiii) bearing the title "The Relativity of Natural Law Theories" should cause, if not consternation, at least mild surprise. Wherein does this relativity of natural law theories lie?

Although every major culture has, at least in its classical phase,   a natural law jurisprudence, the *content*   of these vari-

---

[71] To give the interested reader some idea of the other topics (by chapter) Northrop discusses and that will not be addressed in this chapter I list the following: (iv) Cultural Values and Recent Legal Theory; (v) Legal Positivism, Intuitive Ethics and Sociological Jurisprudence;   (vi) Petrazycki's Psychological Jurisprudence; (vii) The Method of Recent Cultural Anthropology; (viii) The Method and Neurophysiological Basis of Philosophical Anthropology; (ix) Cultural Dynamics and Historical Jurisprudence; (x)   European Political Experience Since World War II; (xi) Philosophical Anthropology and International Law; (xvi) Comparative Ethics and Epistemological Theory; (xvii) Common Law, Roman Law and the Civil Law; (xviii) Concerning the Sociology of Knowledge, etc.

ous theories is different. One major distinction arises from the very meaning of nature itself. Is the "nature" referred to by these theories nature as known through concepts by postulation or nature as known via concepts by intuition. In the latter, nature is an all embracing undifferentiated oneness (Eastern philosophy) whereas for the former (Western philosophy) we have quarks, n-dimensional space-times, atomic triangles, etc.

Nor is the relativity of natural law restricted to those global differences between East and West. Northrop mentions the differences between pre- and post-Kantian natural law theories in the West wherein the former understood science to give ontological meaning to some of its terms, the latter did not. And if that weren't enough, pre-Kantian theories were hardly unanimous about "nature". Contrast Locke with St. Thomas. And no one would be so foolish as to believe that when Jefferson, who referred to Bacon, Newton and Locke as his three gods, declared for natural law in the opening paragraphs of the *Declaration of Independence* he was enunciating a natural law doctrine with an Aristotelian, Thomistic Roman Catholic content.

Nor are these intramural squabblings confined to the West. Certainly one of Northrop's points in this essay is to expose the equivocity of the concept of natural law in the East as well as the West. Consider only India and China as examples. Northrop quotes with approval Dr. Hu Shih who notes that "The conception of . . . nature as taught by Lao-tze and accepted by Confucius was too naturalistic and too radical to please the vast majority of the people who were followers of the traditional Sinitic religion, . . ."[72] He also mentions the well known

differences and incompatibilities between the Hindu laws of
Manu and Gandhi's extreme pacifist interpretations of the
Hindu classics, especially the *Bhagavadgita*. With such extreme
relativity cropping up wherever one looks, it is no wonder that
Northrop pronounces modern natural law theory a failure.   Yet
he is an exponent of natural law.   Thus Northrop must account
for the modern failure and suggest a remedy if there is to be
an answer to the ethical and legal relativists.

Northrop's explanation for the failure is startling.   It is
that "natural law jurisprudence . . . has yet to be pursued in the
contemporary world."   And studies like the Notre Dame study
cited above are evidence for this claim.   The shortcomings of
this collection of essays on natural law (faults espied and noted
by Father Hesburg in his concluding remarks) is that it (1) ignores radical differences in the conception of nature across
cultures and, within its own Western culture, it (2) implicitly
assumes the concept of nature pervasive since Kant.

Since the first problem has already been touched on
above, let us look at Northrop's view of Kant.   Before Kant, natural law meant precisely that--law derived from nature, not
the humanities, via natural science, specifically physics in the
Stoic sense of that word.[73]   Science gave conclusions that were
valid ontologically.   All of Aquinas' arguments for the existence
of God begin with nature known by common perception and
thematized by means of Aristotle's physical and metaphysical
categories.   But since Kant's Second *Critique* it has become a

---

[72] CLEE, 170. Northrop cites the essay Hu Shih contributed to the University
of Notre Dame Natural Law Institute Proceedings, University of Notre Dame
Press, Notre Dame, Vol. 5, 1953.

[73] For the Stoics, physics means any study of non-man-made nature. Compare
the Vorrede of Kant's "Grundlegung zur Metaphysik der Sitten" where he
mentions the Stoic division of all the disciplines into the three broad categories of
Physics, Ethics and Logic.

commonplace that "the empirical knowledge of nature, either of common-sense, scientific or empirical philosophical inquiry, does not give ontological conclusions." (167) From this follows the obvious inference that "ethics and law cannot be grounded in the philosophy or methodology of nature and the natural sciences, but must be treated as autonomous subjects." (Ibid.)

What is Northrop's solution to these two problems? First, we today know that the concepts of science are not categorically a priori they are hypothetically a priori.[74] Since Kant is wrong in this regard, there is no reason to continue to accept the autonomy of ethical and legal science. (PAPP, 259. See also Chapters V and VIII of MEW.) This means that when we know space, time, causality etc. we are not merely knowing the constitution of a transcendental ego, but rather "ontologically existent nature."[75] If this be true, we have a trans-cultural ground upon which to build our ethics and law.

When Northrop goes on to state that natural law jurisprudence, in its root meaning, has yet to be pursued in the contemporary world, we can begin to appreciate his four point program and how much of that program he has realized in his own writings. In order to pursue natural law jurisprudence-- i.e., in order to measure the "philosophy exemplified in the ethical and legal norms of man-made traditional culture" by "the philosophy implicit in the empirically verified theories of God-made--that is, non man-made nature" we must accomplish four major tasks:

---

74 But cf. p. 49 of PRO where he writes that "all verifiable human knowing . . . in natural science . . . [is] a posteriori.

75 See Northrop's essay "Natural Science and the Critical Philosophy of Kant" in The Heritage of Kant, Whitney and Bowers eds. (Princeton University Press), 1939, 62.

first, the determination of the respective philosophies of nature of the different natural law norms
of the world's major modern, as well as ancient,
cultural traditions second, the analysis of the
empirically verified theories of contemporary
natural science to determine the epistemological
and ontological philosophy involved this will require the facing and meeting of Kant's critique of
ontology third, the measuring of the philosophies of
the former against the latter fourth, the
specification of a philosophy of nature which has
the capacity to account, within a single consistent
set of assumptions, for all the facts which brought
into existence the diverse culturally relative and
limited theories of traditional natural law, . . .(171-
2)

Northrop accomplished the first of these tasks in MEW and one
half of the second (the facing and meeting of Kant's critique) in
chapters V and VIII of that same work and the other half of
the second (the analysis of contemporary natural science) in
SFP.   As for three, most philosophies adumbrated in one fail to
meet the requirements of the latest verified theories of contemporary science.   This allows us to pronounce them inadequate for a founding of natural law due to the fact that their
conception of nature is inadequate.   Take the philosophy of St.
Thomas.   To the extent that it rests on Aristotelian physics and
its doctrine of motion it is incorrect.   Or consider communism.
To the extent that it rests on a "self-contradictory, naively realistic and material-dialectically deterministic[76] natural philosophy of Marx and Engels" (159) it is false.   The only solution, as

---

[76] For details on why any, not just Marx's, material-dialectically deterministic
natural natural philosophy must be false, see chapter ix of CLEE, especially pp.
120-1. In brief, the refutation is founded on the fact that any thesis can be
negated in many ways, not just one, as would have to be the case if dialectical
materialism were deterministic.

Northrop indicates above as the fourth major task of current thought, is to construct a philosophy that can account for all the facts which brought the many partially correct but now defunct theories into existence. Such a theory is radical empiricism epistemically correlated with logical realism. Such a doctrine is, of course, Northrop's.

Hence Northrop is a natural law theorist in his jurisprudential thought. To see this in some detail, let us turn to chapter xx, where he defends his conception of natural law jurisprudence.

Although chapter xx bears the title "Ethical Relativism in the Light of Recent Legal Theory," its intent is to refute the relativist position. Before looking at this refutation, let's note how it arises from recent legal theory. After showing how legal positivism gives rise to sociological (or anthropological) jurisprudence,[77] he then proceeds to how it gives rise to the need for natural law. The major reason is the obvious one. "One must judge the living law as well as the positive law." (253) At times this judgment is trans-cultural, e.g., when the living law of Hitler's Germany or Stalin's Russia is condemned by those not of those nations. At other times, the judgments are intracultural. Northrop refers to those nations in Africa and Asia that are reforming their own living law. They want something better, but better presupposes a standard for judging current living law. It is obvious that the "is" of current living law cannot produce such a standard without falling into circularity. Nor can sociological jurisprudence. Its forte is judging positive law based on how well it accords with the living law. What we need is an objective standard by which to judge and measure

---

[77] The pattern is similar to that given above in chapter 4, pp. 71ff, where the relationship between positive law and living law was discussed.

the living law.   "Natural law ethics and jurisprudence is the thesis that there is such a   standard."   (253)

What is the method of natural law?   A hint is to be found in the method of sociological jurisprudence itself.   It consists in making explicit the philosophy underneath the legal and ethical customs of a given culture.   The meaning and concepts by which any given culture conceptualizes "the raw unconceptualized data of anybody's experience" has two parts, viz., the concepts and the data.   If one focuses on the former you generate sociological jurisprudence and its attendant relativity of philosophy to culture.   Obviously there are different cultures with different ways of conceptualizing the data.   If however, one focuses on the data, one "generates natural law jurisprudence and the relativity of culture to natural philosophy." (254)   In order to make this distinction clear, Northrop, in true philosophical fashion makes another distinction, viz., the distinction between two kinds of facts, first-order and second-order facts. Northrop first introduced this distinction in an essay printed in the 1951 collection entitled "Essays in East-West Philosophy" and reprinted as chapter xix of CLEE.   In that essay he also dubbed them natural and cultural facts respectively.   First-order or natural facts "are antecedent to scientifically verified philosophical theory" and are neither good nor bad. Cultural or second-order facts are consequent to scientifically verified philosophical theory and are good or bad.   But their goodness or badness is due, not to their being facts, but because "they derive their character and existence in part at least from human behavior based upon beliefs in scientifically verifiable propositions about nature and natural man which are true or false." (245)   What makes these first order facts objective is that they are "given in anyone's experience [introspectively or extrospectively] in any culture."   Consider the following examples of first- and second-order facts.

> That there are biological animals called 'cows' is a first-order fact, the same for Hindu Indians as for Americans. That the orthodox Hindus have a religious belief which prompts them frequently to slay anyone who kills a cow or a bull, whereas the Mexicans are transported into frenzied raptures of ecstasy over the slaying of such animals in a bull fight and most North Americans experience pleasure rather than sacrilegiously laden irritation and pain, over the eating of a juicy beefsteak--these are second order psychological facts. (264)

"It is a first-order fact that any person in any culture directly inspects colors, sounds, odors, flavors, pains, pleasures and the images of dreams," but it is second-order fact that different cultures have different epistemological, ontological and psychological beliefs concerning these first-orderfacts. Consider epistemology. About the first-order facts of direct inspection, one can be a radical empiricist, a naive realist or a logical realist etc. If one is, say, a naive realist, and believes that all directly inspected qualities are qualities of a physical or mental substance, then one believes a dualist mind-body ontology. These are all second-order facts.

Given this distinction, what use does Northrop make of it? He asks us to suppose a society that accepts a naive realistic epistemology and a dualistic body-mind ontology. Such societies have a predilection for identifying the good and the just "with directly sensed color-of-skin biologically bred familial and tribal man." (264) This gives one an ethics and politics of the law of status as opposed to a law of contract type. Now suppose, Northrop asks us, that the empirical scientists came to the conclusion, as was actually the case in Greece and Rome, that "the genetic traits of people are transmitted to the next generation only by the male, the female serving merely as a receptacle." (265) Given their naive realistic epistemology, these people must locate all ethical and political responsibilities, rights, and privileges with the male.

Note that we have second-order cultural beliefs based on first-order scientific beliefs. According to the modern science of genetics, we know that both "sexes make their contributions to the genetic characteristics of the offspring." (265) This provides us with a way of judging the "living law of any patriarchal law of status community to be a false second-order factual ethical, political and legal state of affairs since the theory of first-order genetic facts which it assumes as the justification for its specific norms is false." (265-6) If Northrop is correct, it seems as if we have a method for judging the living law and hence for "affirming some of the living law of the contemporary world to be bad and unjust." (268)

But it is one thing to realize that a living law is bad and must be replaced it is quite another thing to know the "substantive content of the good and the just new positive law which is the criterion for creating a new good and just living law to replace the old. (268)

After referring the reader to chapter twelve of MEW and chapters five, six and ten of TON for more details, he then goes on to note the following two suggestions. Since both (1) classical Oriental and the modern radical empiricists and (2) The Western mathematical physicists reached the conclusion that a naïve realistic epistemology . . . is a false theory of scientific knowledge . . . ." no positive law should be based on such a spurious foundation. We need for our foundation something that escapes "relativity to different percipients and to the different sense organs of the same percipient."

Here both East and West have a contribution to make. The reader should already be familiar with the undifferentiated aesthetic continuum. This common factor, since its escapes all perceptual relativity, provides a foundation for the treatment of all humans beings as the same. This is due to the fact that "according to this field theory of first order facts, all human beings are, in their elemental, irreducible selves, not merely equal but identical. It follows that any positive and living legal community which is compatible, therefore, with this theory of first-order facts would seem to be one which is egalitarian in its most primitive and basic criterion of the good and the just." (270) Obviously this theory resonates with much in the "old living law and positive legal procedures of Asia which is good and just." (Ibid.)

The West also has its contribution to make. Since the Greeks, the West has had at its disposal theoretical constructs (= Northrop's concepts by intellection) which, because they allow the knower to know the world imagelessly, provide for another manner of escaping perceptual relativity. Positive laws can be constructed that "define laws governing the related individuals which hold universally for any individual whatever which instances the entity variables of the theory." (271)

CHAPTER 6

PHILOSOPHICAL ANTHROPOLOGY AND PRACTICAL POLITICS

This book describes several important recent discoveries in different natural and social sciences,
submits the concepts of each to a careful epistemological analysis, thereby arriving at an empirically
verifiable theory of what a human being is and
what groups of human beings called nations are,
and then applies this theory and the political methods which it prescribes to the description and suggested solution of some major political problems of
today's world. (v)

Thus Northrop begins his preface to PAPP. One of the
sciences referred to is cultural anthropology, especially the
then recent discoveries of Paul Radin and Clyde Kluckhohn that
seemed to indicate that even people without a written language
nevertheless have a complex philosophy which grounds, and
therefore makes explicable, their cultural habits and daily living patterns. Thus the first two words in Northrop's title.

> Two recent discoveries in neurophysiological psy-
> chology receive special attention in Chapters 3 and
> 4. They are (1) the McCulloch-Pitts theory of the
> neuro-physiological correlate of introspected mem-
> ory and ideas and (2) the cybernetic character of
> human nervous systems. Their importance derives
> from the fact that, unless we have a complete and
> correct conception of what an individual person is
> we are likely to have a mistaken theory of what
> any nation is and thereby fall into faulty political
> methods for either understanding nations or mak-
> ing trustworthy domestic or foreign policy decisions
> with respect to them. (v-vi)

Since practical considerations were given pride of place in
chapter four on TON, we shall ignore all but one chapter
(fourteen) from "Part Two: Some Applications" and concentrate
on the more theoretical chapters from part one, viz., one
through eight. The chapter will close with a few words on
chapter eighteen from part three.

Chapter one restates and updates Northrop's plea for
those in power to acquaint themselves with the findings of recent cultural anthropology and sociological jurisprudence.

Chapter two begins by cashing in some of the results of
chapter one. Specifically, we are told that today's political
problems require the following:

> (1) The determination of the specific normative
> content of the living law in any particular nation (2)
> the effective implanting of a new positive law in an
> old living law (3) the evaluation of what in the old
> living law is to be retained and what discarded in
> such reform of an old society. (21)

Obviously (1) and (3) necessitate that one distinguish between description and evaluation. Since chapters six and seven are entitled "The Descriptive Method" and "The Evaluative Method" respectively, some of what Northrop says in this chapter has the quality of a promissory note that I will not try to pay off until I deal with those chapters in their proper sequence.

The reasons for requirement (1) are those given in TON, viz., that positive law must be grounded in living law in order to be effective. But how can we determine the living law? Northrop takes a hint from Eugen Ehrlich. The hint has to do with the fact that since we are interested in normative content we need to learn from the social scientist the *independent variable* in any society that specifies the normative factor in any political constitution or legislative statute. What is the independent variable? It is the normative "inner order of the associations of human beings." (26) What does this mean?

To answer this question Northrop has recourse to Pitirim Sorokin's concept of logico-meaningful causality. Unlike systems of inorganic nature wherein the causality is solely mechanical, systems of human beings are to be known in part by the meanings they consider important. Hence the term "logico-meaningful causality." In other words, ideas do make a difference. Man has "free will."

Notice what happens when one ignores logico-meaningful causality. From a purely inorganic natural scientific point of view, man is nothing but an instance of a Newtonian mass. Because the causality in such a system is mechanical, the future inner order can be determined by Newton's laws provided external forces can be neglected. When this happens and man is considered only from an inorganic point of view, a power-political theory like Hobbes' will result. Hobbes tells us that freedom, which for him means the absence of external impediments to motion, is a concept that "may be applied no less to

irrational, and inanimate creatures, than to rational." (34)
Northrop replies:

> Clearly, this confuses freedom in the concept by
> postulation realistic epistemological sense of a mass
> in public space-time moving according to Newton's
> first law of motion when that mass is not acted on
> by an external force, with the quite different
> meaning of the freedom of a "rational creature," i.e.,
> a person in the concept by intuition meaning of the
> word "person" who introspects himself as freely as-
> senting to a legal or political goal value principle to
> which he commits himself. (34)

We can now answer the question asked three paragraphs back.
By "inner order of the associations of human beings" we mean
"shared meanings" between members of any human group.
These shared meanings are the independent variables mentioned above and they define the inner order or state of any
human being and of any social and political system to which
these humans may belong.

Take the following example. One does not need recourse
to Newton's laws or to their generalization by Einstein to explain why one group of human beings goes to a synagogue
while their neighbors go to a Roman Catholic Church. While
variations in the initial positions and momenta of these two
groups no doubt exist, they would hardly be sufficient to explain or *cause* the behavioral differences between them. Nor it
this failure to find a causal connection between physics and sociology due to the immature state of either discipline. Since
Newton's laws are couched in terms of concepts by postulation
and socio-cultural phenomena (like synagogue or church atten-
dance) in terms of concepts by intuition, one commits world of

discourse   nonsense[78] if one tries to establish a mechanical causal connection between them.   According to Northrop, the proper relation is an epistemic correlation.   Meanings do matter, and are, in some sense, irreducible to their epistemic correlates.

To determine the shared meanings of the inhabitants of any nation ultimately requires the discipline whose very function lies in finding such elementary concepts, viz., philosophy, and specifically philosophical anthropology.   To concretize this, Northrop concludes chapter two with a brief exposition of Kluckhohn's discussion of the philosophy of the Navaho Indians.[79]

Chapters three and four deal with two recent scientific discoveries and their impact on practical politics.

(1) Dr. Warren S. McCulloch and Walter Pitts' indirectly confirmed theory of neurologically "trapped universals." (2) Arturo Rosenblueth, Norbert Wiener and Julian Bigelow's distinction between non-teleological and teleological mechanisms, together with the demonstration that all human nervous systems are mechanisms of the latter type.   (42)

The title of chapter three, "The Neurological Epistemic Correlates of Introspected Ideas,"   perspicuously signals its contents.   The theory of "trapped universals"[80] as the epistemic

---

[78] World of discourse nonsense occurs when for example, the subject of a sentence is a concept by postulation (or intuition) and the predicate is a concept by intuition (or postulation).   Northrop gives the following examples: "electrons are pink."   "Sensed objects are public objects."   "Political power causally determines normative political decisions."   etc. (32-3)

[79] For details the interested reader is directed to "The Philosophy of the Navaho Indians" in Northrop, ed., Ideological Differences and World Order, Yale U. P., New Haven, 1949, pp. 356-384.   Reprinted by Greenwood Press, 1971.

[80] "Trapped universals" is, of course, elliptical, as Northrop points out. Otherwise one would have world of discourse nonsense because "trapped" refers

correlate of   introspected ideas was developed by Warren S.
McCulloch and Walter Pitts. The theory integrates their study
of the brain with Northrop's "theory of epistemic correlations
for escaping the pseudo-body-mind problem and bringing the
data of neurological behavioristic, introspective, and psycho-
analytic psychology into an epistemologically meaningful relation to one another." (47)

The question McCulloch[81] asked himself was what must
the brain be like in order for us to have ideas.   Or more technically, what must the concept by postulation brain be like to enable me to introspect concept by intuition ideas.   Specifically,
how do we remember?   What is the epistemic correlate of
memory?

The clue came from the experimental research of Lorente
de Nó, which gave evidence that the nerve cells in the cortical
neural nets were not only ordered in throughways, but also in
circles.   McCulloch realized that this permitted memory.   How
so?

Had the orderings in the neural net been only throughways, no impulse could ever be trapped in the brain.   Then any
sensory stimulus would simply fire a series of cortical neurons
that would eventually fire a motor neuron giving rise to motor
behavior.   All behavior would model the reflex.   But if some
cortical neurons were ordered in a circle, then the neurons
could pass the impulse around the circle[82] for an extended period of time, thus serving as the epistemic correlate of memory.

---

to a concept by postulation physical impulse whereas "universal" refers to a
concept by intuition mental introspection. Naively combining these produces the
same world of discourse nonsense found in such expressions as "Meanings are
spatially extended" or "Ideas are in the brain." The explication of "trapped universals" follows in the body of the text.

[81] From here on I will use the proper name McCulloch as a shorthand for he,
Pitts and even Northrop where appropriate.

In addition to accounting for memory, McCulloch also noticed another formal property of the circular nets, viz., that not only is the "trapped impulse" the effect of an outer past event, E^1, but also it uniquely[83] represents that event and so has the formal properties of a symbol. (54)

The actual truth of the details of the McCulloch theory of "trapped universals" is not as important as the fact that some such theory must apply if we are to move beyond the global epistemic correlations between the concept by postulation person and the concept by intuition person Northrop talked about on pp. 194-5 of LSH. All that is needed if McCulloch's theory proves deficient is a formal equivalent. This we can leave to the future developments of the science of neurophysiology.

Chapter four, "The Self-Regulation of Human Behavior by Means of the Epistemic Correlates of Ideas" applies the findings of Rosenblueth, Wiener and Bigelow's famous paper "Behavior, Purpose and Teleology" to the issue of practical politics. The chapter opens with several paragraphs that reveal why so many politicians, philosophers and scientists "came to the conclusion that ideas were "mere epiphenomena" incapable of having any significance for the motor behavior of human beings and hence irrelevant to what they actually do." (64) This conclusion was based on two errors. The first has to do with a naive realistic interpretation of Newton's physics and can be corrected by the application of Northrop's distinction between postulation and intuition.[84]

---

82 I ignore here scientific niceties such as "refractory phase times", "simultaneous firings" etc. for which the interested reader is directed to the book. For a rigorous mathematical presentation of the above the interested reader is directed to J. Simoes da Fonseca, ed. Signification and Intention, Lisbon, (Gulbenkian Foundation), 1970.

83 This uniqueness condition is established if and only if one assumes that "only the sensory nerve cell s^1 can fire the cortical nerve cell c^1."

The second error was the assumption that the mechanical causality of all physical systems was non-teleological. If that were true, and if humans were physical systems, then the "ideas are impotent" conclusion follows. But this mistake rests on a failure to make a distinction between two kinds of physical systems, one non-teleological, the other teleological in its behavior.[85] (68) What makes the latter teleological is the presence of a negative feedback mechanism from its target to the motor response to the target. Examples of such systems include an anti-aircraft gun, the furnace thermostat and the human nervous system.

But there are obvious and numerous differences between thermostats and human beings, the crucial one for our purposes being that while thermostats must have their target selected for them by some human being, "human beings self-select their own targets and . . . self-select in part the data and information that is fed into them and also the normative procedural rules for not merely describing but also for evaluating this data. How can this be?" (71) It can be if the target is one's cognitively true or false philosophy. Or to put the point more fully, it can be if "the target of the negative feedback mechanism which is a particular human nervous system be the hierarchically ordered, cortically trapped persisting impulses that are the epistemic correlates of that particular person's set of elemental concepts and postulates, i.e., his cognitively true or false philosophy." (71)

---

[84] Even one of Northrop's best students makes a similar error. See my "Northrop and Grünbaum on the Newtonian Concept of Relative Space" in appendix one.

[85] For a criticism of this very distinction, the interested reader is directed to Harry Binswanger's The Biological Basis of Teleological Concepts, (Los Angeles, Ayn Rand Institute Press) pp. 68ff.

We can see once again the importance of McCulloch and Pitts. By combining their theory of trapped impulses with the cybernetic interpretation of the nervous system, we can begin to understand how philosophy can and must have consequences in the world of nature and politics.

Since the topic is politics, it becomes necessary to ask what is a nation? Northrop again uses the chemistry analogy first employed in TON to motivate the reader concerning the importance of knowing the elements to be mixed in foreign policy decisions.

Chapter five asks two questions: what is a nation and how can one determine the specific properties which distinguish one nation from another?

What is a nation? But surely everyone knows what a nation is! Look at any map. Or read the list of members to the United Nations. On that list we find the Soviet Union. But the Soviet Union has ceased to exist. Surely the former territory is there. We know the weapons and the people are there, but the nation has ceased to exist. "Any theory of what a nation is must provide meaning for a nation passing out of being when the concrete people, the concrete geography and the concrete military soldiers and weapons with which it was previously associated remain." (75)

Although all the concretes remain, the nation is gone. Perhaps a nation is not a concrete. Perhaps we have committed "the fallacy of misplaced concreteness." This does not mean, pace positivism, that the concept nation is meaningless, but rather that the concept nation does not refer to any naive realistic concrete and furthermore, there exists some urgency in discovering exactly what a nation is. After all, the politicians now making foreign policy have some very dangerous weapons at their disposal and we had better get it right before its too late.

What makes a nation one?   To determine this, Northrop
suggests we compare the anatomical unity of a human being
with the quite different unity of a nation.   The body of a human is held together by "physical bones, nerves, muscles and
tendons." To move one's leg is to pull at the rest of one's body.
The unity of a nation is obviously not like this.   "Nevertheless . .
. a unified response is what occurs when any people form a nation or when a majority of them or any group of them respond
with a common domestic or foreign policy.   How is this possible?"   (77)   Thirty years ago (since the book was copyrighted in
1960, Northrop is referring 1930) an answer could not have
been given.   But since the discovery of cybernetics and the theory of "trapped universals," an answer is at hand.

> Stated as briefly as possible, a "nation" is any group
> of concrete, particular human beings who possess in
> the hierarchically ordered neural nets of their
> brains a similar set of elementary trapped impulses
> (which are the physiological epistemic correlates of
> consciously or unconsciously memorized elemen-
> tary ideas and postulates) for firing or inhibiting
> their motor neurons and thereby mechanically
> causing a similar cognitive behavioristic living law
> response to any given stimulus. (77)

Certainly this "definition" could have been given thirty years
ago in terms of the radical empirical concepts by intuition
items contained above.   The advantage of the epistemically correlated concepts by postulation language is identical to the advantage of "mathematical electromagnetic theory with its
spectrum of electromagnetic waves, extending far beyond the
so-called visible range."   (78)   It also provides an operational
test to determine if one has inferred correctly the ideas, behind
the smiles and handshakes,   held by a "given culture, people or
nation."   (78)

We now can understand how a nation can act as a unit. The tie holding a nation together is not that of bones and sinews, but rather the shared meaning or ideas of its people. These ideas are efficacious when and if they are epistemically correlated with trapped impulses in the neural nets (or their formal equivalents) of the citizens. These ideas of a people are its philosophy, or at least the predominant philosophy of the majority.[86]

In chapters six and seven, Northrop turns to the problem of method. The problem arises when one confuses the objective description of a nation with the evaluation of that nation. This occurs due to the intuitive and nebulous descriptive judgments used by most social scientists. He therefore is willing to spend a chapter on each--one on descriptive philosophical anthropology follow by a chapter on evaluative philosophical anthropology.

The descriptive method has two distinct parts, one operational, the other theoretical. As to the first, chapter six acknowledges the validity, at least to a first degree of approximation sufficient for most practical purposes, of determining the covert or overt postulate set of any nation by the method of "interrogating its citizens [and] reading the philosophical or other classics of any nation or political party and their positive legal constitutions and consciously expressed political policies." (89) Northrop also mentions two other operational tests that need not detain us. (90)

He then considers the theoretical part of the descriptive method. The theory involved is mathematical logic, especially its key notion that systems have formal properties. What this

---

[86] This does not necessitate, nor does Northrop imply, a theory of unlimited majority rule. If the majority, or active minority, espouse a philosophy of, say, limited government with a bill of rights guaranteeing the protection of minority rights, then this will be the political system adopted.

means is that individual propositions can only be fully understood when their formal relatedness to all the other propositions of the system in which it is embedded is understood.   If
this sounds familiar, it should.   It is the application of the definition of a concept by postulation to propositions, or what I,
not Northrop, might baptize as propositions by postulation.

> Certainly, if a proposition is in a deductively formu-
> lated theory, any concept in the proposition is ei-
> ther a logical constant, a primitive concept, or a de-
> fined concept--that is, a concept that is defined in
> terms of primitive concepts and logical constants
> and, since any primitive concept in a deductively
> formulated theory depends for its essential, syn-
> tactically given meaning upon all the postulates
> within which it is a term, it follows that the attempt
> to find the complete meaning of any proposition
> merely by analyzing it in isolation is incompatible
> with the way in which the primitive and defined
> concepts of a deductively formulated   theory get
> their meaning.   (91-2)

The cash value of this is that no proposition of any (actual or
potential) deductively formulated theory can be analyzed or
understood apart from a consideration of all the primitive
propositions of the theory in which it occurs.

In addition to giving us a systematic conception of science
and philosophy, it also reveals the essence of these disciplines
as the "definition and resolution of the theoretic problems to
which the different postulate sets of the different deductively
formulated theories are different answers." (94)

Northrop then proceeds to apply the theoretical part of
the descriptive method to the social sciences.   Before doing so,
however, he divides social theories into factual and normative
social theories.   The former attempt to describe their objects as

they in fact are. Few such sciences exist even today. Northrop instances Jevons' formulation of economics and the Austrian school.

On the other hand, normative social theories abound, although most of them, Northrop admits, are written in ordinary prose which does not facilitate understanding of their logical structure. Northrop mentions Roman legal science, Marxist ideology, Thomistic philosophy and Hume's philosophy, as worked out by Bentham, Austin and Jevons, as examples of normative social theories. (96)   He then concludes the chapters by stating that

> the objective social scientist is the one who makes sure that the conceptualization of the facts of a foreign culture which he portrays is the conceptualization of the people in that culture, rather than his own.   To do this, he must,   by conversation with them and by reading their written documents, discover their basic covert and overt concepts or ideology, as well as observe their overt behavior and institutions and he must supplement induction with deductively formulated theory presenting each culture as its particular observable data conceptualized by its particular set of primitive concepts and propositions.   (97)

Most of what Northrop says in chapter six is generally recognized.   Few doubt that we have a cognitive method for describing different cultures.   "The crucial question is whether there is a cognitive method for evaluating such normative judgments, customs and political ideals once they are objectively described."   Such is the task chapter seven sets for itself to answer, and answer it does,   in the affirmative.   Since cultural relativism has been not only a popular but pervasive

topic, Northrop's answer may prove enlightening. [See chapter
XXI of CLEE]

What does Northrop mean by a "cognitive method of
evaluating normative judgments?"   He means a method usable
by anyone at any time from any culture that produces true and
false statements about any given culture.   He believes that if
one sat down with, say, a Hitlerian and after perusing *Mein
Kampf* and comparing what Hitler said with what he did, we
could produce a list of statements that both of us could agree
were either true or false.

Northrop believes that we can do likewise for evaluation.
Note however that the method cannot be the obvious but
fruitless one of judging a foreign culture by one's own.   From a
Nazi point of view, a free democratic society with its legal Bill
of Rights protecting minority groups is evil.   And vice versa.

The deeper question asks whether "there is a cognitive
method which, when applied to both of them, enables one to
say *in a sense which anyone anywhere can confirm* that the
philosophy which correctly describes one of these nation's goal
value beliefs and behavior is true and the quite incompatible,
different philosophy of that of the other nation is false?" (99)

Northrop cautions that the italicized words quoted above
are to be taken with the utmost seriousness.   No one doubts
that we all condemn (or laud) other cultures from the vantage
point of our own.   What Northrop has designed is an approach
that allows the kind of judgments based on repeatability we
assume to be part of the "harder" sciences.   He is not after the
"intuitively convincing" but rather the scientifically confirmable, and confirmable by "anyone anywhere."

Before exposing his method, Northrop deals with and
dismisses, in whole or in part, the pragmatic, the intuitive, and
the hedonistic evaluative methods. (100-104)   Northrop then
reminds us of the salient points he made in chapters three and
four, especially the fact that one's overt behavior is a function

of "(a) the stimulus of the moment and (b) the feedback from the inner target, [which] approximates nearer and nearer to the hitting of the target." (111) In radically empirical language, one's sensed behavior is the result of one's focus of attention and one's ideas. "The crucial point to note with respect to the evaluative method in ethics and politics is that any trapped impulses[87] whatever which define this inner target will have this *prescriptive* effect upon motor behavior." (111, emphasis mine) And this prescriptiveness obtains whether one's introspected ideas are normative or non-normative.

In order to make this clear, Northrop supplies the following example. Adam and Eve, being the first human beings, have no cultural (or second order)[88] facts trapped epistemically in their brains. All of their ideas refer to non-man made nature and those aspects of humankind that have nothing to do with cultural beliefs. The ideas of the original couple would obviously be "non-normatively worded and hence cognitively testable by anyone anywhere by appeal to first-order factual data given by [the] senses and introspectively." (112) That is, their ideas would be either true or false. But if we consider these ideas "relative to the motor side of their nervous systems," they would be prescriptive, specifying an ought or ought not, inhibiting or reinforcing certain motor responses.

It seems that Northrop is drawing an analogy between the cognitive and the affective domains. Propositions that are true or false when considered cognitively are, when considered affectively, prescriptive oughts or ought nots.

---

[87] The phrase "trapped impulses" is less confusing than "trapped universals" which Northrop sometimes uses. One must remember that the latter phrase is elliptical for "the neurologically trapped impulses that are the epistemic correlates of introspected ideas."

[88] For more on first and second order facts, the interested reader is directed to chapter XIX of CLEE.

It is because non-normatively worded first-order factual theory is prescriptive with regard to the motor side of any person's public self and cognitively true or false in a way that can be tested by anyone anywhere by appeal to the first-order factual data on the introspective and sensory side of anyone's nervous system, that an evaluative, as distinct from a merely descriptive, method for ethics and politics is possible and can be specified with operational as well as theoretical exactitude. (112-3)

This means that all ethical and political theories are based on non-normatively worded theories of nature and man.

Skipping some philosophical niceties, lets consider the two ways Northrop gives for evaluating any ethical or political theory. They are (1) logical and (2) empirical. One first examines the epistemological and psychological non-normatively worded premises of the national philosophy in question for logical consistency. If the premises contradict each other, the theory is false and the national philosophy is bad. If said philosophy passes the logical test, one then examines it for empirical correctness. Here we find that the theory must not only be necessary but "sufficient to account for all the first-order factual, introspected and sensed data." (115) Compare two theories, T1 and T2. To say that T1 is false is to say the one can find a first order fact that is incompatible with the deductive consequences of T1. On the other hand, if one can find no fact incompatible with either theory and T2 "accounts for every first-order fact for which T1 accounts and also for at least one such fact for which T1 does not account" then T2 is "confirmed with a greater degree of probability." (115)

Let's concretize with some examples. Northrop asks us to contrast a

patriarchally tribal law of status nation [which] affirms as a non-cognitively worded postulate of their
empirical theory of heredity that all the inherited
qualities of people pass to the children only through
the male line, the mother being merely a passive
receptacle, and that they present this as the justification for affirming that any person's political
rights [etc.] have nothing to do with their being
'born free and equal' as the American Declaration of
Independence affirms, but are instead determined
temporally antecedent to anyone's birth by the patriarchal line of breeding. (115-116)

Let us call this theory T1. With the development of modern
genetics and any political theory based upon such a science, we
have a theory, T2, that is incompatible with a premise in T1.
Such a premise can be cognitively demonstrated to be false by
anyone anywhere and therefore any political argument based
on such a cognitively false premise is unsound. Here we have
an empirical refutation of T1 based on an incompatibility with
T2.

Let us keep T1 as our example and show the logical
method at work. Suppose that by using the descriptive method
from chapter six, we discover that T1 is based on a naive realistic epistemology. Since naive realism is a self-contradictory
theory, we need no appeal to facts to show it to be a false theory. The proof is simple enough. Naive realism asserts that a
given object of knowledge exists and possesses a certain property independently of its relation to any perceiver but then
goes on to define said object in terms referring to properties
which are relative to the perceiver. In Northrop's technical
terminology, concept by intuition red, (to take a secondary
quality as an example) is a multi-valued relation and the perceiver is one of the indispensable relata. Hence it does not and

cannot exist apart from the perceiver. Sensed red only exists
when someone is sensing it. The *esse* of sensed red is *percipi*,
as Bishop Berkeley would say.

If Northrop is correct, and I doubt that many moderns
would agree with him on this issue, cultural relativism is a
false relativism. One can evaluate, in a manner verifiable by
anyone anywhere, various cultures, normative judgments and
political ideals.

What follows is Northrop's summary of the first seven
chapters.

A person (and hence a nation) is an epistemologically complex item of knowledge. One exemplifies
not merely (1) one's private introspected covert
and overt non-normatively worded theory of first-
order factual man and nature, but also (2) its one-
one epistemic correlate which is the inner hierarchically trapped target of one's public teleologically
mechanical nervous system and its motor behavior
as mechanically inhibited or reinforced prescrip-
tively by this target. Hence, although by itself the
philosophy of (1), being non-normatively worded,
does not imply an ought for human behavior, nevertheless, when considered in its one-one epistemic
relation to its formal equivalent (2), it does.
Normative prescriptive words refer therefore not to
items of knowledge, but to the relation between
non-normatively described items of knowledge and
their epistemically correlated target effect upon
human behavior. Consequently evaluative, as well
as descriptive, morality and politics is a science. Its
method consists in finding the non-normatively
worded first-order factual assumptions of any personal or national philosophy, apart from which its
normative words are devoid of content, and then
examining these assumption with respect both to
(a) their logical consistency and (b) empirical data

inspectable *by anyone anywhere*, to test their truth
or falsity. (120)

CHAPTER 14

Let us now turn to two later chapters. Northrop writes
on modern technology in chapter fourteen. There he addresses
the question of man's relation to the earth, specifically "what
effect has man's role in changing the face of the earth had on
his aesthetic sensitivity and creativity, his ethical, political and
legal standards for determining whether his tools are used for
good or for bad ends?" (238) This suggests that man's relation
to the earth has changed with the advent of modern technology.

What makes for a technological civilization as opposed to
a non-technological one? And what cultural changes does such
a civilization entail?

A technological civilization, in Northrop's sense, is one in
which most of the tools that are used have their source in a science that is constituted, in whole or in part, of concepts by
postulation. On the other hand, tool making and using civilizations based on concept by intuition (or at best concept by perception) sciences are non-technological. Perhaps this is why,
when Western technology is introduced into African or
Southeast Asian cultures, the natives "feel that they are confronted with something baffling which they do not understand
and which to them seems destructive of all values." (239) In a
sense they are right. For man's relation to nature is different
in a technological civilization and hence his cultural values are
different.

It is important to understand that Northrop does not endorse the view that the technological countries are scientific
while the non-technological ones are not. As was said above,

the difference is epistemological, not scientific. Non-technological societies can certainly have science, but it is a science, the
fundamental concepts of which are all concepts by intuition.
All these sciences are purely descriptive.   Natural history biology of the species-genera type or Charvakian materialism and
Vaiseshika dualism are examples.   (240) All of the fundamental entities of these sciences are defined in terms of sensed
qualities.

The case is otherwise with a technological society. It discovers new tools, not by moving sensed materials about in the
manner of the proto-man of Kubrick's *2001*, but rather by reference to a concept by postulation theory.   The atomic bomb is
a tool the discovery of which presupposes the mass-energy
equation of Einstein's special theory of relativity.

One can see that the difference between a technological
and non-technological society is equivalent to the difference
between a concept by intuition and a concept by postulation
society.   Northrop then goes on to describe how this epistemological difference manifests itself.   Beginning with the concept
by intuition society he notes the various consequences that re-
dound in its physics, scientific method, grammar, aesthetics,
ethics, metaphysics and religion. (242-251) He then does the
same for concept by postulation societies.   Since space does not
permit a detail recapitulation, let us single out music for examination.

The music of a concept by intuition society or culture has
melody and rhythm but lacks harmony and counterpoint.   It is
neither recorded nor controlled by a written text as is the music of a technological society.   Typically the melody is played
against a background drone.

> The drone also symbolizes something immediately
> experienced. [It] expresses both the dynamism of
> the going-on-ness and the relatively undifferenti-

ated character of the vast spreadoutness. It sym-
bolizes, therefore, the infinite timelessness out of
which each sensed particular thing, including
sensed particular man himself, arises and to which
it returns at death.   (246-7)

Music of a technological society differs in many ways.   The
drone is no longer a necessary standard background to the
melody.   In its place we find the "ratios of the deductively formulated, mathematical acoustics of the Greek Pythagoreans and
Democritus."   (252) These ratios are, of course, concepts by
postulation.

Melody also changes.   Instead of a cyclically repeatable
melody we find the ratios mentioned above also governing it.
This eventually gives rise to harmony and counterpoint.   Such
vertical considerations presuppose a "precise musical scale."
Without such a mathematically imposed precision, the "simultaneous ordering of sounds in harmony and counterpoint would
become chaotic, as would also the uniform, temporal ordering
of sound in melody."   (253)   Think of the conductor counting
beats, one, two, three, four, etc.   Their job is to impose mathematical order on what otherwise would be chaos.   That is, to
subject the sensuous musical materials to a "mathematically
formal and intellectually prescribed *logos* of proportion and
perfection," and thus giving rise to a new technologically based
concept of the beautiful.   And this concept of the beautiful not
only pertains and constrains the composer, but even the *techne*
of the instrument maker.   The mathematical ratios must be
built into the instruments in order for them to produce the exact notes the composer requires.

The actualization of these aesthetic potentialities "came to some of its richest formal fulfillments in Bach and Beethoven."[89]

Nevertheless, these new aesthetic (as well as ethical, legal, economic and religious) values, constructed as they are on concept by postulation theories, give rise to the following two problems in politics. First, just as it is possible to construct more than one theory to account for the concept by intuition sensed world, so also one may construct different and even incompatible constitutions for ordering human relations. This means that in addition to the problems encountered in any clash between the values of technological and non-technological societies, conflicts can also occur among the constructed contractual constitutions of different technological societies. Northrop has discussed his solution to this problem in TON.

The second problem has to do with the tendency of those who live in a technological society to place all value in it and degrade the concept by intuition world to one of mere appearance. "This has created a modern man who has become so absorbed by the intellectual imagination, its technological tools and its abstract legal codes that he is starved emotionally and with respect to aesthetic immediacy."

A similar but inverse problem plagues the non-technological cultures. They are starved physically and produce millions of children who die each year.

---

[89] For more details the interested reader is directed to "Toward a General Theory of the Arts" in The Journal of Value Inquiry, Vol. 1, #2, Fall, 1967; "The Relation between Naturalistic Scientific Knowledge and Humanistic Intrinsic Values in Western Culture," in Contemporary American Philosophy, 2nd Series, ed. J. E. Smith, Allen and Unwin, London, 1970, pp. 107-151; and "The Relationally Analytic and the Impressionistically Concrete Components of Western Music," Journal of Research in Music Education, Vol. 19, #4, Winter 1971, pp. 399-407.

The resolution of the latter two problems lies, in general philosophical terms, in "specifying the relation between these two components of complete human knowledge, supplementing the one with the other," thus integrating these two half-men into a whole.   Man is an aesthetically (known entity) in epistemic correlation with a theoretically known entity.   Northrop goes on in chapter19 to merge these two halves into a whole, recapitulating much of what he wrote on pp. 436-478 of MEW. Since MEW has already been discussed, a look at chapter 18 is warranted.

CHAPTER 18

PAPP's penultimate chapter, and the last we shall consider,   contains what Northrop considers to be the six postulates of any free society: (1) aesthetic, (2) epistemological, (3) psychological, (4) mathematical and (5) mathematical physical and (6) Jeffersonian.   Let's consider them in this order.

(1)   Aesthetic: a free society needs to embody and hence educate its citizens in "the cultivation of radically empirical sensitivity."   This aesthetic education (and experience) is designed to "never leave one with a legal and political person who is regarded as nothing but an aggregate of unconscious material substances for which political freedom means the inevitability of physical collisions[90] with other unconscious material substances after the manner of Hobbes and Marx." (314)   Aesthetic sensitivity insures that we will know our own souls (in the only true sense of that term, i.e., the concept by intuition sense) and bodies in all their emotive, immediately felt intuitiveness.

---

[90]   I think but cannot say for sure that what Northrop meant here was that for Hobbes freedom means the absence of physical collisions. See p. 34 of PAPP, Hobbes' Leviathan, Part II, ch. xxi and the text to note 1 above.

(2) Epistemological: This postulate needs little elaboration since most of this book is devoted to a working out of the
implications of Northrop's concept by intuition epistemically
correlated with concept by postulation epistemological theory.

(3) Psychological: This postulate, covered in the review
of chapters three and four above, is the theory of circular neural nets functioning as a negative feedback system in epistemic
correlation with radically empirical introspected ideas.

(4) Mathematical: All of pure mathematics is analytic
and true tautologically. All of pure mathematics is composed of
concepts by postulation.

(5) Mathematical Physical: This postulate is merely the
most recent truths of indirectly confirmed mathematical
physics of which Northrop has written about in great detail in
SFP and elsewhere.

(6) Jeffersonian: Northrop spends 12 pages (312-323)
on the first five postulates, but he devotes the next 15 pages to
this last postulate, the ethical and political postulate he calls
the Jeffersonian principle. The remainder of this chapter shall
be devoted to this principle.

What is this principle or postulate? To ask this is to ask
for "the elementary postulate of contractual legal science."
(323) It is expressed in ordinary prose in, for example, the
Declaration of Independence--hence the name "Jeffersonian
principle." Expanding on what Northrop takes to be Jefferson's
elliptical words, he writes: "We hold these truths to be self-
evident, that all men are born free and equal with respect to
their religious, moral, legal and political rights, privileges, obligations and duties." (324) In other words: no contract, no
contractual obligations. So much for Northrop's statement of
the principle.

How do we know it is true? It's self-evident. Jefferson
used those very words and Northrop agrees. Yet he realizes
that the English prose of Jefferson, based as it is on an erro-

neous naive realistic epistemology, may mislead those who read it, and therefore Northrop removes the postulate from its imageful context by couching it in the notation of symbolic logic.

Before looking at the Jeffersonian principle in its symbolic clothing, it might profit us to ask What makes it self-evident? It is self-evident in the sense that Peano's mathematical postulates are self-evident, viz., that they are tautologically true. What makes it true is that it is the "basic tautologically true proposition of any contractual legal and political system whatever." There simply are no "legal or political obligations, duties, rights and privileges until . . . the parties concerned specify these legal and political rights and duties." (325) So at birth, all persons are equal with respect to any political obligation, duty or right. At birth, they have no political[91] obligations, duties, rights, etc.[92]

"Or put more exactly, just as Peano's Fifth postulate specifies the substantive property which differentiates the class of all natural numbers from the class of all real numbers in the science of mathematics, so Jefferson's principle gives the differentiating property of any legally contractual nation." (325)

It might be objected that Northrop is being provincial in taking as the fundamental principle of contractual legal science a principle from a Founding Father of his own country and generalizing it for the rest of the human race. He answers this

---

91 But, I take it, they do have natural rights. To enter into a contract presupposes those natural rights outlined by Jefferson.

92 Northrop also regards the above as true empirically. Anyone anywhere can vouch for the truth of the statement that neonates are not born pledging allegiance to any political system. But this would seem to make the proposition both analytic and synthetic. Since he nowhere elaborates on this point, I prefer to confess my confusion in a footnote.

charge by recalling the words of Jefferson to the effect that "*all* men are created equal" not just Americans.   In fact, the implication is from the universal to the particular, i.e., all men are not equal because Americans are equal; Americans are equal because all men are equal.

We are now in a, position to examine the Jeffersonian principle as Northrop embodies it in the notation of symbolic logic.[93] Let p = any person x = any object of intrinsic goal-value legal and political judgment l = any law which is a maxim, i.e., a hypothetically normative imperative and s = the substantive content of any l.   Then the Jeffersonian principle looks likes this:

(p) (s) (x) (l): x is intrinsically good or just iff x is an instance of an l such that for (p)l and (p)s of l.

This reads that for all p, s, x and l, x is a good or just aim or goal if and only if x is a law that applies to all people and applies the same substantive content of the law to all people.

Consider the following example.   The pre-Brown v. Board educational system of the South certainly satisfied the (p)l condition.   *Every* child was required and afforded access to a grade and high school education.   Nevertheless it failed the (p)s condition by assigning the white kids to the best schools and the blacks to poor schools.   Hence one could conclude that the educational school system of the South was bad because self-contradictory, violating the tautologically true Jeffersonian principle.[94]

---

[93] Those unfamiliar with symbolic logic may skip this and the next two paragraphs.

[94] This is a complicated. For example, it is not obvious if the p(s) condition would rule out "separate but equal" schools.

One additional example may help concretize this principle. Take the Constitution of the former Soviet Union. Since this document does not define the obligations and duties of its "citizens in terms of biology of birth. . .its codified law is that of contractual legal science." (335) This means that any law granting privileges to one citizen or group of citizens, like the Communist party, must grant them to all or run afoul of the (p)s condition of the Jeffersonian principle. Obviously it did not do this. Hence, one can conclude that said Constitution is self-contradictory constitutional law, violating the very principle "upon which any legally contractual nation rests." (335)

Northrop writes that since all of the postulates have been verified (postulates (1), (2), (3) and (5) being synthetic have an empirical verification whereas (4) and (6) being analytic are tautologically true), they might be placed at the beginning of any nation's constitution, "with the explicit provision that the synthetic propositions (1), (2), (3) and (5) are subject to revision should further empirical observations and theoretical reconstructions, that are experimentally and cognitively confirmable by anyone anywhere, indicate this to be necessary." (337)

One word of warning of a technical nature must be made before concluding this chapter. Northrop expresses a reservation concerning whether his symbolic logical formulation of the Jeffersonian principle is complete enough to rule out as illegal certain things that the principle requires to be ruled out. Although he doesn't go into any detail, declaring it to be " entirely too complicated a question to pursue and settle here" he does suggest that perhaps s must be universally quantified to read (s). With that tantalizing tid-bit, this chapter concludes.

CHAPTER 7

MAN, NATURE AND GOD

In MNG, Northrop further *generalizes* his theology. As the last word in the title indicates, Northrop returns to the theme of God after an absence of nearly thirty years.[95] In SFP, Northrop developed his two God theology.[96] One God, identified with the single physical, formal and psychical macroscopic atom the other with the *order* of the many physical, formal and psychical microscopic atoms.

In MNG, the physical and the psychical are de-emphasized and the formal takes center stage. In addition to this emphasis on the purely formal, Northrop also spends a lot of time on the intellectual or concept by postulation component of God's nature. So before looking at this in greater detail, it would pay us to recall the other component of God's nature, i.e., the aesthetic component. Northrop identifies the aesthetic component of God's nature with the undifferentiated aesthetic continuum. That is Northrop's Western terminology for point-

---

[95] I am going to restrict my analysis of MNG to God since (1) we have just finished chapter six which was much ado about man from a scientific or natural point of view and, (2) the contrast between MNG and SFP is a fascinating one.

[96] These two gods are concept by postulation gods and it must be remembered that they are epistemically correlated with the undifferentiated aesthetic continuum. For purposes of this chapter, nothing will be lost if we just refer to the macroscopic atom exclusively and ignore the order of nature God.

ing to the Eastern conception of the divine, variously named Tao, chit consciousness, Nirvana etc.   Here one can see that Northrop is quite traditional vis-a-vis the Eastern conception of the divine.   In fact, he has merely given it a Western name. Since the Divine is undifferentiated, it is hardly possible to give it a new characterization, because all characterization depends on the positing of determinate qualities which by definition, (actually by experience) the undifferentiated does not have. It's not even an *it*.   An "it" is too definite a substantive to apply to the undifferentiated aesthetic continuum.

The situation is quite otherwise when we turn to the traditional   Western conception of God.   Since the typical Western notion is a concept by postulation, it can only be known tentatively (hence the appeal to faith) and is subject to revision, as are all concepts by postulation, when our data changes.   It is to this Western conception of God, or God as theoretically known, that we now turn.

Northrop states that *any* modern Western theology must identify God's nature with "the only nonself-contradictory interpretation of the irreducible concepts by postulation in contemporary mathematical physics" i.e., "the Limit, or organically related lawful Logos that is approached asymptotically by the changing, logically realistic constructs of Western mathematical physics." (230)   Once again it is apparent how Northrop keeps to the tradition.   The concept of the Logos[97] has a venerable history in Philo, the Stoic natural philosophers and John of the Fourth Gospel.   All use the term Logos (λόγος).

Northrop's "keeping to the tradition" is revealed not only in his use of the term Logos, but also in his understanding of how the (at least Catholic) tradition itself understood the rela-

---

[97] Note that Northrop's two god theology in SFP is merely one possible specification of the Logos.

tion between theology and science.   Consider the following
paragraph from MEW.

> [A]ccording to contemporary Catholic doctrine, it is
> quite erroneous to suppose, as do so many Protes-
> tant Christians, that by independent, purely reli-
> gious modes of information and knowledge one
> knows what the words "soul," "God," "grace," and
> "revelation" mean.   Clearly none of these items is
> given with self-evident immediacy in experience.
> It is precisely because this is the case that Christ
> had to come into the world, the point being that God
> himself, immediately, in his own nature, is not here.
> Thus St. Thomas and the Roman Catholics see very
> clearly that the traditional words of Christian doc-
> trine are by themselves quite meaningless noises
> unless they are identified, or by the accepted
> methods of logic, connected with the specific con-
> tent of scientific knowledge.[98]   Thus, what St.
> Thomas did was to take the conception of man and
> nature precisely in the form which Greek Science,
> as made philosophically articulate by Aristotle, in-
> dicated it to possess, and to identify the traditional
> words of Christian doctrine such as "soul," "God,"
> "perfection," "grace," and "revelation" with certain
> factors in this generally accepted and, for its time,
> scientifically verified theory.   Thus there is no jus-
> tification whatever, even in the doctrine of revela-
> tion in Roman Catholicism, for the contemporary,
> erroneous supposition that the doctrines of the
> Christian religion and one's moral ideas of perfec-

---

[98] See. Summa Theologica, II, II, Q.2, ART. 4 where St. Thomas writes "the
science to which it pertains to prove the existence of God is the last of all to offer
itself to human inquiry, since it presupposes many other sciences. . . ." Cf. also
the first of his five ways (ST, I, Q2, Art. 3) to prove the existence of God where
he starts from the premise that "it is certain and evident to our senses that some
things are in motion." But what is motion. He tells us that it is "the reduction of
something from potency to act."   That this is different from what Descartes or
Newton would say is obvious.

tion can be validated independently of systemati-
cally developed philosophical theory that is grounded in the empirical content of our knowledge of
man and nature, as this content is specified by the
methods of natural science.   (279)

Returning to the "Logos," let us ask What exactly does the term
"logos" mean for Northrop?   The quick but probably unin-
formative answer is that to which mathematical physics refers.
This subject is taken up in detail in chapter 15.   It refers to a
"logically realistic ontological object of knowledge, the same for
all knowers and, hence, appropriately called reality, . . ."   (224)

But this object(s) is "at the Limit" for Northrop.   What
does this mean?   To speak religiously, it means that we can
never know God perfectly.   To speak scientifically, it means we
can only know, say, the macroscopic atom, asymptotically, with
ever higher and higher degrees of approximation.   He draws a
comparison with Eastern philosophy.   Just as the undifferentiated aesthetic continuum is known "only to a higher and higher
degree of approximation as [one] . . . eliminates one after another of the differentiations within his existential immediate
experience, so erring human mortals, with their partial factual
knowledge, know the logically real, in the sense of Principle of
Relativity invariance for all facts and for everyone, only by
asymptotic approximation."   (225)

Since God is at the logically realistic limit and approached
asymptotically in terms of concepts by postulation, we can now
understand why our concept of God is subject to change.   This
parallels historical fact.   When Aquinas come into possession of
the scientific and philosophical achievements of Aristotle,   God
got defined, at least in part,   in terms of the unmoved mover of
Aristotle's physics. In this sense, Northrop is the Aquinas of the
modern age, defining God in terms of his macroscopic atom, or,
if that fails to achieve empirical confirmation, in terms of the

currently confirmed content of contemporary theoretical physics. We can *formally* equate this with the logos.

Let us now examine how Northrop's logical realism impacts upon other traditional Western theological notions. Such an examination will also permit a comparison with the notion of God discussed in SFP. Northrop begins with omniscience. This is particularly interesting because no sooner does he attribute omniscience to God, than he finds it necessary to qualify his statement. (231) This is illustrative of the tentativity of concepts by postulation. They are subject to change with the appearance of new evidence. Prior to the discovery of quantum mechanics, one could say that God was omniscient, since contemporary natural science had achieved a theoretical dynamics relating entities and their states at one time to all other times. But since quantum mechanics we have discovered, much to the shock of Einstein and other contemporary religious thinkers, that the Newtonian type of determinism is too strong when we approach the very small. "God does not play dice" said Albert Einstein, to which Werner Heisenberg replied, "Yes, he does."

What does this mean? In terms less suited to heaven or Las Vegas and more appropriate to physics, Northrop reminds us that in the theories of both Newton and Einstein, "chance and its derivative concept of probability appear only on the concept by intuitional, nominalistic, and operational side of modern physics." (251) Chance only enters on the operational side. Only man plays dice.

But in order to account for black-body radiation, scientists "found it necessary to introduce chance and its concept of probability into the logically realistic definition of the state of any naturalistic system an any moment of time." (252) This means that God as well as man is a gambler. But like us, God must pay for his fun and the price he pays is the surrendering of omniscience.[99]

Before leaving this attribute, the reader might recall that in SFP God (=macroscopic atom) was stated to be omniscient, since it was a physical item whose form contained, quite literally, all possible forms for all eternity. Since Northrop, following the Greeks, identifies form with rationality, the obvious conclusion follows, viz., that God is omniscient. (SFP, 275) He literally has all forms within him. This despite the fact that all of chapter three is devoted to quantum and wave mechanics![100] So much for omniscience.

As for omnipotence, the position articulated in MNG is equivalent to SFP. Northrop denies, in SFP, that God is omnipotent due to the fact that the microscopic atoms possess energy and therefore are not totally controlled by the big atom. Although less explicit, MNG agrees.

Likewise with creation. The macroscopic atom "is the creator of all complex things. For creation is a rearrangement of the eternal microscopic particles into stable or partially stable systems. This, the macroscopic atom does." (SFP, 270)
In MNG, Northrop writes as follows.

> Another implication of this logically realistic meaning of the intellectual component of the word God is that His creation of nature is a many-termed

---

[99] One curious result is to make God more like the Hindu conception of God that Northrop talks about in the last chapter of MNG. He reminds us that the Hindus express God's playfulness in the poetic concept by intuition image of a carefree child in a swing. See 247.

[100] To be perfectly fair to Northrop, he does not use the word "omniscience" in SFP but rather refers to the macroscopic atom as the most perfectly and unequivocally clear headed of all real objects." (SFP, 275) One might call such a God "asymptotically omniscient." If, however, one assumes that omniscience and omnipotence mutually imply each other, then, since the macroscopic is not the latter, then he can't be the former.

relational *logical* creation *within which first-order factual man, able to commit error as he eats from the tree of natural knowledge,* is one of the relationally specified terms.   The phrase in italics is what distinguishes theism from pantheism.   God's creativity is, therefore, not a temporal act committed long ago in the infinite past.   The latter type of creator is the product of the misleading poetry of either an anthropomorphic carpenter or a long-bearded, snooping old man in an apple orchard whom Occam should have shaved with his razor and disposed of long ago. (231)

This notion of creation is similar to the one outlined in SFP. The word "logical" is in italics to emphasize the fact the creation is not a physical process.   It is a logical or formal process of re-arrangement of eternal physical stuff.   This is not to deny that energy is required to accomplish such a re-arrangement, but rather to underscore the fact that we are not dealing with creation *ex nihilio*.

In addition, it must be noted that creation is not a past event, but an eternal one, i.e., one that occurred, is occurring and will always occur.   This is nothing more than an implication from the principle of being (the real doesn't change its properties) coupled with the primacy (i.e., irreducibility) of motion. To say that God's creative acts are eternal is equivalent to proposition that the rearrangement of the microscopic atoms will never cease.

Finally, let us try to get clear about what Northrop means when he calls God "the Limit, or organically related lawful Logos that is approached asymptotically by the changing, logically realistic constructs of Western mathematical physics." (230) What is meant by the limit?

The limit is an imageless concept by postulation.   To understand the concept of the limit one must understand the concept of serial order. This concept is also a concept by postulation and Northrop defines both serial order and limit in chapter 4 of MNG, to which we now turn.

There are four postulates that found the notion of serial order. Even if the reader is unfamiliar with modern symbolic logic, it would be best if one read the following to get some idea of Northrop's God.

Postulate I (x, y) : x R y,   [x is related to y]

Postulate II (x) : not (x R x), [x is not related to x by R]

Postulate III (x, y) : (x R y) and not (y R x), [x is related to y by R but not vice versa].

Postulate IV (x, y, z) (x R y) and (y R z) implies : (x R z). [If x is related to y and y to z by R then x is related to z by R].

Northrop elaborates these four postulates as follows. Postulate I merely establishes the fact that, in any particular domain of discourse to which it applies, the objects to which the variables refer are not chaotic, disconnected objects; they are related. Take any two natural numbers. R merely states that they are connected. Postulate I states that for any two natural numbers you pick, those two numbers are related by some connective law. R is equivalent to a universal field equation.

To find out more about this field of objects requires positing additional postulates. One cannot find out anything by directly predicating properties of them as is done in naive realistic substance-property thinking. We do this by assigning additional imageless properties to R.

Consider Postulate II. It tells us that R is not a reflexive relation, i.e., a relation that any given object has to itself. "Father of" is Northrop's example of such a relation. No one is their own father.

Postulate III asserts asymmetry. R only goes one way and if, as is the case with the symbols we have given, R holds between x and y it doesn't hold in reverse, i.e., between y and x. Again we could use "father of" as an example from ordinary life. If John is the father of Darnell, then Darnell cannot be John's father. "Father of" is an asymmetrical relation. Thus far the three postulates tell us that R is connected, irreflexive and asymmetrical. What does postulate IV tell us.

Postulate IV tells us that R is a transitive relation. Here father of will not work as an example. But "earlier than" will. If x is earlier than y and y is earlier than z, then x is earlier than z.

All entities that obey the foregoing four postulates are serially ordered entities. Noticed that nowhere was reference made to any immediately sensed objects. "It is by this means that man is able to arrive at the concept of an object which exists independently of sensed images which are relative to perceivers." (82)

Northrop then goes on to show how the concept of serial order is an elementary idea in the concept of the limit. He tells us that

> [A]ny term in the serial order is not the term that is the limit. Instead, within the field of any serially ordered relation, its entities may be divided into two classes, which we shall call A and B. When class B has a first term and is approached asymptotically (i.e., never reached) by the unending serially ordered entities in class A, then the first term in class B is the limit of the series of terms in class A.
> (83)

This limit is the logos which Northrop identifies with God in later chapters of MNG. This Limit "is approached asymptotically by the changing, logically realistic constructs of Western mathematical physics." (230)

Northrop then points out that the placing of the entity variables within parentheses is the convention by which the mathematical logicians express universal quantification. What this means is that "the relation R holds not for some of the "epistemic correlates" of these entities, but for all of them."

This means that the language of contemporary science is not that of Aristotle but of Plato. If Aristotle had been right on this issue, then such directly sensed qualities as wet, cold and yellow would be persisting predicates of "supposedly directly sensed substances or external objects." It would also be true that we could have no ideas in our minds that were not first in the senses. That this is false is easily realized. No one has ever perceived a four dimensional space time continuum yet we not only have such an idea, but within the context of contemporary confirmed scientific theory, it is a true idea.

But if the language of science is not Aristotelian two termed subject-predicate language, what is it? It is the logic of many termed relations, most adequately expressed in symbolic logical and/or mathematical notation.

What are the implications of this excursus into physics and language for theology. Taking the latter discipline first we discover that unless all our talk about God is to be restricted to poetic metaphor, we must talk scientifically and philosophically. This means that we must realize that attributing predicates to a cosmic substance simply will not do. God is not a substance, but a relation. This doctrine is hardly revolutionary nor artificial. Roman Catholics, for example, will simply have to shift from the naïve realism of Thomas Aquinas to "William of Champeaux with his Stoic logically realistic concept of God and His logically relational creativity." (232)   In other words, Catholics already have a thinker in their tradition that sees God as a relation.[101]   Christians in general have long proclaimed that God is Love and Love is, of course, a relation, not an entity.   Now they have scientific as well as religious reasons for their proclamations.

Northrop, after showing the inadequacies of the theologies of Descartes, Leibniz, Locke, Berkeley, Hegel and Marx, goes on to state that the main cause of these errors is a confusion on the part of the thinkers just mentioned between "metaphorical religious poetry with realistic scientific prose." (235) He then applauds McTaggart's explication of God as love, specifically as a determinate relation between beloved persons. If one accepts this characterization of love, then Jesus' second great law of love, viz., "thou shalt love thy neighbor as thyself" follows tautologically from the first law, i.e., "Thou shalt love the Lord thy God with all thy heart, with all thy soul and with all thy mind."   (Matthew xxii, 37-39 and Luke x: 27 for a slightly different wording.)   (235)

Northrop then reiterates his point that God is love and love "is neither a naïve realistic substance nor a causal relation between such substances but is a logically realistic relation." (236)   Notice that we have arrived at the same negative conclusion as the Buddhists, albeit from a different epistemological direction.   The Buddhists, and *mutatis mutandis*, other Eastern philosophies, would tell us that Nirvana or Divine Blissfulness is neither a determinate naïve realistic entity nor a mechanistic causal relation between such entities.   To conclude this part MNG and lead into the last two chapters, Northrop writes the following summary:

.

_____

101 This has an epistemological parallel in Augustine. Augustine countenances concepts by postulation as opposed to the naive realism of Aquinas. Cf. City of God, Book II, ch. 2 and On Christian Doctrine Book I, ch. 7

Religion has to do with . . . two first-order factors in ourselves and in all things which are eternal. The part of God's nature which is radically empirically and existentially experienced, when its transitory and relativistic differentiations are approximately neglected or abstracted away, meets this condition. Only its differentiated particulars are temporary and transitory. The same eternally-now timelessness characterizes the Limit as approached asymptotically by man's imageless, intellectually known, theoretically dynamic, logically realistic theories of what It is. As shown just above, this Limit remains invariant through all the transitory events of all space-time that are its items. Such would not be the case were the theories of modern mathematical physics merely statical, rather than dynamical theories whose laws relate the present state of any natural system to its past and future states, thereby timelessly embracing the whole of cosmic four-dimensional space-time. (237)

Of course, the relation between God as approximately experienced as the undifferentiated aesthetic continuum and God as intellectually known is one of epistemic correlation. Epistemic correlations are needed simply because one cannot deduce either way of knowing God from the other way of knowing God, for the same reason that one cannot deduce sensed yellow from intellectually known yellow. This fact leads Northrop into a discussion of mysticism.

It may seem incredible to some that after all this talk about four-dimensional space-time continuums, serial orders and limits, words that are preeminently suggestive of the scientific, Northrop would turn his attention to mysticism. Our age has certainly been described by some as, if not a scientific age, at least an age when science is the dominant epistemological expression. Yet Northrop claims, following Wittgenstein,[102] that there is no knowledge "that is not, in its elements, mystical. Furthermore, since the compound items of knowledge, defined in terms of its elements, are meaningless, except as its elements are meaningful, this entails that all knowledge is mystical." Naturally a flat out statement like that calls for an immediate elucidation of the word "mysticism." Northrop tells us that mysticism is a type of knowledge that "has to be known by immediate intuition independently of the language which tries to, but cannot, say it." From this definition, it should be obvious that Northrop does not mean anything "noncommon-sensical, unscientific, or nonsensically esoteric about mysticism." (239)

Since there are two ways of knowing the world, there are two variants of mysticism. Consider concepts by intuition first. They are all mystical in the sense that they are denotative and cannot be meaningful to anyone who has not had the experience, say, of green, in question. They are pointer words that can only point, but never say or self-show (more on this expression below) what something is.[103]

The other type of mystical knowledge is to be found in concepts by postulation. "Serial order," "number," "limit" and "God" are such examples. "The timelessly invariant, eternally-now factors in these two species of mystical knowledge give, respectively, the two inseparable components of the first-order

---

[102] Most of Northrop's remarks on mysticism occur in chapter 17, "Language, Mysticism and God." I will, however, be ignoring Wittgenstein, but the interested reader is, of course, encouraged to seek further.

[103] Since I will have more to say about Northrop's theory of language in the next chapter, a note on the three functions of language is what I will limit myself to here. Language can either (1) point to, (2) say or (3) self-show its meaning. Northrop will argue that only (1) and (3) are legitimate.

factual eternal nature of ourselves and all other natural creatures that is the complete mystical knowledge of God." (242)
All concepts by postulation self-show but cannot say or point.
I am not sure I understand what "self-show" means but for our
purposes this much is at least clear.   First, the way concepts by
postulation mean is different from the way concepts by intuition mean.   Second, self-showing must refer to something that
cannot, in principle, be sensed.   Third, like pointing, self-showing is not to be confused with the traditional subject-predicate
proposition.   It would have been the proper function of the
traditional subject-predicate proposition to *say* what
something is.[104]   But that function is intimately connected with
naïve realism, which Northrop has shown to be self-
contradictory.[105]   Hence, of three possible functions of language, viz., pointing, self-showing and saying, only the first two
are valid.   But much of ordinary language is spoken and
written as if one could "say" something, hence the importance
of the advice Alfred North Whitehead gave to Northrop in 1922
"One cannot be too suspicious of ordinary language in science
and philosophy, the reason being its single entity-property
syntax."   We shall have more to "say" on language in chapter
eight.

   Let us recall that this is a chapter on God.   I don't know
what is accomplished by making all knowledge mystical, but if
it be so, then naturally all knowledge pertaining to God is mystical knowledge.   According to Northrop, we come to know God

---

104 Northrop is in agreement with H. Veatch who in the title of chapter one of
his book Two Logics refers to mathematical logic as "a logic that can't say what
anything is." Of course, Veatch means this as a shocking criticism; Northrop does
not.   Veatch, as is well known, believes there is a vital, in fact, fundamental role
of the subject-predicate sentence. Northrop thinks it nothing but a snare and a
delusion. Of this, more in due course.

105 See above p. 129.

in coming to know (by pointing or self-showing) the timeless invariants of "first-order factual eternal nature."

The final chapter of MNG is devoted to the poetry of God's playfulness. How is God playful aesthetically? What is the concept by intuition cash value of this notion? "[W]hen God playfully creates the unsayable aesthetically imageful, differentiated transitory sensing selves and their relativistic objects that Maya-mask both Himself and His-Self-in-each-one-of-us, He has no determinate laws to guide Him." (And remember, He's not even a him!) This is but another way of saying that everything, even our consciousness of everything, comes out of and retreats into the undifferentiated aesthetic continuum. But we already knew that. The emphasis here is on the fact that God is always playing games; that he is full of fun. This "purple prose" simply means that not even God can deduce the "unsayable, mystically experienced differentiation that is a perishing particular "yellow" from the eternally-now undifferentiatedly Blissful existential love of God." (247) And since deduction is impossible, there is no sense in which such "creation" islawful. In keeping with the playfulness of God Northrop writes

> The Hindus are right
> Who can't say, but do see
> That a gay child in a swing
> Is like God's creativity. (248)

The phrase "a child in a swing" is an allusion to the fact that in a large traffic circle in the heart of Bangkok the city has erected "two tall, upright poles with a crosspole at the top to which the ropes of a carefree child's swing are attached. [T]his object is the religious symbol of God's playful creativity" according to Princess Poon whom Northrop visited in the early '50s. (247)

God's playfulness is also evident in the West. When
Einstein tells us that God does not wear His heart on His sleeve
he is telling us that God likes to play games. One way God
plays the game can be seen in the existence of beings with free
will, viz., humans. We can see this in the Spanish bull fights,
and the English cricket matches.

> God's creation of human beings, who may and do
> err as they play the game within its lawful rules, is
> present also, in the Americans' baseball. Otherwise,
> there would be no "booting of the ball" after the
> manner of a clumsy and aesthetically crude,
> Brooklyn bum. Hear his religious language: "Jesus
> Christ. This burns me up like Hell." Nor would one
> in the next inning have the unsayable experience of
> seeing that same sinful, very human soul, the vul-
> gar crowd still trying to boo him out of Flatbush,
> scoot, Peeweelike, back to his right, deep into the
> hole between Short and Third, to come up with the
> ball in the smooth single motion over to First that
> has the Divinely Creative Omniscient Anticipation,
> Beauty, and Grace of a Rizzuto as he nips Eddie
> Collins at First by an eyelash when the Umpire
> there, his ear on the ping in the baseman's mitt, his
> nose in the dust, and his eye on the runner's foot by
> the sack, snaps up his right arm, its Englishlike
> thumb pointing outward, with a shout that *means*
> "Out!" If this be not Heaven and its Judgment Day,
> what is? God has Spoken![106]   (249-50)

Northrop then appends a stanza that parallels the one cited
above for the Eastern playfulness of God.

---

[106] I have taken the liberty of substituting the religious name "Jesus Christ"
for Northrop's "blankety-blank" as this seems to make the player's language
more religious--as was Northrop's intent.

The Yanks too are right
When they show and so-see
That to be without baseball
Is not to Be

The foregoing seems to reveal three aspects of God's playful nature: (1) the aesthetic concept by intuition playfulness, (2) theoretic concept by postulation playfulness, and (3) the creation of first order factual creatures that "are capable of committing errors and the inclusion of them in His game."

But God is not only present on a child's swing or in baseball. It seems He has been to Las Vegas. He must have been there if quantum mechanics is correct. God is a Divine gambler who does take a turn at the tables. He must do this if He is to create humans with free will and hence with the capacity for good and evil. This means that there exists in nature "irreducible chance, [and hence] a naturalistic meaning for the Devil."

This also gives a meaning to the theological notion of "natural evil." But this evil should not be confused with moral evil. Most of us have experienced a "tragically painful misfortune" and know the difference between it and "personally responsible moral guilt." Natural evil is a first-order factual occurrence which no human being is responsible for but has negative effects on human beings. Man made evil is "the deposit of self-responsible, second-order artifactual human behavior, which is the mechanical effect of false human beliefs concerning first-order factual man, nature and Nature's God." (255)

If this be true, historians should find, when looking at the past, a mix of the true, the good and the beautiful alongside the false, the bad and the ugly. This is hardly a controversial finding. What is controversial is Northrop's claim that only the naturalistic scientists and philosophers are in a position to tell what cultural facts and artifacts are sinful or not. This is done by testing first-order factual beliefs "against the first-order facts of the non-manmade part of man, nature and Nature's God." (255)

Northrop concludes his quest for God and life's meaning (and the book) with the following poem which is reproduced in its entirety.

That unshaved patriarch told a fib
Such snooping silly rot, about a rib.
The gay Virgin is God, She aswinging
Beauty everywhere from the beginning.

Man was a dead stone.
So God said:
"Let there be error."
Thus moral man was born.

A mortal man then said:
"Blessed be the merciful
For they asymptotically
Shall see God."

Later than Man shocks:
"My human asymptotic
Limit is errorless.
Hence, isomorphically
I am both man and God."

Here endeth our paradox.

CHAPTER 8

"AND IN THE END"

I want to do three things in this final chapter. First, I want to direct the interested reader to several publications that are important in their own right but have not made it, for whatever reason, into the previous chapters of this book.

Second, I want to summarize what I take to be Northrop's major and manifold achievements. And finally, I want to say a few more words about his philosophy of language as I promised in note 9 of chapter seven.

SOME ADDITIONAL PUBLICATIONS

1. *European Union and United States Foreign Policy: A Study in Sociological Jurisprudence*, New York: The Macmillan Company, 1954. In chapter five, I gave short shrift to Northrop's ideas on sociological jurisprudence simply because I knew then that I would refer the interested reader to this work, which is an application of that very theory. Sociological jurisprudence is the science that studies the relation between the positive and the living law of the people to whom the positive law applies. (vi) With this definition in mind it is easy to understand why Northrop has two chapters on positive law (4 & 5) followed by two chapters on the living law of the European nations under consideration.

2. *The Prolegomena To a 1985 Philosophiae Naturalis Principia Mathematica*, Ox Bow Press, Woodbridge, Conn. 1985. This book is only for the advanced student of Northrop. Although only 70 pages in length, they are some of the most dense pages in Northrop whole corpus. His tendency to pile up adjectives reaches its apogee with this work. The reason for the word "Prolegomena" in the title has to do with the fact that he was projecting a four volume work (in addition to PRO). Succeeding volumes were to bear the titles (1) *1985 Philosophiae Naturalis Principia Mathematica* (2) *et Aesthetica* (3) *et Jurisprudencia* and (4) *et Summa Theologica*.

3. "An Internal Inconsistency in Aristotelian Logic," *Monist*, Vol. 38, No. 2 (April, 1928), pp. 193-210. This essay has to do with the problem of existential commitment of the universal affirmative proposition of Aristotle's logic. One has to remind oneself of this essay's date to appreciate Northop's insights.

4. "The Mathematical Background and Content of Greek Philosophy" was originally written for *Philosophical Essays for Alfred North Whitehead* published in 1936. Northrop's précis of this article is concise enough to warrant full quotation. He tells us that the essay "correlates all the ancient Greek Scientists, Philosophers and Humanists from Anaximander through Parmenides, Anaxagoras, Democritos, Archytas, Plato, Eudoxos, Aristotle and the Stoics with the respective Thirteen Greeks Books of Euclid's *Elements* in which the respective *First Principles* . . . of each are defined with their respective deduced theorems proved." (PRO, 64) Actually he misremembers, a forgivable *faux pas* if one considers that nearly fifty years separate this essay from PRO. The essay ends with Plato; Aristotle and the Stoics hardly play but a passing role. Despite this caveat, the work is crucial for understanding Northrop and

was presaged somewhat in the first chapter of SFP. Recall SFP literally means science and philosophy.

5. "The Relation between the Natural and the Normative Sciences" appeared in volume 1 of the *Delaware Seminar in the Philosophy of Science* for 1961-1962. I include it here not only for its intrinsic importance, (it contains a good discussion of the is/ought problem, but also for the fact that *inter alia* Northrop makes passing references to chapters in his other books so as to, inadvertently at least, expose what he thought he was doing in those works.

6. "Toward A General Theory of the Arts" appeared in the Fall 1967 issue of *The Journal of Value Inquiry*. As its title indicates, the purpose of this article is to provide a general theory of the arts, a project begun in chapter IX of LSH, "The Functions and Future of Poetry."

7. "The Relation Between Naturalistic Scientific Knowledge and Humanistic Intrinsic Values in Western Culture" (Hereafter NSKHIV) was published in 1970 in *Contemporary American Philosophy: Second Series*. In this long article, (nearly 45 pages) Northrop deals with the relationship between science and two (of many) humanistic intrinsic values of Western Culture, viz., music and legal science.

8. While NSKHIV paints with a broad brush, "The Relationally Analytic and the Impressionistically Concrete Components of Western Music" focuses on music. This article can be found in the vol. 19 #4 (1971) of the *Journal of Research in Music Education*. Northrop argues for the thesis that sciences establishes the criterion of beauty for music. I think he establishes a much weaker thesis, viz., that the science of acoustics provides a necessary, but not sufficient, condition for the beautiful.

9. "Natural Science and the Critical Philosophy of Kant" in *The Heritage of Kant*, Whitney and Bowers eds. (Princeton University Press), 1939.   In this essay, Northrop endeavors to show that from the first of his pre-critical writings until about 1768, Kant had a "physiologically and neurologically based" theory of the *a priori* conditions of experience.   (48)   It was only with certain discoveries by Euler and Kant that the latter felt compelled to posit the existence of a transcendental ego and develop his more famous epistemological theory of the *a priori* in the First Critique.   Northrop also points out that an examination of Kant's essay on Euler indicates that Kant had good reasons for distinguishing two kinds of concepts, those obtained by abstraction from the senses and those not so obtained.   This essay is delightful simply from the point of view of the insightful rehearsal of Kant's early physical writings.

NORTHROP'S ACHIEVEMENTS

I have decided to list Northrop's achievements according to the following categories: Metaphysics, epistemology, philosophy of science, ethics, politics, aesthetics. We shall give metaphysics pride of place since it had such seminal position in the thought of Northrop himself.

METAPHYSICS

Northrop's foremost achievement (in this area) is the postulation of the macroscopic atom.[107]   This solution to the problem occasion by Einstein's rejection of absolute space has no found acceptance in the scientific community due mainly to the

---

107 Notice here the inevitable overlap among categories--the macroscopic atom is as much an achievement in metaphysics as in science.

highly confirmed Hubble expansion theory.   As of this writing there has appeared no thinker either concerned or capable enough to construct a crucial experiment to adjudicate between Hubble and Northrop.   Nevertheless, one can only marvel at the number of problems in disparate disciplines that the postulation of the macroscopic atom solves.

Besides Northrop, only Einstein and Whitehead seemed even remotely aware of the problem that arises within Einstein's theory when absolute space is jettisoned.   Needless to say, no other thinkers have attempted to solve this problem One needs an integrative approach even to be aware of the dilemma, and the twentieth century has been short of that kind of philosopher.

Among additional accomplishments in metaphysics, I would name the problem of organization in biology, the electro-dynamic theory of life, the definition of the physically embod-ied psychical as bare indeterminate experienced quality.

EPISTEMOLOGY

I'm torn here between the concept by postulation/concept by intuition duality on the one hand and the discovery of epistemic correlations on the other.   Both have predecessors.   In fact, much of it can be found or re-found in Plato, and even in Parmenides.   Consider Plato.   In his famous divided line the main division is between opinion and knowledge, roughly congruent with concepts by intuition and concepts by postulation respectively.   He even tells us that the uppermost portion of the line contains a knowledge that "makes no use of images."[108] This would of course be almost identical to Northrop's concepts by intellection.

We   find a similar parallel in Plato's philosophy between what he calls "participation" and what Northrop calls "epistemic correlation."   The complaint[109] against Plato, viz., that he never really made clear the nature of "participation", cannot be made against Northrop.   He devotes chapter seven of LSH to its explication,   and he constantly talks about it in his other works. If I had written this book in a few years earlier, I would have chosen the careful explication of the two main types of concepts as Northrop's major epistemological achievement, but lately I have come to appreciate the profundity of his notion of epistemic correlation.   The fact that it solves it the mind-body problem would be achievement enough.   But it does more than that.   If Northrop is correct in chapter 12 of MEW, it solves the basic problem of how to relate the cultures and philosophies of

---

[108] Quoted by Northrop in LSH p. 90. The line occurs at Republic, 510. Cf. Phaedo, 100.

[109] To cite but two commentators: Fr. Copleston in Vol. 1, Part 1, ch. 20 p. 205 of his A History of Philosophy; Windelband's A History of Philosophy, vol. 1, p. 120. The locus classicus for this criticism of Plato goes back to his best pupil, Aristotle. Cf. Metaphysics, Book I, ch. vi, 987b11ff.

East and West, Latin and Anglo-Saxon, democracy and communism, medieval and modern, and the more general problem of the sciences and the humanities.

> The answer to the basic problem underlying the ideological issues of these times is, therefore, as follows: the aesthetic, intuitive, purely empirically given component in man and nature is related to the theoretically designated and indirectly verified component, not as traditional modern Western science and philosophy supposed, by a three-termed relation of appearance, but instead by the two-termed relation of epistemic correlation. (443)

PHILOSOPHY OF SCIENCE

Here I can be brief. SFP is Northrop's major achievement in this the philosophy of science. Chapter one alone is brilliant in its outlining of all possible approaches to this particular discipline. Second to SFP, I would place the following chapters of LSH; I-VIII, XI, and XII.

ETHICS

One of Northrop's major achievements in ethics comes from an understanding of the dangerousness of severing ethics from physics and philosophy, (e.g., seeKant who attempted to make these respective disciplines autonomous.) Since such a separation was unwarranted, Northrop was able to solve the is-ought problem as we saw above in the chapter on PAPP. See the Delaware Seminar article and chapter 12 of MEW as well.

AESTHETICS

Northrop began to develop his two function theory of art as early as 1941 in an article that appeared in <u>Furioso</u> and later was reprinted at chapter ix of LSH bearing the title "The Functions and Future of Poetry." Briefly what this theory does is announce two epistemological purposes of art. Art can function in and for itself and when it does it is mainly concerned to convey to the spectator the concept by intuition materials of that art in and for themselves without any thought of a didactic message. This Northrop calls the art in its first function. MEW provides a picture illustrating first function art in Plate XI.

Second function art is art that does have a message to convey, a message beyond the beauty of the aesthetic materials themselves. Any "Madonna and Child" illustrates this type of art (Plate XII of MEW).

I would also point to "Toward a General Theory of the Arts" and NSKHIV, especially the section on music. He elaborated his theory of music in "The Relationally Analytic and the Impressionistically Concrete Components of Western Music" published in vol. 19, 1971 of the *Journal of Research in Music Education.* The thesis of these works (and I will restrict myself to music) is that the humanistic, concept by intuition felt beauty is, for Westerners at least, related by epistemic correlations to the mathematical ratios of Euclidean geometry and its later extrapolations. To give but one example, since the time of Bach and the well tempered scale, "the immediately successive notes . . . are related by the nonarithmetical Eudoxian ratio of one over the twelfth root of two." (404)

So much for some of the major achievements of Northrop. I would now like to conclude by formalizing some of his final thoughts on language.

NORTHROP'S LAST THOUGHTS ON LANGUAGE

In chapter seven, I promised to say something about Northrop's final thoughts on language. Northrop, as early as LSH, was keenly aware of the problem of ordinary language, but his treatment was *en passant*. But in a paper published in 1970,[110] as well as in PRO, he tackles the problem in a systematic way. Recall the problem with ordinary language. It possesses a subject-predicate structure capable of misleading all but the most wary into the dogmatic slumberland of naive realism. This two termed syntax was read back into both God-made and man-made nature. Thus arose the modern distinction between *Naturwissenschaften* and *Geisteswissenschaften*, the latter literally meaning the science of persons conceived as Ghosts. Modern thinkers fell over themselves in a frantic effort to rename these Ghosts. From the more mundane mind or spirit, they moved onto such neologisms as windowless monad, Id, Ego, Superego, blank tablet, *Cogito*, *Dasein*, transcendental ego, regulative moral ego, etc. (NSKHIV 113) Meanwhile scientists, not to be outdone, also had their little subjects, called atoms or corpuscles, so that properties like mass and momentum could have a subject of predication. Inertial mass got talked about as if it were a property of an atom instead of the many-entity-termed concept that mathematical physics revealed it to be.

But the biggest problem of all was specifying the common denominator factors for meaningfully relating the material atoms and the spiritual atoms, i.e., the mind-body problem. But this was not the only relational problem. What, for example, was the relation between one introspective knower to an-

---

110 "The Relation Between Naturalistic Scientific Knowledge and Humanistic Intrinsic Values in Western Culture" in Contemporary American Philosophy, 2nd Series, ed. J. E. Smith, Allen and Unwin, London, 1970, pp. 107-151. Hereafter NSKHIV.

other the introspected knower to what is objectively known naturalistic scientific knowledge with humanistic knowledge etc. Three hundred years of argument has produced no solution.

Northrop suggests that we desperately needed some epistemological house cleaning. He calls for the systematic replacing of "the purported directly observed two-termed entity-property persisting entities with nominalistic sensuously qualitative disjunctively relational radical empiricism in epistemological correlation with speculatively discovered deductively formulated, indirectly and experimentally confirmed many-entity-termed logical realism, in which the epistemic correlations implicit in the theory's deduced operational definitions and accordingly constructed instruments are two termed, but not one-one two termed." (Ibid. 119-20)   In this same article he was able to formulate his solution to the problems of ordinary language in terms of three maxims and two corollaries.   Unfortunately, Northrop's tendency to pile up adjectives, coupled with a text that could have used some judicious editing, makes reading these maxims even more difficult than it usually is to read the grammatically compressed, nay vexatious, prose of a maxim.   Northrop manages to be, per impossible, both wordy and compressed at the same time.   What follows is my own wording Northrop's original wording will be found in the notes.[111]

Maxim I: When referring to the differentiated aesthetic continuum, all words are to be understood *only* in their concept by intuition meaning. [The "pointer" words of chapter 7]

---

[111] I mainly rely here on the wording in PRO.

Maxim II: When referring to the world as it exists independently from all perceivers, all words are to understood *only* in their concept by postulation meaning. [The "self-showing" words of chapter 7]

Corollary I: All two-termed entity-property symbols of Principia Mathematica must always be interpreted as many-termed, relationally defined entities.

Corollary II: An irreducible (at least) three-entity-termed logic of relations must be completed.

Maxim III: (This is not recorded by Northrop in the formal way given above, but can be found on p. 47 of PRO.) When referring to the undifferentiated aesthetic continuum, all words that attempt to qualify it must be met with the Asians' Neti-Neti (not this differentiated quality, not that differentiated quality) logic.[112]

---

[112] Maxim I: When referring to the [differentiated aesthetic] component of cognitive knowledge, all its words must be thought of, written, and read <u>only</u> in their nominalistic radical empirical meaning, as described best for the so-called 'outer' sensed qualities by Berkeley, and for introspected qualities by the skeptical Hume of Volume I of <u>The Treatise</u> and in William James's <u>Radical Empiricism</u> and other essays on the self.

Maxim II: When referring to [the logically realistic factor in warrantable knowledge of human and cosmic nature] , the noun in our ordinary sentence must be an irreducible many-entity-termed relation and its predicate the substantive content of that relation.

Corollary I: Applied to the two-termed entity-property $F_x Y_x$ symbols of Principia Mathematica, it entails that the F_s and Y_s must always be many-entity-termed relationally defined.

Corollary II: Necessary, too, is the construction [accomplished, at least according to Northorp, by J. S. da Fonseca et al in <u>Signification and Intention</u>, (Lisbon, University of Lisbon) 1970] of an irreducible at least three-entity-termed logic of relations.

Maxim III: When referring to the undifferentiated aesthetic continuum, one's logic must be of the Neti-Neti type (it isn't this differentiated quali<u>ty</u>, it isn't this differentiated quali<u>ty</u>. [I do not know why Northrop underlines 'ity' in quality.

It should be obvious that these maxims and corollaries reflect the application of Northrop's epistemology, especially his theory of possible concepts, to the problem of concept meaning.   And with that we end (or more hopefully, initiate) our journey.

Northrop quotes Corollary II twice in PRO, 45-6 and 49 respectively. On 49 he omits 19 words, those following "Necessary too is . . ." I suspect a typo.

APPENDIX A

Grünbaum On Newton's Conception Of Relative Space And Time

(This essay originally appeared in Vol. 1, #6 of *Objectivity*)

The purpose of this appendix is to examine Grünbaum's interpretation of the Newtonian conception of relative space (and time) as elaborated by the latter in his *Philosophiae Naturalis Principia Mathematica.* My text will be Grünbaum's "Geometry, Chronometry and Empiricism" which first appeared in vol. 3 of the *Minnesota Studies in the Philosophy of Science* and was later reprinted in his 1968 book, *Geometry and Chronometry in Philosophical Perspective.* [Hereafter GCPP] I will be focusing on pp. 7-11. These five pages must have satisfied Grünbaum since he reproduced them without redaction as pp. 4-8 of his 1973 book, *Philosophical Problems of Space and Time,* a much enlarged version of an earlier work of the same title. (All quotations are from the former work.) Specifically I will be concerned to examine Grünbaum's claim that F. S. C. Northrop's interpretation of Newton's concept of relative space is incorrect and that his reading is the correct one. The theses to be defended in this study are the following: (T1) Grünbaum is wrong in his understanding of Newton's concept of relative space, but (T2) Northrop's own analysis, albeit correct, is nevertheless vitiated by an epistemological ambiguity. Let us begin with (T1).

I. Grünbaum   on   Newton

It will be profitable to have before us the text in question, viz., the famous Scholium from Newton's *Principia* which is reprinted below as quoted by Grünbaum.

the common people conceive those quantities [i.e., time, space, place and motion] under no other notions but from [1] the relation they bear to sensible objects.   And thence arise certain prejudices, for the removing of which it will be convenient to distinguish them into absolute and relative, true and apparent, mathematical and common. . . . because the [2] parts of space cannot be seen, or distinguished from one and another by our senses, therefore in their stead we use sensible measures of them.   For from the positions and distances of things from any body considered as immovable, we define all places and then with respect to such places, we estimate all motions, considering bodies as transferred from some of those places into others.   And so, instead of absolute places and motions, we use relative ones and that without any inconvenience in common affairs but in philosophical disquisitions, [3] we ought to abstract from our senses, and consider things themselves,   [4] distinct from what are only sensible measures of them.   For it may be that there is no body really at rest, to which the places and motions of others may be referred. . . . those . . . . . defile the purity of mathematical and philosophical truths, who confound real quantities with their relations and sensible measure. . . .

I. Absolute, true, and mathematical time, of itself and from its own nature, flows equably without relation to anything external and by another name is called duration: [5] *relative, apparent, and common time, is some sensible,*   and external (whether *accurate or unequable*) *measure*   of duration by the means of motion, which is commonly used instead of true time such as an hour, a day, a month, a year.

II. Absolute space, in its own nature, without relation to anything external, remains always similar and immovable. Relative space is some movable dimension or measure of the absolute spaces which [6] *our senses determine by its position to bodies* and which is commonly taken for immovable space such is the dimension of a subterraneous, an aerial, or celestial space, determined by its position in respect of the earth. [7] *Absolute and relative space are the same in figure and magnitude but they do not remain always numerically the same.* For if the earth, for instance, moves, a space of our air, which relatively and in respect of the earth remains always the same, will at one time be one part of the absolute space into which the air passes at another time it will be another part of the same, and so, absolutely understood, it will be continually changed. . . . Absolute time, in astronomy, is distinguished from relative, by the equation or correction of apparent time. For the [8] *natural day are truly unequal, though commonly considered as equal, and used for a measure of time* astronomers correct this inequality that they may measure the celestial motions by a more accurate time. It may be, that there is no such thing as an equable motion, whereby time may be accurately measured. All motions may be accelerated and retarded, but the flowing of absolute time is not liable to any change. The duration or perseverance of the existence of things remain the same, whether the motions are swift or slow, or none at all: and therefore this [9] *duration ought to be distinguished from what are only sensible measures thereof* and from which we deduce it, by means of the astronomical equation. (Grünbaum, 1968, pp. 6-9. Emphases and numbers in square brackets are mine.)

According to Grünbaum, Newton is making two points here, viz., (1) that absolute space and time are autonomous and (2) that it has an intrinsic metric from which he concludes that "what Newton is therefore rejecting here is a relational theory of space and time." (Ibid. p. 9)

Now while it is true, as Grünbaum notes, that Newton would likewise reject any identification of absolute space and time with psychological space and time, he also wants to insist that one is seriously mistaken if one assumes that Newton means to identify the latter with the relative space and time referred to in the Scholium. [This is Grünbaum's charge against Northrop of which more in due course.] According to Grünbaum, the important contrast is between two kinds of public space and time, one absolute and the other relative and both having nothing to do with any conception of private spaces and times. Newton is, in effect, saying that hitherto natural philosophers have known only the public space and time that he calls relative space and time. Against such a view he wants to suggest that absolute space and time is (the only) real public space and time while relative space and time is merely the way the "common people conceive" these notions. He rejects the ultimate reality of relative space and time, i.e., that "bodies and events first *define* points and instants by conferring their identity upon them," and he further rejects the notion that absolute "space and time are metrically amorphous." (Ibid.)

II. Grünbaum on Northrop

So much for Grünbaum's reading of Newton. How, according to Grünbaum, does Northrop read this text. Northrop sees Newton as attempting to differentiate absolute from relative space and time as per Grünbaum, but Northrop would have us believe that Newton identifies the relative space and time with the private "psychological space and time of conscious awareness whose respective metrics are given by unaided ocular congruence and by psychological estimates of duration, . . ." (Ibid. p. 10) But this, according to Grünbaum, is wrongheaded and causes Northrop to miss Newton's essential point which is that "relative space and time are indeed . . . public space and time which is defined by the system of relations between material bodies and events, and not the egocentrically private space and time of phenomenal experience." (Ibid.) As for the "sensible" measures that Newton discusses in the Scholium, they are "furnished by the public bodies of the physicist, not by the unaided ocular congruence of one's eyes or by one's mood-dependent psychological estimates of duration." (Ibid.)

As evidence for these charges against Northrop's interpretation Grünbaum offers three references (direct and indirect) to the Scholium which he claims renders Newton's position on this matter "unambiguously clear." (Ibid.)

III. Northrop's Epistemology

(Readers who don't want to read another exposition Northrop's epistemology can skip this section without loss. Most of it appears in chapter 2 above.)

Before checking these references, we must briefly expose Northrop epistemology, at least in outline, since it is against this backdrop that he analyses the Scholium. We shall return to Grünbaum's attack in section six. If this exposition is successful, it will also discharge our thesis (T2) concerning an ambiguity in Northrop's epistemology. What follows is a broad, general presentation of Northrop's epistemology as contained in LSH and MEW. These texts have been chosen for two reasons: they contain the most detailed expositions of Northrop's epistemology, and Grünbaum is familiar with both of them he quotes MEW as his source throughout the passages under consideration and he reviewed LSH for the Yale Law Journal in 1948.

Northrop is an epistemological bifurcationist, i.e., according to him there are two ways of knowing the world, sense and reason. These two sources of knowledge give rise to two major types of concepts those concepts that have their origin in sense Northrop calls concepts by intuition while those whose origin is reason are called concepts by postulation. Concepts by postulation have their meanings postulated for them theoretically by the "postulates of the deductive theory in which" they may or do occur, whereas concepts by intuition get their meaning denotatively from the immediate data of either sensory or introspective experience. The following are examples from LSH of both types of concepts. "Blue" in the sense of the blue we experience when we look at a blue sky or lake is a concept by intuition whereas "blue" as it is employed in electromagnetic theory is a concept by postulation. To know what Newton, qua theoretical physicist, means by a "physical object" one does not immediately apprehend the colored shapes of tables, chairs and the like; rather one examines the postulates and the theorems of his *Principia*. On the other hand, the yellow of Van Gogh, the pounding, insistent rhythms of Beethoven, or the odor of freshly brewed coffee must be experienced to be known. It is by way of concepts by postulation that science and philosophy go beyond the immediately given to entities and relations that are in principle unobservable. [If fact, Northrop defines metaphysics as the "thesis that there are concepts by postulation" (LSH p. 87 -- a thesis denied Berkeley, Hume and positivism, to mention just three dissenters.] The following chart contains Northrop's exhaustive list of concept by postulation.

Concepts by postulation are divided by Northrop into three subcategories and defined as follows:

I. Concepts by Intellection: = Concepts designating factors which can neither by imagined nor sensed.

II. Concepts by Imagination = Concepts designating factors which can be imagined but cannot be sensed.

III. Concepts by Perception = Concepts designating factors which are in part sensed and in part imagined. (LSH p. 94)

In order to clarify the above, let us look as some of Northrop's own examples from each of the subcategories.   Starting with III, the concepts by perception, Northrop instances tables, chairs, other people, the moon with its backside that we do not see and its presented side that we do see and, most important for what we are about, *the public space of daily life.* (LSH p. 93)   For II, Northrop lists the ether concept of classical pre-relativistic field physics or the atoms and molecules of classical particle physics.   The size of these atoms prohibits the reflection of light and so they cannot be sensed but they can be imagined, e.g., the Bohr atom pictured as a miniature solar system.   Finally the space-time continuum of Einstein's field physics or Plato's atomic ratios are given as examples of group I, as are, to move to a completely different discipline for contrast purposes, individual property rights and the equality Jefferson mentions in the *Declaration of Independence.* Since these concepts and their referents are not only not sensible but unimaginable, they can only be known in their symbolical logical relatedness.

Concepts by intuition, i.e., concepts "which refer to the aesthetic component of anything for their complete meaning, are also divided into three sub-categories.   In MEW Northrop characterizes these as follows:

There is the totality of the immediately apprehended. This is the aesthetic component of all
things in its entirety, with nothing neglected or
abstracted. It is more accurately described as the
differentiated aesthetic continuum. Within this total differentiated aesthetic continuum attention can
be directed . . . upon the continuum in its all-embracing continuity and indeterminacy neglecting
the transitory differentiations or it can be directed,
as it has been by Hume and the modern Western
positivists, upon the specific determinate differentiations (images and sense data) neglecting the continuum. The former method leads to Jen, Tao,
Nirvana, Brahman, Atman and Chit the latter to the
specific particular colors, sounds, odors and their
transitory relative sensed relations of Galilei's and
Newton's sensed space and time and to the introspected wants and preferences of Anglo-American
economic theory. (MEW p. 447. Emphasis mine.)

Summarizing we have: I. The differentiated aesthetic continuum II. the undifferentiated aesthetic continuum and III. the
differentiations.

IV. The T2 Ambiguity

But here an ambiguity arises, the ambiguity referred to
in my initial characterization of (T2) on p. 1. If one looks at the
quotation from LSH given by Northrop on p. 6 above, relative
space is given as an example of a concept by postulation that is
a concept by perception whereas the quotation from MEW on p.
7 would have us believe that it is a concept by intuition that is
a concept of the differentiations within the aesthetic continuum. One is led to ask "Is relative space and time a concept by
postulation that is a concept by perception or is it a concept by
intuition that is a concept of the differentiations?"

[In answering this question it is perhaps advisable to note that the identification of relative space and time as a concept by perception occurs only in LSH and not in MEW. But although the copyrights on MEW and LSH are 1946 and 1947 respectively, the actual chapter from LSH is which the identification under consideration occurs is taken from a talk written for a conference on East-West philosophy given at the University of Hawaii in 1939. (LSH p. 100) There is a possibility that during the intervening years Northrop changed his mind as to the epistemological status of relative space and time.]

Given that Grünbaum only quotes MEW, one could simply ignore the LSH doctrine and regard relative space and time as a concept by intuition, as per MEW. But this would leave the supposed change of opinion on Northrop's part unexplained, to say nothing of the seeming paradoxical nature of the "privateness of public" space and time. Take the latter first. Grünbaum would have us believe that Newton means by his relative space and time public space whereas Northrop thinks relative space is, in some sense, mind dependent or private. If there is to be a genuine disagreement here, public space must exclude private space. Grünbaum makes such an assumption.

Yet many thinkers have not held these two to be mutually exclusive. Alexander, for example, writes that "[If] relativism means philosophically . . . that Space-Time for each observer is his own, it inevitably leads on to a total Space-Time which combines these worlds." (90-1) Or consider Russell who regards public space as simply "the system of private spaces themselves. (1960, p. 74 and 1954, pp. 207-210) And finally, D'Abro, one of Grünbaum's favorite authorities in this area, writes, in a book listed in the bibliography of the essay we are examining, ". . . the three-dimensional space of experience appears to have arisen as the result of a synthesis of private views. . ." (p. 83) If these views are correct it would appear that the notion of the exclusive natures of public versus private space is something to be argued for and not simply asserted. If Alexander, Russell and D'Abro are correct, there is a sense in which both Grünbaum and Northrop are right! Grünbaum is simply focusing on space after "the synthesis of private views" that D'Abro mentions. Northrop's focus is on space prior to the synthesis.

To see this via Northrop's terminology, recall the definition of a concept by perception it is a concept designating factors which are in part sensed and in part imagined. Public space and time is such a concept since, although its spread-aboutness can be sensed, its (1) independent extramental existence cannot nor can (2) its infinite extension. We cannot sense (1) since it is simply impossible to sense what unsensed space and time is like when we're not sensing it and we cannot sense (2) since all sensing is finite and limited. We can only imagine or guess what these unsensed properties are like. For example, we can imagine that these properties are exactly what they are like when we are sensing them. It is done all the time by the man of common sense and that species of philosophers (and scientists) known as naive realists. Grünbaum is focusing on the "imagined" part of relative space and time, i.e., the part thought to be independent (hence the adjective "public") of any sensing subject and therefore he feels justified in taking Northrop to task for his privatization of relative space.

Northrop, focusing on the relationship that every concept by perception has to the sensing subject, feels equally justified in calling relative space and time private. But when this focus becomes paramount Northrop is led to conceive relative space and time as a concept by intuition, instead of a concept by perception. This would explain the MEW analysis as well as Grünbaum objections.

V. The Ambiguity Resolved

Now I would like to suggest a solution to the ambiguity mentioned above concerning whether, for Northrop, relative space and time is a concept by postulation that is a concept by perception or a concept by intuition.   It seems that the latter is the more suitable candidate and the argument for this is as follows.   All concepts by postulation that are concepts by perception buy into the philosophical position known as naive (or direct realism) and since Northrop has demonstrated [or will in PAPP] that this position is self-contradictory one is led to conclude the following: if one construes Newton's concept of relative space and time as a concept by postulation that is a concept by perception then it is a contradictory notion on the other hand, if read as a concept by intuition, then not only is it non-contradictory, but it can be epistemically correlated [epistemic correlation is a technical term in Northrop's epistemology and is defined as "a relation joining an unobserved component of anything designated by a concept by postulation to its directly inspected component denoted by a concept by intuition" (LSH p. 119)] with absolute space in its concept by postulation that is a concept by intellection meaning to provide a more complete explication of this important concept.   Since the proof is short I close this section with a full quotation from Northrop.

> [A]ny naive realistic epistemological concept of the public self or any public object is self-contradictory. The mark of such an epistemology is that it attempts to define the purportedly public substances in terms of directly sensed or introspected properties.   But all sensed or imagined items of knowledge are imageful and all images are relative, not merely to the observer's frame of reference and to the percipient, but even, as Democritus, Galileo, Newton and Berkeley pointed out, to different sense organs and moments of perception of the same percipient. The naive realist means, however, by his public substances something that exists. . . independently

of its relations to any observer. Clearly, therefore, it is self-contradictory to define an object existing independently of its relation to the observer in terms of sensed or introspected imageful properties all of which are relative to the perceiver. (PAPP p. 66)

From this I conclude that Northrop's considered position is the interpretation given in MEW, viz., that relative space is a concept by intuition.

VI. Grünbaum contra Northrop I

With this rough sketch of Northrop's epistemology in hand, we can begin payment on the promissory note that was issued at the end of section two. Grünbaum's criticism of Northrop would be correct if and only if Newton's own conception of relative space were such that it was independent of all sensing subjects. To see that this is not the case one has merely to consult the longish quotation with which we began this study. [The numbers in square brackets are from that quotation.] [3] tells us that in order to arrive at the concept of absolute space we must "abstract from our senses" and [6] states that relative space is a measure of absolute space made by "our senses". That the conception "common people" have of relative space is percipient relative, can be gleaned from [1] where Newton writes of the "relation they bear to sensible objects." Note the switch Grünbaum makes in GCPP when he attempts to tell us that for Newton relative space and time "is defined by the system of relations between material bodies and events. . ." (p. 10) By emphasizing "material" as Grünbaum does, he makes the conceptual switch even more blatant. Newton says "sensible" not "material". And on the same page, Grünbaum would have us believe that the "sensible measures"

Newton talks about are furnished by the "public bodies of the physicist" but Newton, in introducing his notion of relative space and time talks about "the common people" and how they conceive time, space, motion etc. Notice also how Grünbaum prefers to use the qualifying adjective "relative" when referring to the common people's conception of space, whereas Newton typically employs three different adjectives, as if he we trying to make himself perfectly clear.   In addition to "relative" he uses "apparent" and "common" e.g., in between [1] and [2] as well as in [5] itself.   If Grünbaum was correct in his interpretation, "apparent" space, the space that appears to ordinary people, would be "apparent" to no one since he wants to eliminate all reference to "the unaided ocular congruence of one's eyes. . ." (Ibid.)   To see this in full relief, consider an argument Grünbaum gives in support of his position, bearing the number iii.

> iii. Newton illustrates relative motion by reference to the kinematic relation [note the jargon of the physicist and not that of the common man] between a body [sans sense organs] on a moving ship, the ship and the earth, these relations being defined in the customary manner of physics without phenomenal space and time. (GCPP p. 11)

But the body on the ship is not a body without sense organs miraculously calculating kinematic relations but a common sailor as Newton himself tells us in the fifth last paragraph of the Scholium.   In fact, Newton refers to the example as the "example of the sailor" whereas reading Grünbaum, one would think Newton had a theoretical physicist in mind.   So much for the third argument which Grünbaum proffers against Northrop.

VII. Grünbaum contra Northrop II

Next we need to deal with Grünbaum's other (number ii will not be dealt with here since it deals with time and what is said below applies mutatis mutandis to it) argument against Northrop.

> i. "Absolute and relative space are the same in figure and magnitude," a declaration which is incompatible with Northrop's interpretation of relative space as "the immediately sensed spatial extension of, and relation between, sensed data (which is purely private space, varying with the degree of one's astigmatism or the clearness of one's vision)" (LSH p. 10 & MEW p. 76)

Strictly speaking, there is no argument offered here merely a declaration of incompatibility. Grünbaum apparently felt that his own "interpretation of Newton is fully attested by . . . specific assertions of [Newton] . . ." Lacking any argument, let us nevertheless try to be clear on what Grünbaum is saying. He is claiming that absolute space and time and *public* relative space and time "are the same in figure and magnitude" and that such a commonality of characteristics is impossible on Northrop's reading, wherein absolute space and time is contrasted with *private* relative space and time, neither of which can have *anything* in common, especially figure and magnitude. And yet if we look at Newton's description of the process by which we move from the notion of relative to absolute space and time which occurs between [2] and [4] we find statements that are simply incompatible [tu quoque noted] with Grünbaum's account. Newton tells us that since we cannot distinguish parts of space "by our senses" we use "sensible measures of them" instead. In order to accomplish this we take an object that we sense to be immovable (perhaps the earth) and define all places with respect to this sensible immovable. But because of the relationship between this object and our senses we produce relative instead of absolute places, motions etc. Now comes the crucial question for our purposes -- how, according to Newton, do we get to the absolute from the relative? [3] and [4] tell us.   We abstract from our senses.   We "consider things themselves" apart from or in abstraction from our senses.   This is the way Newton suggests we proceed in order not to "defile the purity of mathematical and philosophical truths."   What is left after the process of abstraction occurs?   It must be admitted that what any individual thinker claims to remain behind after we have abstracted from our senses depends on where he is on the continuum that extends from naive realism at the one extreme to the more rarefied variants of scientific realism at the other. [It is curious to note that both Grünbaum and Northrop are both scientific realists in some sense of that term.   In that respect, the dispute here is between family members.]   A naive realist believes that the relationship between the properties of absolute and relative space is one of identity, i.e., they share all their characteristics.   [This is an extremely naive realist.]

Newton is on that continuum, and while his epistemological position calls for a distinction between sensed and postulated space, such a position does allow for a sharing of some but not all of the properties of sensed and absolute space and time, e.g., figure and magnitude.   What Grünbaum seems to be unaware of is what epistemological theory is presupposed by Newton's distinction between absolute and relative space that permits a sharing of certain characteristics, viz., Galileo's distinction between primary and secondary qualities.   Or as one might phrase it to bring the distinction home immediately, absolute and relative qualities.   Secondary or relative or apparent qualities have no existence without the mind, or, to quote from Galileo's *IL Saggiatore*, if the observer (say, Newton's sailor) "were removed . . . nothing of them" would remain. (MEW p. 78

& Burtt, pp. 85-6.) Burtt writes that it is of "utmost importance" to realize that for Galileo "secondary qualities were subjective." (p. 84)

What happened after Galileo is old news. The game of
listing and altering the list of primary and secondary qualities
became an industry. For Galileo, "number, figure, [and] magnitude" (among others) were primary for Berkeley, none were for
Newton figure and magnitude were primary while he seems to
shift number to relative or secondary status. By the time we
arrive at Hutton we find him writing that even "magnitude and
figure have no other existence than in the conceiving faculty of
our mind." (McQuire and Heimann, p. 115) What emerges from
this brief account of the debate is how no one questioned the
mind dependence of the relative qualities. In this respect,
Northrop is more historically accurate than Grünbaum.

Even one of Grünbaum's favorite authorities is in agreement with Northrop on this issue.   D'Abro writes that mathematical space is "an abstraction from the space of experience"
(p. 47) and that the space of experience has its definition of
congruence provided by man's "sense of sight" (What
Grünbaum calls "the unaided ocular congruence of one's eyes").
In chapter II D'Abro is even clearer concerning the mind dependence of Newtonian relative space. He tells us that "our
understanding of space as a three-dimensional continuum had
arisen from a synthesis of our various sense impressions" especially " visual experience." (Ibid. p 32) Relative space is a
"synthesis of private views" albeit simplified to neglect, say,
the "focusing effort" and" convergence" etc. (D'Abro, pp. 32, 33,
33* and 58)   Northrop's only difference from D'Abro is that he
can be read as including focusing, convergence etc. as his reference to "astigmatism [and] the clearness of one's vision" (MEW
p. 76) makes obvious. So much for the mind dependence of
relative space.

As for Grünbaum's opening declaration in (i) above, viz., that the mind dependent and the mind independent can have nothing in common, one can only reply that many participants in the primary-secondary quality debate allowed for the commonality of certain qualities.   In fact, Locke held that what separates the primary from the secondary is that the latter qualities are not copies of their extramental producers, while the idea in our mind of, say, solidity, is such a copy. Therefore, absolute and relative things could have solidity in common.

Or to return to Newton, figure and magnitude could be a common element between absolute and relative space even if the latter is mind dependent in Northrop's sense.   Grünbaum needs more than a bald assertion that the absolute and relative [when the latter is construed as mind dependent] can have nothing in common if he would be convincing.

VIII.   One   final   problem

In addition to the above, another problem remains if we accept Grünbaum's interpretation, viz., how do we get from relative to absolute space and time?   Recall Newton's answer to the question.   In [3] he tells us that we ought to "abstract from our senses", which would seem to imply that the relative space is sense dependent.   Obviously this reply is not open to Grünbaum.   For if he mentions the process of abstracting from the senses, as both Newton and Northrop do, he makes his public space into private (at least in the sense of relative to somebody's sense organs) space and that would be the end of the discussion, since such relativity is what he is at pains to deny in his reading of Newton and criticism of Northrop.

If the above is roughly correct, it would seem that Northrop's interpretation of the Newtonian conception of relative space and time is the correct one.   In addition, it would also seem that relative space and time is a concept by intuition and not a concept by postulation that is a concept by perception.

[References for appendix A only]

Alexander, S. (1966) *Space, Time and Deity*, vol. 1, New York: Dover.

Burtt, E. A. (1980) *The Metaphysical Foundations of Modern Science*, Atlantic Highlands: Humanities Press.

D'Abro, A. (1950) *The Evolution of Scientific Thought From Newton to Einstein*, New York: Dover.

Grünbaum, A. (1947) "Critical Study of F. S. C. Northrop's *The Logic of the Sciences and the Humanities* ," *Yale Law Journal*, 57, 1331-1338.

Grünbaum, A. (1968), *Geometry and Chronometry in Philosophical Perspective*, Minnesota: University of Minnesota Press.

Grünbaum, A. (1973), *Philosophical Problems of Space and Time*, Dordrecht: Reidel.

Hutton, J. (1794) *Investigations of the Principles of Knowledge, from Sense to Sciences and Philosophy*, 3 vols. Edinburgh.

McQuire and Heimann, (1978) "The Rejection of Newton's Concept of Matter in the Eighteenth Century", *The Concept of Matter in Modern Philosophy*, E. McMullin, ed. Notre Dame: University of Notre Dame Press.

Newton, I. (1947), *Philosophiae Naturalis Principia Mathematica*, vol. 34, Chicago: Encyclopaedia Britannica.

Northrop, F. S. C. (1946) *The Meeting of East and West*, New York: MacMillan.

Northrop, F. S. C. (1947) *The Logic of the Sciences and the Humanities*, News York: MacMillan.

Northrop, F. S. C. (1960) *Philosophical Anthropology and Practical Politics*, New York: MacMillan.

Russell, B. (1954) *An Analysis of Matter*, New York: Dover.

Russell, B. (1960) *Our Knowledge of the External World*, New York: Dover.

APPENDIX B

NORTHROP ON RUSSIAN COMMUNISM

(This is a shortened version, mainly due to the excision of a presentation of Northrop's epistemology, of my article "Northrop on Russian Communism" which appeared in *Studies in Soviet Thought* 32, (1986) 133-154.)

Northrop authored three essays on Russian Communism. These articles appeared over a period of 12 years from 1946 to 1960. The first, entitled "Russian Communism" appeared in 1946 in MEW the second, "The Theory and Practice of Soviet Russian Communism" was printed TON in 1952 and the last appeared in 1960 in PAPP and bore the title "The Present and Likely Future Success of Russian Communism." The purpose of this study is to examine each essay in order to ascertain Northrop's understanding of Russian Communism and his method of analysis. Since Northrop's analysis of Russian Communism is in terms of the fundamental concepts that found the system of communism and since there are various kinds of concepts, some of which cannot be combined without generating world of discourse nonsense, this exposition presupposes that the reader is familiar with Northrop's theory of possible concepts. This theory is discussed in chapter 5 of LSH and in chapter 2 above.

Given this familiarity, we may now begin a reading of Northrop's essays which in chronological order.

THE MEETING OF EAST AND WEST

In 1946, Northrop published his MEW which, in attempting "An Inquiry into World Understanding", contained a lengthy chapter of 33 pages on the subject of Russian Communism. The chapter is divided into six sections: (1) The Philosophy of Karl Marx (2) Feuerbach's Realism and Materialism (3) The Labor Theory of Economic Value (4) The Communistic Theory of the State (5) The Communistic Attitude toward Democracy and (6) Communism and Science. We shall now examine each of these sections in turn.

I. The Philosophy Of Karl Marx

Quoting Lenin, Northrop stresses that the three chief ideological influences on Marx were German philosophy, French socialism and English political economy. Of these, the philosophy of Hegel was paramount since it was through the lenses of the dialectic that Marx viewed the other two. As Lenin wrote in his *Teaching of Karl Marx:* "Marx and Engels regarded Hegelian dialectics . . . as the greatest achievement of classical German philosophy." (223) This enabled Marx to regard the democratic rights respecting culture of Locke and Hume, not as the final telos of western political development, but as the antithesis of the thesis known as medieval aristocracy and in need of real revolution in order to achieve the ultimate synthesis in communism.

II. Feuerbach

The next major German philosophical influence Northrop mentions is the realism and materialism of the German theologian Ludwig Feuerbach, although he discounts this influence in two important respects. Positively, Marx took from Feuerbach his realism and substituted it for Hegel's idealism. Since Feuerbach designated as real the material, Marx's new found realism became dialectical materialism. But the difference between dialectical idealism and dialectical realism is not as great as one would think given the radical gulf the tradition sees between idealism and realism in themselves. The reason for this is not far to seek. There are three major developments that can be determined by the dialectic -- nature, man and culture --and both Hegel and Feuerbach and therefore Marx apply the dialectic to all three. Since these developments are completely determined under either dialectical idealism or dialectical materialism, the end result is the same and the change, at least in this area, is more verbal than real. Also the dialectical materialism of Marx has little in common with the materialism of traditional science and philosophy. Not only was the latter non-dialectical, it ignored as irrelevant history and culture as factors in the analysis of nature. "For the Marxian, however, history, and in particular economic history, is the fundamental thing, tending even to determine and define one's scientific theories of nature. Thus, even the materialism of Feuerbach and the Marxians is more like the Idealism of Hegel than it is like the traditional materialism." (226) For all practical purposes, when we turn to examine the influence of English economic theory, it is Hegel's dialectic that will be emphasized.

III. The Labor Theory Of Economic Value

According to Northrop, Marx's use of the word 'economic' has two meanings a less technical one based on the Feuerbachian analysis of historical process and a more technical, Smithian-Ricardian sense which founds the work of the more mature Marx. Influenced early by Feuerbach, Marx was led to look not only at the dialectics of historical process, but also behind the social institutions to note that man must wrest from material nature the sustenance his body requires. In so doing, man co-operates with other men (production relations) and creates new tools and entire industries (forces of production). This constitutes the non-technical sense of the term "economic".

The second, more technical sense of 'economic' Marx de-rived, in part at least, from the English economists, especially Ricardo. The qualifying phrase "in part at least" is necessary since Northrop maintains that while Smith and Ricardo used la-bor as the measure of value, Marx used labor to define the essence of exchange value itself. It was labor that was to pro-vide the answer to the question as to what different commodi-ties had in common that permitted them to be compared and exchanged. In this sense, Northrop claims that only Marx had a labor theory of value whereas economists like Smith and Ricardo has a theory of labor as the measure of value. Unfortunately, Marx's labor theory of value fails to explain the autonomy of economics vis-a-vis historical circumstances, types of government or cultural heritage. (Given Marx's histori-cal determinism it is easy to see how he missed this fact.) That people have wants and order them in an introspectively known hierarchy is true under any regime, at any historical time. However, those who raise their economic theories on such radi-cally empirical (in the concept by intuition that is a concept by introspection sense) principles, as do e.g., the Austrians, must necessarily pay a price that most economists, including Marx, have usually not been willing to pay. This price is a loss of predictive power. Only an economic statics is achievable for any concept by intuition economic theory. Marx sought rather for an economic dynamics, a dynamics that would permit any Marxian anywhere to predict economic change and all that is attendant thereto -- which for Marx is just about everything. And since economic transactions are meaningful for Marx only as part of systematic production relations in an organically con-ceived social whole, the theory is actually an organic, social labor theory of value boasting both a statics and a dynamics. Given this theory, "...the value of the commodity is determined not by the total demands for it or the sum total or aggregate of psychological preferences for it in the free market, but by the amount of physical energy and labor which went into its production." (223)   And unless the laborer is paid a wage equal to the value (or any portion thereof) of the commodity, he is a victim of exploitation.   "Surplus value" is the well known name Marx gives to the difference between what the laborer earns and what he actually receives.   Plowing the surplus value back into the means of production augments the capitalist's capital and brings about unprecedented advances in industry.   Quoting Marx (I presume this is Marx, although a reference is not provided by Northrop) he writes "The advance of industry, whose involuntary promoter is the bourgeoisie, replaces the isolation of the laborers, due to competition, by their revolutionary competition, due to association. The development of modern industry, therefore, cuts from under its feet the very foundation on which the bourgeoisie produces and appropriates products." (233)   But the capture by the proletariat of the means of production is not accomplished by economic but by political means.

IV. The Communistic Theory Of The State

Marx accepts from Hegel the distinction between "society" and the "state." Society, defined as " . . . the organic system of individuals determined by the production relations in the dialectical process of history . . ." has always existed, whereas the state, defined as   "a more restricted social organization within society, arising out of the dialectical conflict of class interests by means of which those who control the means of production oppress those who do not . . , " (234) has not, at least in its modern, oppressive and increasingly alienated form.   Since the capitalists will not hand over the reigns of the state willingly, revolution is dialectically logically required. This will bring the proletariat, or more correctly the party vanguard, into power and constitutes the first stage of the revolution eventuating in a stateless and classless society. But why is the first stage necessary at all -- why not simply move to the stateless condition -- what need have we of the dictatorship of the party vanguard and the state control which is its necessary manifestation? If Marx had been simply a power political thinker, seizure of the apparatus of power would have been sufficient and the revolution would have been a one-step procedure. But Marx knew that positive law and all the guns in the states' arsenal are not enough to insure acceptance of what Sir Henry Maine has called "the living law" which must found the written code. But any change in the living law requires time and re-education. As soon as the habits and beliefs of the masses are brought into line with Marxian theory, (and this is one of the most important functions of the communist state) the second stage will appear and the state will automatically wither away.

IV.   The   Communist   Attitude Toward   Democracy

Northrop writes for nearly seven pages on this topic, the essence of which is to dispel the notion that the 1936 Russian Constitution represents a softening of the Marxist-Leninist attitude toward democracy. That attitude was grudging as Lenin writes: "Democracy is of great importance for the working class in its struggle for freedom against the capitalists. But democracy is by no means a boundary that must not be overstepped it is only one of the stages in the process of development from feudalism to capitalism, and from capitalism to communism." (233-4) Democracy also has a post revolutionary sense, but it represents an evanescent state at best. Lenin writes of it thusly:

> Only in communist society, when the resistance of
> the capitalists has been completely broken...will
> really complete democracy, democracy without any
> exception, be possible and be realized. And only
> then will democracy itselfbegin to wither away . .
> . Communism alone is capable of giving really
> complete democracy, and the more complete it is
> the more quickly will it become unnecessary and
> wither away of itself. (238-9)

If Northrop is correct and democracy has only these two
senses, pre- and post-revolutionary - neither of which have
their meaning derived from Locke, Hume or Jevons - then
when "democracy" is bandied about at high level conference
tables, our politicians are in never-never land if they think
they have gained a victory when the communists agree to
democratic reforms, democratic processes etc. for a pre-revolutionary country since democracy for the communists means a
withering away of democracy in a post-revolutionary communist state. Nor is the Constitution of 1936 evidence of a move
toward the Lockean conception of democracy and away from
the Marxian, with its guarantees of various economic and political rights notwithstanding. Northrop cites two articles from
the Russian Constitution to show this Article 131 and 141.
Article 131 concludes as follows: "Persons makings attacks
upon public socialist property shall be regarded as enemies of
the people." (241) According to Beatrice Webb this means that
"No criticism of the living philosophy of the Communist party is
permitted in the Soviet Union . . . (There is an sic.) absolute
prohibition within the USSR of any propaganda advocating the
return to capitalist profit making, or even to any independent
thinking on the fundamental social issues about possible new
ways of organizing men in society, new forms of social activity,
and new development of the socially established code of con-

duct." (242) So much for freedom of speech. Northrop is also concerned about the meaning of Article 141 as it affects "guaranteed freedoms".   "Candidates for elections shall be nominated by electoral districts. The right to nominate candidates shall be ensured to public organizations trade unions cooperatives organizations of youth cultural societies." (243)   Stalin himself expands this to mean: "In the Soviet Union, in the land where the dictatorship of the proletariat is in force, no important political or organizational problem is ever decided by our soviets (the elected legislative bodies, sic.) and other mass organizations, without directives from our party. In this sense, we may say that the dictatorship of the proletariat is substantially the dictatorship of the party, as the force which effectively guides the proletariat." (243)   Since political power rests with the party and not the people, membership becomes a necessity - yet as the Webbs have written, the party is very selective in its recruitment (2 1/2 million members from a nation of 192 million in 1946) the main criterion being acceptance of "an ideology of the nature of a creed,"   the creed of Karl Marx.   That creed "will have nothing to do with the supernatural. It admits nothing to be true which cannot be demonstrated by the "scientific method" of observation, experimentation, ratiocination and verification." (244)   After raising the rhetorical query whether Marxism itself passes this test, Northrop moves to the closing section.

VI.   Communism And Science

That the Marxists claim to be scientific in their philosophy there is no doubt, but Northrop reminds us of the influence
of Kant and Fichte on Marx Kant separated science from morality and Fichte gave unequivocal primacy to the latter.
Henceforth, "instead of the theory of man and nature discovered by a factually controlled scientific study determining
man's beliefs and evolving historical, cultural institutions, the
process of history itself became the determining factor" (244)
Couple this with the Hegelian presupposition that nature obeys
the logic of the dialectic and the claim that the communists "are
realist, scientific empiricists looking objectively at the historical
process and merely reporting what is happening to it as a
whole is a sheer pose." (246) The magnitude of the pose is eloquently revealed by the fact that science and dialectic are incompatible, as an examination of the scientific theories and the
nature they expose indicate. "Certainly in none of the theories
of the natural scientist - Newton, Maxwell, Gibbs, Einstein or
Max Plank is nature exhibited as obeying Hegel's dialectic.
Thus at this basic point, as Sidney Hook has shown, communistic philosophical theory is unequivocally false." (247) Nor is
the nature revealed by these theories a revolutionary one--
rather biological nature appears evolutionary. In addition,
"...the advent of a new species does not involve the wiping out
of the preceding species by a logic of negation after the manner
in which the proletariat is supposed to wipe out the bourgeoisie. The dialectic does not even apply, in toto, to the reconstruction of cultural institutions. When a new philosophy
replaces an older one, e.g., when Thomas Aquinas moved the
Catholic Church from Augustine and Plato to Aristotle. If
Northrop is correct, one is confronted with the following alternative science or dialectic. Science excludes dialectic and
revolution, whereas dialectic excludes, or at least ignores, the

results of Newton, Gibbs, Maxwell et al.   Had science been the determining factor, the logic of identity would have replace the logic of dialectic and an evolutionary approach to world communism would have replace the revolutionary method.   That some contemporary Marxists are advocating at least the evolutionary theory of development places them in the pro-science wing of modern day Marxism.

The Taming Of Nations

In TON,   Northrop includes as Chapter 12 "The Theory and Practice of Soviet Russian Communism" and from this essay we will examine three topics:

(1) The overwhelming importance of ideas for Russian Communism

(2)   The relationship between the masses and the party

(3) The role of force as a political tool.

1. Ideas

As in MEW, so in TON, ideas are crucial not only in Northrop's enterprise, but also, as he demonstrates, in the theory and practice of Communism.   TON contains no radical departure from the analysis given in MEW, but rather an addition of the ideas of the Luther to the collection of concepts necessary for an understanding of Russian Communism. The dialectic is still derived from Hegel and the materialism from Feuerbach, but now the influence of Luther is mentioned.   "When Luther struck his blow for the German people, he shifted man's conception of nature and the relation of himself to nature as known through the universal laws of deductively formulated scientific theory to nature as given inductively." (246) To employ Northrop's technical terminology, this means the virtual elimination of concepts by postulation (and a fortiori concepts by intellection) as an instrument of understanding man and replaces them with radical empirical concepts by intuition, effectively restricting the intent of Jesus and the New Testament to the interpretation of each individual German reader rather than to a corps of scholastically trained experts.   Henceforth, man could not be known as a citizen of the universe but ". . . mere citizen of the German folk." (246)   German nationalism replaced the Stoic Roman legal and moral conception of man and nature.   Marx continued this fractionating process by replacing the nation with the small class of oppressed factory workers.   "Thereby moral man was corrupted from being a citizen of the universe, under determinate laws the same for all men, into being the leader of the members of a small class in society guided by a restricted and arbitrary concern with nothing but material clothes, shoes, technological tools and other purely material values.   The disastrous effect of this type of thinking is exacerbated by the fact that although the communists, following Marx, regard ideas as a mere by-product of the forces of production and the relations engendered thereby, they are careful to exempt their own ideology.   For example, in distinguishing the vanguard of the proletariat from the proletariat itself, the most important factor is to arm the vanguard with an ideology.   This according to Stalin.   In *Foundations of Leninism* Stalin tells us on p. 90 that the crucial task of the party during its formative years is the establishment of an all-Russian illegal newspaper to prepare the conditions for ideological unity.   Or consider Lenin's pronouncement that the "proletarian vanguard has been ideologically won over.   This is the most important thing.   Without this, we cannot take even the first step towards victory." (250)   And finally Vishinsky tells us that "We shall win the world with ideas." (250)

II.   The   Party

The speed of light is not propagated at an instant through space, but rather requires a finite amount of time to traverse a given distance. So too with ideology. Since the party is to be composed of the ideologically pure, one might conclude that the relationship between the ideologically aware party members and the masses would be a simple one which albeit two-tiered would nevertheless be egalitarian. Nothing could be further from the truth. With extreme sarcasm, Northrop writes

> So great is [Stalin's) devotion to the removal of class distinctions that even the fissioning of the Russian people into the vast masses and the proletariat minority class, the division of the proletariat into the non-Party members and the Party, and the division of the Party into its tail dragging portion and its vanguard is not sufficient. Even the vanguard protected by its revolutionary theory must have a General Staff, separated from the vanguard, which in turn is separated from the proletariat of urban workers, which in their turn are set apart from the masses, is not sufficient to win the revolutionary battle for the removal of all class distinctions. (250-1)

What is required, according to Stalin following Lenin, is a necessary unity of will and it takes little wit to know that this unity resides in the person of one man.

III.   Force

The use and importance of force to the Russian Communists has never been hidden. In the final paragraph of "The Programme of the Communist International" we read "The Communists disdain to conceal their views and aims. They openly declare that their aims can be attained only by the forcible overthrow of all the existing social conditions." (288, Northrop is quoting from *The Handbook for Marxism*) Stalin has seconded this notion in both *Dialectical and Historical Materialism* and in a series of lectures given to the students of the Sverdlov University in 1924 and entitled *Foundations of Leninism.* He talks of ". . . ruthlessly suppress(ing) the counterrevolutionary activity of the ecclesiastical organizations . . ." and he quotes Marx approvingly when he advises men to "fight it out . . ." and to expand the scope of the Russian revolution to the international arena and ". . . smash social-chauvinism and social-pacifism." (233, 241, & 247) Force is needed in order to give to the revolutionary the opportunity to ". . . crush, to smash to bits, to wipe off the face of the earth the bourgeois state machinery . . ." (253) Echoing these sentiments of Lenin, Stalin advises the victorious proletariat of one country to send   ". . . its military forces against the exploiting classes and their states." (253) The implications of such a policy in international affairs is obvious: ". . . a General Staff which . . . insists that recourse to force is a moral necessity for the salvation of its own people will (have no) moral scruples about the use of force against foreigners." ((253) Protection against such a nation guided by such an ideology is according to Northrop, ". . . an alternative ideology backed with the police power necessary to protect its adherents." (254)   But what about recourse to an effective international law?   In the closing pages of the essay Northrop examines this possibility.   Korovin, one of Russia's authorities on the subject of international law has written that such a law among nations of the world . . . presupposes some common evaluation, unity of conviction-- legal, ethical and political . . ." and this simply means that international law requires that the countries in question share the same ideology.

Any beginning student knows that this condition is not met by the two major powers and should not be surprised when Korovin concludes that   ". . . *an intercourse on the basis of*

*intellectual unity (ideological solidarity sic.) between countries
of bourgeois and socialist cultures, cannot exist as a rule, and
hence the rules of international law covering this intercourse
become pointless."* (255)

But if any beginner can know this, it takes a more informed student of Soviet Communism to realize that international law is impossible even between Russia and other
Communist nations since Article 14 of the Constitution ". . . lists
those matters reserved to the Soviet Union and hence not
within the jurisdiction of the 'sovereign autonomous republics.'"
Almost every single important state function is listed and one
can only conclude that the ultimate end of Soviet Communism
is not peace through international law but rather unity under
Soviet domestic law. This is the not very optimistic conclusion
of the essay.

Philosophical Anthropology & Practical Politics

Northrop's last full length essay on Russian Communism, "The
Present and Likely Future Success of the Soviet Union" appeared in PAPP and its title may be usefully contrasted with
the chapter which immediately follows it viz., "The Remarkable
Short-Run Success of Mao's China." However much observers
may disagree concerning Russia and China, most would concur
that today (1985) China has moved further from Mao than
Russia has moved from Khrushchev.   [Today, 1993, the same
observers might conclude the opposite.]   The differences between the titles (future success of Russia vs. short-run success
of China) has to do, I would suggest, with Northrop's ideological approach to politics and in particular, his typology of concepts.   In the case of the Soviet Union the intellectual heritage
is, like most modern nations, one employing concepts by postulation that are concepts by intellection.   Northrop notes a dual
source of concepts by intellection "[l]ong before the origin of

the modern world, two things went into Russia from Constantinople. The first was Greek Orthodox Christianity; the second was the contractual legal science of Stoic Rome which came to its most perfect codified formulation under Justinian." (264)

It must be remembered that both of these disciplines require concepts by intellection. The Russian mind, unlike the Chinese, is no stranger to these most esoteric intellectual tools. Such minds, with some of its best representatives living in St. Petersburg -- a few miles from Koenigsberg -- had no difficulty absorbing Kant's epistemological theses concerning scientific knowledge. Except for the fact that Kant regarded the categories of scientific knowledge as categorically *a priori* whereas our contemporaries know them to be hypothetically universal and necessary, there is little to distinguish between the two. Applying the *a priori* notions of his analysis of scientific nouns to issues in morality, Kant discovered his ". . . famous categorical imperative: Act as if one were an instance of a universal law." (260)   The gulf between Kant's scientific epistemology and his morality is too well known to require comment here. The gap gave rise to . . . Russian Romanticism, Fichtean voluntarism . . ." etc. It required a mind as vast as Hegel's to bring Eastern and Central Europe back under ". . . thoughtful and logical control by keeping Kant's idealistic epistemology but replacing his logic of identity with the dialectic logic of negation which he (Hegel sic.) erroneously concluded to be causally deterministic, thereby fallaciously identifying the 'ought' for evaluating any correctly described humanistic or political "is" with the dialectically deterministic historical evolution of that 'is'." (261)   The result is the fundamental proposition of Russian Communism, viz., that since the ". . . facts of both nature and culture are under the deterministic lawful control of a dialectically deterministic logic. . . the assent of individuals is irrelevant."   (261) While on the subject of individual consent, it would be appropriate to consider Northrop's acceptance of Sir Henry Maine's dichotomy of societies into law of status vs. law of contract types (most are mixed). Law of status societies are based on radical empirical (or at most naive realistic) epistemologies whereas law of contract societies require at least some concepts by postulation that are concepts by intellection and hence are in part logically or scientifically realistic in their theories of knowledge. Being based on concepts by intuition, law of status societies are caste societies and one's radical empirical skin color, sex and birth order determine one's position in the community. A law of contract society, however, is based on consent.

> In the ethics of the law of contract society, consent is of the essence. A law has no validity unless those to whom it is applied give their consent. In a contract, nothing is binding unless the parties to the contract have consented to accept it. Furthermore, with respect to consent, and hence with respect to the obligation to obey any law of contract, all men are born free and equal. (251)

Russia is a law of contract society with a written constitution which must not oppress its citizens without their consent. That massive oppression is the rule in Russia is not discussed by Northrop, but the reasons, both historical and philosophical, behind this ubiquitous inhumanity are. According to Northrop, although the Russian mind readily accepted Kant's categorical imperative, its purely formal character allow the universality that Kant sought for in his supreme ethical principle to be undercut by filling in the formal mold with a substantive content that would legally permit the dictatorship of the majority by the minority or vice versa. To prevent this, the substantive content of the law must be universally quantified. To capture this in the language of *Principia Mathematica* Northrop writes "(p) (s) (x) (l): x is intrinsically good or just iff $\underline{x}$ is an instance of an $\underline{l}$ such that $(p)l$ and $(p)s$ of l." (333) In this statement $p =$ any person of any country $x =$ any intrinsic goal-value $s =$ the substantive content of l and $l =$ any law. We may replace this mathematical formulation by a more poetic one which Northrop calls the Jefferson principle. Jefferson, never having read Russell and Whitehead, but intimate with the concepts by postulation that are concepts by intellection of Sir Isaac Newton said it this way "All men are created equal." But Karl Marx rejected any ranking by birth law of status society -- therefore he must accept the only possible alternative, i.e., a law of contract society whose first principle is a categorical imperative, analytic and hence tautologically true. Societies, like the Soviet Union, which rear themselves on Marxian principles must likewise conform to the Jefferson principle. Since the constitution of the Soviet Union does not define the rights and obligations of its citizens in terms of "biology of birth" its law is the law of contract type. Yet this same document, as we saw above, gives the goal value policy decision making power into the hands of a very small elite--in some cases one man--and therefore runs afoul of the second quantification, (i.e., (p)s of the Jefferson principle). From this it follows that Soviet Union constitutional law is self-contradictory constitutional law, violating the analytic tautologically true proposition upon which any legally contractual nation rests.

We saw above how Northrop exposes the contradiction of the dialectical logic which is the first premise in the Communistic Philosophy. Premise two can now be examined. It derives from Feuerbach (probably from Holbach and Helvetis) and involves the shift from the Idealism of Hegel to a naive or direct realism. Before dealing with Northrop's treatment of Feuerbach and in order to appreciate the differences between it and its counterparts in the earlier essays, the reader should be familiar with what Northrop calls the evaluative method and to which he devoted chapter 7 of PAPP.   First, Northrop takes the method to be a cognitive device for evaluating any set of normative judgments, customs and political ideals once they are objectively described.   The method of objective description Northrop outlines in chapter 6. In chapter 7, we are told what a cognitive method is: "By a cognitive method is meant one which, when applied to the living and positive legal norms of a given person, people or nation, gives a conclusion of which it is significant to say that it is true or false in a sense which can be confirmed by anyone in that or any other culture or nation."   And on p. 120, Northrop summarizes this method as follows: "Its method consists in finding the non-normatively worded first-order factual assumptions of any personal or national philosophy, apart from which its normative words are devoid of content, and then examining these assumptions with respect both to (a) their logical consistency and (b) empirical data inspectable *by anyone, anywhere* to test their truth or falsity."

To return now to Feuerbach. Northrop finds that one does not have to check the empirical data to refute naive realism, because such an epistemological theory fails to pass criterion (a).   The logical refutation of naive realism occurs on p. 66 in a chapter entitled "The Self-Regulation of Human Behavior" and will be quoted in full.

> any naive realistic epistemological concept of the public self or any public object is self-contradictory. The mark of such an epistemology is that it attempts to define the purportedly public substances in terms of directly sensed or introspected properties. But all sensed or imagined items of knowledge are imageful and all images are relative, not merely to the observer's frame of reference and to the percipient, but even, as Democritus, Galilei, Newton

and Berkeley pointed out, to different sense organs and moments of perception of the same percipient. The naive realist means, however, by his public substances some-thing   that exists . . . independently of its relation to any observer.   Clearly, therefore, it is self -contradictory to define an object existing independently of its relation to the observer in terms of sensed or introspected imageful properties all of which are relative to the perceiver.

Northrop's refutation is not as important as the fact that naive realism is a fundamental premise of Russian Communism which makes readily understandable Lenin's furious attacks on Mach, who did for particle physics what Bishop Berkeley did for tables and chairs.

We now have in hand the three postulates of Russian Communism according to Northrop's analysis.   They are as follows: (1) modern Soviet Russia is a law of contract society, not a law of status society.   In the main it employs a (2) naive realistic epistemology for determining the nature of reality and the nature of man, and finally (3) it reject the law of identity for the deterministic dialectic of negation which, according to Northrops analysis, obviates the need for consent of the governed.   (277)

After pointing out the arbitrariness of identifying the thesis, antithesis and synthesis with businessmen, labor and the dictatorship of the Communist Party, Northrop claims that all three postulates are false.   Now we have seen that (2) and (3) are self -contradictory, i.e., false on logical grounds--but surely (1) cannot be false.   In fact, Northrop uses the truth of (1) to establish its incompatibility with (3). That is, if Russia is a law of contract society requiring the true consent of its citizens to validate any legal obligation, then the determinism of (3) stands in direct contradiction with (1) and its requirement of free consent.   But if both (1) and (3) are false no such incompatibility, at least of a kind interesting to political thought, exists. Let us, *pro temp*, grant the truth of (1) and see if we can figure out Northrop's point. On p. 278, after claiming that (1) entails the Jefferson principle, Northrop goes on to show that the substantive content of the political ideals of Soviet Communism is incompatible with (1). I take Northrop to be saying, not that (1) is false simpliciter, but rather the substantive content specification of (1) by the Soviets is incompatible with its other formal properties. "It is as if a pure mathematician put substantive content in a theorem of arithmetic which is logically incompatible with Peano's Fifth Postulate concerning what any arithmetical number means." (278)

What are some of the practical implications of Northrop's analysis? Surely the leaders of the CPSU are not going to close up shop even if they were to agree and accept Northrop's analysis of the self-contradictory state of their basic principles - nor does Northrop suggest that they will. Rather he makes four predictions concerning the likely future success of the Soviet Union, hence the chapter's title. What are these predictions?

(1) *No popular revolt of the masses in the near future.* Popular revolts presuppose a difference between the overt and covert philosophy of the people and their leaders. There is no evidence of any systematic educational popular movement away from Hegel, Feuerbach and Marx to, say, Locke, Hume and Jevons. To suppose the Russian people are going to reject Communism for Capitalism and express this rejection in a *coup d'état* is to engage in the "most fanciful daydreaming."

(2) *No real peace.* The reasoning behind this prognostication is twofold, empirical and theoretical. On the empirical side, Northrop points to the fact that every time the Soviet leaders sue for peace or demand a summit conference, their demands are accompanied by a threat of war at some place in the world. Moreover, the Soviets refuse to discuss any topic other than the

political battleground of the moment and of their choosing. The theoretical reasons once again have to do with education. Not only are the Communists still teaching ". . . the two basic Hegelian-Feuerbachian materialistic premises of their thinking, but also the third and fourth level, more opportunistic procedural derivative applications which give the instrumental rules for applying the premises to particular circumstances of the moment. " (272-3)   These tactics run the gamut from conciliatory warmongering, from appeal to verifiable international law to lies and threats--all designed with one purpose in mind--world domination by the dictatorship of the proletariat.   We are inextricably led to

(3) *No end to the Cold far.*   Here the reasons Northrop marshals are nearly identical with (2) above and we can skip to the final prediction i.e.,

(4)   *Trade alone will not do it.*   To assume that the West should shrug off their skepticism and engage in profit-making business as usual with the Soviets presupposes the following counterfactuals: (a) The Russians believe in the virtues of the profit-making system, (b) They want peaceful coexistence, and (c) They have rejected Hegel-Feuerbach-Marx-Lenin et al for Locke, Bentham and von Mises.

Despite the fact that some (two and three) of these predictions have been falsified, it may nevertheless prove enlightening to review Northrop's 1960 prescription for doing foreign policy.   One must answer the following questions if disaster is to be avoided in dealing with any foreign politician.

(1)   To what political party in his own nation does he belong?   (2) What are the elementary concepts and propositions which specify the goal-value political aims of this party? (3) To what extent is this set of philosophical beliefs taught universally throughout the educational system or inculcated emotively and covertly in religious or political ceremonies or

by the public press?   What percentage of the people
in his nation vote for his party?   (5) Most important
of all, what *was*   the educational and cultural living
law philosophy of the people of his nation and its
plural religious communities antecedent to his advent to political office?   (274)

These questions have easy answers for a philosophical monolith like the Soviet Union, and they cause Northrop to conclude
with advice both pessimistic and realistic.   First, we must get
our philosophical house in order and decide the goal values for
which our massive weapons are the "necessary defense."   For
Northrop, these include at minimum (1) training in aesthetic
sensibility to enable the student and politician to distinguish
between the concept by intuition radical empirical data and (2)
the concept by postulation meaning he infers from (1).   (3)
Awareness of the neurophysiological nature of man and the directly inspected ideas that constitute their epistemic correlates.
(4) Training in mathematics and symbolic logic as well as (5)
mathematical physics and (6) the concept by postulation
meaning of the Jefferson principle.   All of these notions get
elaborate treatment in PAPP.

Second, we must, in effect, circle the wagons and be constantly on guard against a nation whose fundamental premises
not only permit but encourage aggression in the achievement
of their purposes.   (With hindsight, we can regret that fact that
Northrop did not specify what the United States should when it
won the cold war.)

APPENDIX C

MCALLISTER ON NORTHROP

(This article appeared in a slightly different form in volume xviii, 1993 of the *Journal of Philosophical Research.* I include it as a pedagogic device--I have learned a lot about Northrop's philosophy by trying to defend it and perhaps the reader can do the same by, so to speak, looking over my shoulder.)

Joseph B. McAllister's article "Northrop's concepts by Intuition and Concepts by Postulation" that appeared in *The New Scholasticism* in 1950 attempts to provide both (1) an exposition of the epistemology of F. S. C. Northrop, and (2) a warning that, Northrop's protestations to the contrary notwithstanding, what one finds upon examination of his philosophy comes so dangerously close to Berkeley's "esse est percipi" idealism, that a skepticism, unable to support any morality, cannot be far behind. This paper attempts to review and correct McAllister's exposition and demonstrate that the warning is an unnecessary cry in the dark against a wolf that isn't there.

McAllister's exposition of Northrop's theory is not without its faults (these by omission). His concern over incipient skepticism is unwarranted, and is bound to vanish upon a fuller analysis of Northrop's actual position. This I propose to provide.

Note that this will not be a defense of Northrop's position, but a revealing of those crucial areas and points of detail left unexposed by McAllister's essay. The second part of this article will deal with McAllister's worry about Northrop's supposed "tendency to realism, the charge being that a "tendency to realism" isn't enough to satisfy McAllister since it fails to provide a strong enough connection between human knowledge and reality, and *a fortiori,* morality and reality.

While I cannot object to McAllister's rehearsal of Northrop's distinction between concepts by intuition and concepts by postulation since I believe it clears up much confusion in philosophy in general and comparative philosophy in particular, I cannot forbear to point out that, by selectively focusing on only one of the four main types of the former, McAllister's misses the essence of Northrop's epistemology and creates problems where none exist. Also, by ignoring how the realistic component is adumbrated with respect to the concepts by postulation, McAllister fails to see exactly how much of a realist Northrop is.[113]   To see exactly where McAllister goes astray, let us examine concepts by intuition first.

---

[113] The interested reader is directed to Northrop's article "To What Does Mathematical Physics Refer?" in MNG 216-229 where he juxtaposes the logical realism component of his epistemology with the logical non-realism of Poincare, Duhem, Cassirer and Margenau. McAllister's article originally appeared in The New Scholasticism, 24, 1950, pp. 115-134.

On page 99 of *The Logic and the Sciences and the Humanities*, Northrop presents the following chart[114] that I reproduce in full.

I   The Concept of the Differentiated Aesthetic Continuum = The totality of the immediately apprehended with nothing abstracted away.

II The Concept of the Indeterminate or Undifferentiated Aesthetic Continuum = The immediately apprehended continuum apart from all differentiations.

III   The Concepts of the Differentiations = Concepts by Inspection = Atomic Concepts by Inspection = The specific inspected qualities or differentiations considered apart from the continuum.

(a)   Concepts by Sensation = III given through the senses.
      (b) Concepts by Introspection = III given introspectively.

IV Field Concepts by Inspection = Any instance of III considered as inseparable from II.

It is, I believe, McAllister's exclusive concentration on III, the concepts of the differentiations, that cause him. as it caused Berkeley and Hume, to miss the realistic core in II, viz., the undifferentiated aesthetic continuum.   In some fairness to McAllister, it might be mentioned that Northrop does, on page 69 (a part of which McAllister quotes), tell us that *any* concept by intuition ". . . refers to a particular factor within the totality of immediately apprehended fact, . . ." and this would mislead anyone who has not carefully read chapter V of LSH.   What

---

114   Although this chart appears above in the text to LSH, I have reproduced it here for ease of reference.

I challenge is McAllister's method of presenting Northrop's concepts by intuition.   Surely it would have been easier to reproduce, as I have done, the entire chart and append to it such
commentary as space and intention would jointly permit.   And
on page 97 of LSH, Northrop explicitly warns the reader of the
special difficulty for the Western mind in coming to understanding II. For those, like McAllister, concerned with realism,
the big question is, what is II? What is its referent?   Would that
the answer could be phrased in as simple a form as the question.   Part of the difficulty stems from the fact that its character cannot be described[115] although it can be known (read experienced) in at least three ways.[116]

That there is such an undifferentiated aesthetic
continuum is known in three ways, notwithstanding
the fact that what is immediately experienced is
this continuum with its differentiations.   First, the
whole of the immediately experienced continuum is
not differentiated.   As William James pointed out,
and Alfred Whitehead has recently reemphasized,
its periphery is undifferentiated and indeterminate.
Secondly, the undifferentiated aesthetic continuum
can be known even where it is differentiated, by
merely abstracting it from the local limited differentiations, just as the shape of a sensed color can be
abstracted from the color, or the color from the
shape: Thirdly, we can, by certain methods, attempt

---

115   Cf. p. 336 MEW where Northrop writes "a description is possible only by
having recourse to words denoting local specific qualities or differentiations and
since the undifferentiated aesthetic continuum is the all-embracing immediately
apprehended unity apart from any differentiations the recourse to descriptive
terms always brings out the differentiations rather than the undifferentiated
aesthetic continuum.

116   Four are mentioned in MNG but this was published over a decade after
McAllister's article.

> to remove the sensed or imagined differentiations
> from the otherwise completely indeterminate un-
> differentiated aesthetic manifold. (MEW 341-2)

One also can approach the experience of the undifferentiated aesthetic
continuum via art and Northrop refers to Plate XIV in his MEW that reproduces B0AT AT ANCHOR BY REEDS from the Sung dynasty as an example of such a procedure.

Now all this has been by way of an attempt to answer the question asked about concerning the whatness of the undifferentiated continuum. But the crucial point for our purposes is that the undifferentiated aesthetic continuum is the same for all observers, and this is what Northrop means by "independent" in the realist sense. The *esse* of the undifferentiated aesthetic continuum is not *percipi*. No perceiver makes any difference to its nature, it is entirely independent (i.e., the same for all) of any perceiver. The consequences of this will be drawn in section II below.

One additional characteristic of concepts by intuition that is important to remember is that they are known (= experienced) to be <u>certain.</u> In this they differ radically from concepts by postulation that are known *tentatively* and only by checking deductive consequences that the concepts give rise to, especially when those concepts occur in scientific theories. McAllister notes this distinction on page 129 of his article. I mention it here because it will be important in the conclusion.

Now let us consider concepts by postulation. Again Northrop has a chart in LSH dedicated to an exhaustive classification of these concepts. [In fact, I think it represents a bit of philosophical overkill due to the inclusion of a breakdown of the four major types of concepts by postulation into monistic and pluralistic examples, a distinction he never employs. They have been ignored in the chart reproduced below.]

I Concepts by Intellection = Concepts by postulation designating factors that can by neither imagined nor sensed.

II Concepts by Imagination = Concepts by postulation designating factors which can be imagined but cannot be sensed.

III Concepts by Perception = Concepts by postulation designating factors which are in part sensed and in part imagined.

IV Logical Concepts by Intuition = Concepts designating factors, the content of which is given through the senses or by mere abstraction from the totality of sense awareness, and whose logical universality and immortality are given by postulation.

Two short remarks concerning the above classification need to be made before concluding this section.   Northrop emphasizes both the tentative nature of the knowledge provided by concepts by postulation and the fact that those in I were designed to refer to an invariant and independent factor in one's knowledge claims, i.e., to use concepts by postulation is to be, at least implicitly, a realist, in some sense of that term. *Esse est percipi* does not apply to anything designated by a concept by postulation.   I refers to the philosophical position known as direct or naive realism, whereas III to those, like Einstein, Grünbaum and Northrop, to name but three, who embrace logical or scientific realism.

I I

Northrop's epistemology is a marriage of both concepts by intuition and concepts by postulation via epistemic correlations.   What in this theory could possibly give rise either to the worries or quell the fears voiced by McAllister over incipient idealism, corrosive skepticism and moral subjectivism? On p. 133 McAllister gives a partial answer when he writes that "When Northrop follows Locke and Berkeley and Hume . . . he has gone a long way towards idealism . . . . " That Northrop does draw upon the insights of this British triumvirate cannot be denied, but what is enlightening is not the granting of this obvious aspect of Northrop's epistemology, but the precise location in his system where they get their due. And this occurs in category III of concepts by intuition, i.e., the Concepts of the Differentiations. One of the major points of MEW is that Western philosophy is predominantly concerned with concepts by postulation but when Western thinkers do reflect on or employ concepts by intuition, it is almost always the concept of the differentiations, e.g., pains, tickles, itches, reds, etc. Whereas the Eastern thinkers typically concentrate on the "aesthetic continuum in and for itself for its own sake." (MEW 375) Northrop severely criticizes the myopia of Western thinkers about concepts by intuition. Except for the concepts of the differentiations, they hardly recognize the other three types. If there were only the concepts of the differentiations, then the Idealism of Berkeley and Hume would follow. But this is part of Northrop's very critique. For McAllister to criticize the criticizer of idealism as having "gone a long way towards idealism" is a symptom of that very myopia. Since Northrop devotes three large sections of MEW to the undifferentiated aesthetic continuum, (specifically pp. 335-43 pp. 352-7 pp. 366-71), one commits a grave injustice to his thought and risks gross misunderstanding of his position if one sees him as little more than a superficial realist whose subtext is idealistic, since it is the undifferentiated aesthetic continuum alone of all the concepts by intuition that represents the invariant factor constituting the realistic core of this side of Northrop's theory.

On the other hand, *all* concepts by postulation attempt to denote a realistic counterpart of the knowing situation, a positing of an invariant aspect, the same for all observers and thus independent of them. The fact that most concepts fail is irrelevant to the intention founding their employment. One could, albeit provocatively, define a realist as one who countenances the use of concepts by postulation.

In a word, Northrop is a realist in spades. More exactly, but as we shall see a little misleadingly, Northrop's epistemology is logical realism epistemically correlated with radical empiricism. (MNG 210) I say "a little misleadingly" because there is an obvious realistic core within the concepts by intuition themselves, viz., the undifferentiated aesthetic continuum, whereas the name "radical empiricism" surely makes a Westerner think of, say, Hume and James rather that Lao Tse or the Buddha.

Experience has convinced me that one has but to emphasize a part of Northrop's position to misunderstand the whole. When McAllister focuses on the similarity of Northrop to Berkeley and Hume, Northrop seems no different from any radical empiricist. As long as the flavor of that emphasis is fresh upon the palate, the logical realism will seem to be only a "tendency" or a "belief" or an insubstantial hope insufficient to safeguard "man's hold on a real, extra-mentally existing world" (McAllister 115, 134, 133) though assuredly not by intent, cuts off human knowledge from reality." (McAllister 135) Frankly, I do not think that the issue between McAllister and Northrop is one of realism vs. idealism (or skepticism), but rather one brand of realism against another. McAllister wants to defend a form of naive (or direct, to use Wilfrid Sellars' euphemism) realism against Northrop's logical (or scientific) realism. A look at six quotations from McAllister's article should make this clear.

(1)   On page 132 he points out that Northrop agrees with Locke, Berkeley and Hume that "man has no immediate knowledge of concrete things."

(2) On the same page, "l do not have direct, immediate contact with them (things)."

(3) Lower, same page, "But I do not . . . directly know the   object."

(4) Lower still, he asks, "Then how do I know book and man and table and moon or sun or anything else."

(5) Page 134. "We cannot know the thing directly."

(6) Page 134. "indirectly he may form concepts by postulation."

(l), (2), (5) and (6) are all true of Northrop's position and constitute an objection only if one assumes the truth of direct realism.   Northrop believes that Berkeley and Hume have shown the nonsense of that view.   His bow to them is in II of concepts by intuition.   Also, for Northrop as for Sellars,[117] there are no common sense things if these are meant to refer to invariant, independent entities.   This is the position of logical or scientific realism.   But it is *realism*, not idealism.   Nor is there any necessary connection between such a realism and the kind of idealism McAllister attacks.   It is only by regarding logical realism as an insufficient realism (see (4) above) that McAllister's overemphasis on Northrop's radical empiricism component of his epistemology comes to have any force at all. As to a Northropian answer to (4) above, one must first clearly appreciate the fact that most words are ambiguous between a concept by intuition meaning and a concept by postulation meaning.   Once this difference is specified a prototypical

---

[117] See p. 354 of Philosophical Perspectives where Sellars writes "there really are no such things as the physical object of the common sense framework."

answer might be given as follows.   If one means the aesthetic,
concept by intuition (not naive realistic) book (to take only the
first of the objects mentioned in (4) by McAllister then one
knows it, and *knows it directly* every time one feels, smells or
sees etc.   an aesthetic "object" of the kind misleadingly
designated in the common sense framework by the concept by
perception "book."

On the other hand, if one means by "book" the theoretical
book as given by current scientific and philosophical theory
then one knows it to be a collection of physical particles in a
physical field whose chemical details are elaborated in chemistry, whose sociological details are given by that science etc.
Finally, if one means the book in its aesthetic-theoretic completeness, one must synthesize the above two approaches.   In
other words, man knows the book in two ways, aesthetically
and theoretically or, in other words, by sense and by reason.

Now even if the above is wrongheaded or inadequate, it
is *not* Lockean sensationalism, or Berkelean Idealism, but
rather logical realism epistemically correlated with radical
empiricism.   Or more simply, an aesthetic-theoretic theory of
knowledge.

Actually, McAllister's complaint is not against the how
(direct or indirect) of Northrop's theory, but rather with the
object of direct knowledge.   McAllister wants a direct knowledge of common sense objects and tells us on the last page that
"no solution ought to be accepted which cuts men off from the
world of common sense, public objects." Now there is surely a
sense is which Northrop does exactly that.   Why?

To see why we must have recourse to a text not available
to
McAllister, viz., PAPP in which he summarizes his refutation of
naive realism, the position that McAllister in (5) is loath to
have man cut off from.   Although this might seem not only
anachronistic but patently unfair, the text I will quote at length

is in the nature of a "best" summary of Northrop's proof, the roots of which were certainly available to McAllister.   (Cf. LSH 91)

> any naive realistic epistemological concept of the public self or any public object is self-contradictory. The mark of such an epistemology is that it attempts to define the purportedly public substances in terms of directly sensed or introspected properties.   But all sensed or imagined items of knowledge are imageful and all images are relative, not merely to the observer's frame of reference and to the percipient, but even, as Democritus, Galileo, Newton and Berkeley pointed out, to different sense organs and moments of perception of the same percipient.   The naive realist means, however, by his public substances something that exists... independently of its relation to any observer, Clearly, therefore, it is self -contradictory to define an object existing independently of its relation to the observer in terms of sensed or introspected imageful properties all of which are relative to the perceiver. (PAPP 66)

Now we can see, within the limits of a single paragraph, why Northrop would cut man off from the world of "common sense."

The appeal of direct realism is the certainty it provides, or rather promises, vis-a-vis common sense objects.   That Northrop takes this promise seriously is revealed in a back hand sort of way when he regards the "the errors in our perceptual judgments" as conclusive refutations of direct realism. (LSH 91)   As was pointed out in section 1, Northrop finds a place for certainty in concepts by intuition.   To be dissatisfied with this type of certainty, as McAllister no doubt would be, is a piece of fallout from his holding a direct realist position.   The certainty of one's impressions seems too little compensation for the certainty lost by giving up naive realism concerning common sense objects.   But if the theory is self-contradictory, one has also lost an erroneous theory, and that is hardly a loss to be mourned. One should also remember that the undifferentiated aesthetic continuum is a concept by intuition and therefore certain[118] providing an aesthetic (in addition to the theoretic) realistic component to Northrop's epistemology.[119] It is with respect to this aesthetic realism that I would venture to correct Northrop's formulation of his theory as follows: logical realism epistemically correlated with a radical empiricism and an aesthetic realism.   A capturing of the truth of F. S. C. Northrop's complex position more than compensates for the longwinded title.[120]

In conclusion, it should be now clear that Northrop's epistemology is more than just a "tendency to realism," but rather a robust realism (in epistemic correlation with an empiricism, to be sure) -- robust enough to support a natural law approach in both ethics and jurisprudence.   In fact, this is one of the major themes of CLEE.   Such a realism, while not able to satisfy the demands of a direct realism for obvious reasons, is certainly sufficient to allay fears that Northrop's philosophy,

---

118 In Northrop's epistemology all concepts by intuition are known with certainty whereas all concepts by postulation are tentatively known. The recognition of this aspect of concepts by postulation in religion is captured in the necessity for belief. St. Paul explicitly tells us that "eye has not seen or ear heard nor has it entered into the heart of man what things God has prepared for those who love him. (1 Cor. 29) This does not prevent guessing, i.e., concepts by postulation.

119 Northrop hints at this fact in various places but I believe I am the first to explicitly identify it as a realistic part of the concepts by intuition.

120 I believe we all have more complicated epistemologies than we realize. Most direct realists would acknowledge the esse of a toothache pain is percipi, that they don't sense quarks but know them in some other way. Cf. Book VI of Aristotle's Nicomachean Ethics which reveals a similar complexity. According to Aristotle, we know first principles by νοῦς, deduction by ἐπιστήμη, both by σοφία, making things by τέχνη, practical things by φρόνησι" and proper sensibles by αἴσθσις.

and specifically his epistemology, leads to skepticism and eventually to moral and legal relativism.

BIBLIOGRAPHY

This bibliography represents the combined efforts of Dr. Joyotpaul Chaudhuri and Mr. Norman P. Riise with minor corrections and several additions by the writer.

BOOKS

Northrop, F. S. C. *Science and First Principles.* New York: The Macmillan Company, 1931. Reprinted in 1979, Ox Bow Press.

Northrop, F. S. C. *The Meeting of East and West: An Inquiry ConcerningWorld Understanding.* New York: The Macmillan Company, 1946. Reprinted in 1979, Ox Bow Press.

Northrop, F. S. C. *The Logic of the Sciences and the Humanities.* New York: Meridian Books, Inc., 1947. Reprinted in 1983, Ox Bow Press.

Northrop, F. S. C. (ed.) *Ideological Differences and World Order: Studies in the Philosophy and Science of the World's Cultures.* New Haven: Yale University Press, 1949.

Northrop, F. S. C. The *Taming of the Nations: A Study of the Cultural Basis of International Policy.* New York: The Macmillan Company, 1952. Reprinted in 1987, Ox Bow Press.

Northrop, F. S. C. and Gross, Mason W. (eds.) *Alfred North Whitehead: An Anthology.* New York: The Macmillan Company, 1953.

Northrop, F. S. C. *European Union and United States Foreign Policy: A Study in Sociological Jurisprudence.* New York: The Macmillan Company, 1954.

Northrop, F. S. C. *The Complexity of Legal and Ethical Experience: Studies in the Method of Normative Subiects.* Boston: Little, Brown and Company, 1959. Reprinted in 1959, Greenwood Press.

Northrop, F. S. C. *Philosophical Anthropology and Practical Politics.* New York: The Macmillan Company, 1960.

Northrop, F. S. C. *Man Nature and God: A Quest for Life's Meaning.* The Credo Series, Planned and edited by Ruth Nanda Anshen, paperback 1963. New York: A Trident Press Book, Simon and Schuster, December, 1962.

Northrop, F. S. C. and Livingston, Helen H. (ed.). *Cross-Cultural Understanding: Epistemology in Anthropology.* New York: Harper & Row, 1964.

Northrop, F. S. C. *The Prolegomena To a 1985 Philosophiae Naturalis Principia Mathematica.* OxBow Press, Woodbridge, Conn. 1985

ARTICLES, REPRINTS AND UNPUBLISHED MANUSCRIPTS BY NORTHROP

"The Problem of Organization in Biology" Ph.D. Dissertation, Harvard University Library.

"The Theory of Relativity and the Relation Between Science and Philosophy," *Monist,* XXXV, No. 1 (January, 1925), 1-26.

"An Internal Inconsistency in Aristotelian Logic," *Monist,* Vol. 38, No. 2 (April,1928), 193-210. (See also a Reply by Uchenko and a counter-reply by Northrop in *Monist,* Vol. 39, No. 1 (Jan. 1929) 153-159.

"Basic Assumptions of Science in Their Bearing on Religion," *Journal of Religious Education,* XXX, No. 8 (April, 1928), 293-296.

"Concerning the Philosophical Consequences of the Theory of Relativity," *Journal of Philosophy,* XXVII, No. 8 (April, 1930), 197-210.

"The Theory of Relativity and the First Principles of Science," *Journal of Philosophy,* XXV (August 2, 1928), 421-435.

"The Macroscopic Atomic Theory: A Physical Interpretation of the Theory of Relativity," *Journal of Philosophy,* XXV (August 16, 1928), 449-467.

"Einstein's Unitary Field Theory and Its Bearing on the Macroscopic Atomic Theory," *Monist,* 1930. 325-338.

"The Contribution of Philosophy to Area Studies," *Social Science Research Council.* Pamphlet No. 6 edited by Charles Wagley (November 28, 1930).

"The Relation Between Time and Eternity in The Light of Contemporary Physics", *Proceedings of the 7th International Congress of Philosophy* (Oxford 1930), 100-105.

"Two Contradictions in Current Physical Theory and Their Resolution," *Proceedings of the National Academy of Science.* Physics Section, (January, 1930). 55-68.

"The Philosophical Foundations of World Understanding," *The Aryan Path,* India (June, 1932).

"The Present Crisis in Western Culture," *The Aryan Path* (May, 1934).

"Newton and the Modern Age," *Saturday Review of Literature* (February 2, 1935).

"Pareto's General Sociology, *Virginia Quarterly Review,* Vol. 11, No. 4, (October, 1935). Reprinted as chapter XV of LSH.

"The Electro-dynamic Theory of Life," with H.S. Burr, *Review of Biology,* Vol. 10, No. 3, (September, 1935), 322-333.

"The Philosophical Significance of the Concept of Probability in Quantum Mechanics, *Journal of the Philosophy of Science,* (April, 1936).

"Experimental Findings Concerning the Electro-dynamic Theory of Life and an Analysis of Their Physical Meaning," with H.S. Burr, *Growth,* I, No. 2 (April, 1937),   78-88.

"Causality in Field Physics in Its Bearing Upon Biological Causation," *Journal of the Philosophy of Science,* V, No. 2 (April, 1938),   166-180. Reprinted as chapter XII of LSH.

"The History of Modern Physics in Its Bearing Upon Biology and Medicine," *Yale Journal of Biology and Medicine,* X, No. 3 (January, 1938),   209-232.

"The Significance of Epistemic Correlations in Scientific Method," *Journal of the Philosophy of Science,* V, No. 2 (April, 1939),   166-179.

"Discussion of the Problem of Body and Mind," Proceedings of the *Association for Research in Nervous and Mental Disease,* XIX (1939),   99-104. Reprinted as chapter 10 of LSH.

"Evidence for the Existence of an Electro-dynamic Field in Living Organism, with H.S. Burr, *Proceedings of the National Academy of Science,* Vol. 25, No. 6 (June 1939), 284-288.

"Natural Science and the Critical Philosophy of Kant" *The Heritage of Kant,* Whitney and Bowers eds. (Princeton University Press), 1939.

"The Method and Theories of Physical Science in Their Bearing Upon Biological Organization," *Growth Supplement* (June, 1940). Reprinted as chapter VIII of LSH.

"The Functions and Future of Poetry," *Furioso*, No. 4 (1941), 71-82. Reprinted as chapter IX of LSH.

"The Impossibility of a Theoretical Science of Economic Dynamics," *The Quarterly Journal of Economics,* LVI (November, 1941), 1-17. Reprinted as chapter XIII of LSH.

"The Criterion of the Good State," *Ethics,* LII, No. 3 (April, 1942), 309-322. Reprinted as chapter XVII of LSH.

"Literature and Science," *Saturday Review of Literature,* XXVII, NO. 32 (August 5, 1944), 33-36.

"The Complementary Emphasis of Eastern Intuitive and Western Scientific Philosophy", *Philosophy - East and West*, ed. C. Moore (Princeton, 1944, 2nd printing 1946) 168-235.

"El Sentido del Civilicion Occidental," Mexico, D. F., *Filosofia y Letras*, IX, No. 17 (1945), 181-200.

"Las Letras y Las Ciencias, *Asomante*, Puerto Rico (April, June, 1945), 7-15.

"Leibniz's Theory of Space," *Journal of the History of Ideas,* VII, No. 4 (October, 1946), 422-446.

Proceedings and Addresses of the American Philosophical Association, 1945-46. Report of delegate of APA to AAAS, Vol. XIX (1946), 428-433.

"The Physical Sciences and Their Bearing on Philosophy and Human Values," Princeton Bicentennial Conferences. *The Future of Nuclear Science* (1946).

"Education for Intercultural Understanding, *Journal of Higher Education,* XVIII, No. 4 (April, 1947), 171-181. Reprinted as chapter XXI in LSH.

"The Precarious Position of Western Civilization," *Realidad,* Buenos Aires, Argentina, I, No. 2 (March-April, 1947), 181-197.

Proceedings and Addresses of the American Philosophical Association, 1946-47. Report of delegate of APA to AAAS, XX (1947), 532-533.

"The Scientific Method for Determining the Correct Ends of Social Action," XXII, No. 3, *Social Science* (July, 1947), 218-227. Reprinted as chapter XXI in LSH.

"Alfred North Whitehead," *Science,* Vol. 107, No. 2776 (March 12, 1948), 262-263.

"Education for World Understanding," *Proceedings* of 27th Annual Meeting of the National Association of Principals of Schools for Girls (1948), 156-171.

"The Neurological and Behavioristic Psychological Basis of the Ordering of Society by Means of Ideas," *Science,* Vol. 107, No. 2782 (April 23, 1948), 411-417. Reprinted as chapter XIX of *Ideological Differences and World Order.*

"The Implications of Traditional Modern Physics for Modern Philosophy," *Revue Internationale de Philosophie,* VIII (April, 1949), 1-27.

"Jurisprudence in the Law School Curriculum," (See *Lectures and Papers,* December 28, 1948) *Journal of Legal Education,* Vol. I (Summer, 1949), 482-494.

"La Filosofe y el Arte Contemporaneo," published by *Institute Mexicano Norteamericano de Relacions Culturales,* Mexico (March, 1949).

"La Filosofie y Un Orden Juridico Mundial," published by *Embajada de los Estados Unidos de America,* Mexico (March, 1949), 1-21.

"The Philosophy of Culture and Its Bearing on the Philosophy of History," *Philosophy and Phenomenological Research,* IX, No. 3 (March, 1949), 568-574.

"Towards Valid Integrative Concepts," *Main Currents in Modern Thought,* No. 4 (Spring, 1949).

"Los Factores Genericos y Differenciales en la Cultura Panamericana," (Written for Pan-Am. Cong. of Philos., January, 1950) *Filosofia y Letras,* Vol. 38 (April-June, 1950), 393-402.

"Naturalistic and Cultural Foundations for a More Effective International Law," *Yale Law Journal,* Vol. #19, No. 8 (December, 1950), 1430-1450.

"Underhill Moore's Legal Science: Its Nature and Significance," *Yale Law Journal,* Vol. 59, No. 2 (January, 1950), 196-213.

"The Difficulty in Relating the Diverse Spiritual Values of the Orient and the Occident," *The Vedanta Kesari,* XXXVII, No. 6 (October, 1950), 212-217.

"Asian Mentality and United States Foreign Policy," *The Annals of the American Academe of Political and Social Science,* Vol. 276, July, 1951, 118-127.

"Philosophical Anthropology and World Law," *Transactions of the New York Academy of Sciences,* Ser. II, Vol. 14, No. 2 (December, 1951), 109-112.

"The Mind of Asia," *Life,* Vol. 31, No. 27 (December 31, 1951), 39-42.

"Concerning UNESCO's Basic Document on World Philosophy," *Philosophy East and West,* I, No. 4 (January, 1952), 59-67.

"Contemporary Jurisprudence and International Law," *Yale Law Journal,* Vol. 61, No. 5 (May, 1952), 623-654.

"How Can We Defend Free Culture?" (Given as a paper before American Committee for Cultural Freedom, March 29, 1952). *Modern Review,* LXXXXI, No. 5, Whole No. 545 (May, 1952), 357-360.

"The Role of the Philosopher and in Particular the Philosophy of Culture in Preserving Intellectual Freedom and Understanding in the Contemporary World." *El Peligro de la Liberatad intelectual,* 3rd Interamerican Philosophy Congress, UNESCO Round Table, Mexico 1952, 73-77.

"Obstacles to a World Legal Order and Their Removal," *Brooklyn Law Review,* XIX, I No. 1 (December, 1952), 1-10.
"What Should Be the Relation of Morals to Law? A Round Table, II, The Philosopher Speaks," *Journal of Public Law,* I, No. 2 (Fall, 1952), 261-262.

"Philosophy's Statement of the Problem of Creativity," *The Nature of Creative Thinking* (Monograph), Industrial Research Institute, New York, 1953, 16-22 inc.

"The Philosophy of Natural Science and Comparative Law," *Proceedings and Addresses of the American Philosophical Association,* 1952-1954, XXVI (September, 1953), 2-25

"American Education and African Culture," African Student Conference, published by *The All African Students Union of the Americas* (Washington, D.C., 1954), 67-75.

"A New Approach to Human Nature," *The Christian Resister,* Vol. 133, No. 1 (January, 1954), 13-17.
"International Conflict and Means of Resolution," *Naval War College Review,* VII, No. 4 (December, 1954), 1-19.

"Should U.S. Give Military Aid to Pakistan?" *Foreign Policy Bulletin,* XXXIII, No. 11 (February 15, 1954), 5-6.

"United States' Foreign Policy and Continental European Union," *Harvard Studies in International Affairs*, IV, No. 1 (February, 1954), 7-34.

"Comparative Religion in Today's World," *The Christian Century*, LXXII, No. 37 (September 14, 1955), 1050-1052.

"Ethical Relativism in the Light of Recent Legal Science," *Journal of Philosophy*, LII, No. 23 (November 10, 1955), 649-662.

"Great Britain's Relation to the Continent in the Light of European Union, translated by M. Bouvier, "Les Relations de Ia Grande-Bretagne avec le Continent Considerees a la Luminere de l'Union Europeenne," *Comprendre*, Revue de Ia Societe Europeenne de Culture, Vol. 13-14, June, 1955, 88-98.

"The Struggle for Order and Purpose: An Ideological Approach," *Civilizations*, V, No. 4 (1955), 523-539.

"Man's Relation to the Earth in its Bearing on his Aesthetic, Ethical and Legal Values," *The Hyphen*, II, No. 3 (March, 1958), 10-16 (Reprinted from *Man's Role in Changing the Face of the Earth.)*

"Mathematical Physics and Korzbyski's Semantics," *General Semantics Bulletin*, V, Nos. 16 and 17 (1955), 1-8.

"The Nineteenth Century Background of Contemporary Events," *Proceedings of the Centennial Convocation*, Polytechnic Inst. of Brooklyn (1956), 3-8.

"Philosophy in the Modern World," *Yale Alumni Magazine*, XIX, No. 9 (June, 1956), 19-20.

"Neutralism and United States Foreign Policy," *The Annals of the American Academy of Political and Social Science*, Vol. 312 (July, 1957), 42-68.

"Philosophical Problems in Contemporary Law," *Natural Law Forum,* Vol. 2, No. 1 (1957).

"The Mediational Approval Theory of Law in American Legal Realism, *Virginia law Review,* Vol. 44, No. 3 (April, 1958, 347-363.

"Comparative Philosophy and Science in the Light of Comparative Law," (Preliminary report on the 3rd East-West Philosophers' Conf., Honolulu, 1959) *Philosophy East and West,* IX, Nos. 1 and 2 (April, July, 1959), 67-69.

"Technological and Non-Technological Societies," Adapted from "Man's Relation to the Earth in Its Bearing on His Aesthetic, Ethical, and Legal Values, in *Man's Role in Changing the Fact of the Earth. Panorma,* Vol. 1, No. 2 (Summer, 1959), 11 -13.

"What Kind of an American Civilization Do We Want?" *The Annals of the American Academy of Political and Social Science,* Vol. 325 (September, 1959), 1-10.

"The Comparative Philosophy of Comparative Law," *Cornell Law Quarterly,* XLV, No. 4 (Summer, 1960), 617-658.

"Instruments and Ideals," Commencement Address: Rollins College, June, 1960.

"The Human Communicants in Communication Engineering," *The Journal of Communication,* XI, No. 4 (December, 1961), 202-204.

"Law, Language and Morals," *Yale Law Journal,* Vol. 71, No. 6 (May, 1962), 1017-1048.

Burr, H. S. and Northrop, F. S. C. "The Electro-Dynamic Theory of Life," *Main Currents in Modern Thought,* Vol. 19, No. 1 (September-October, 1962), p. 4.

Epistemology in Science. Symposium II: "Field Theory as an Integrator of Knowledge" Williamsburg, VA: Eastern State Hospital, College of William and Mary and Virginia Society of Clinical Hypnosis. Dodge Room, Phi Beta Kappa Memorial Hall, William and Mary, 21 November 1959.

"Epistemology and the Psychiatry of the Unconscious." 21 November 1959. Ibid.

"The Epistemology of Legal Judgements" *Northwestern University Law Review,* Vol. 58, No. 6 (1964), 732-749.

"The Undifferentiated Aesthetic Continuum" *Philosophy-East and West,* Vol. 14, (1964) 67-71.

"The Wedding of the World's Civilizations" *Main Currents in Modern Thought,* Vol. 21, No. 4 (1968), 100-104.

"Commentary on Theological Resources from the Physical Sciences", *Zygon,* Vol. 1, (1966), 22-27.

"Jefferson's Conception of the Role of Science in World History" *Cahiers of History,* Cahiers d'Histoise Mondiale, Vol. 9, No. 4 (1966), 891-911.

"The Present Context and Character of the World's Religions", *Graduate Journal,* Vol. 7, (1966), 47-64.

"Toward a General Theory of the Arts" *Journal of Value Inquiry,* Vol. 1, No. 2 (1967), 96-116.

"From the Kindergarten Onward" *Main Currents in Modern Thought,* Vol. 25, No. 5 (1969), 122-128.

"The Relationally Analytic and Impressionistically Concrete Components of Western Classical Music" *Journal of Research in Music Education* Vol. 19, No. 4 (1971), 399-407.

"The Deeper Meaning and Promise of Today's Events." *Progress. Happiness and Prosperity* Vol. 4, No. 8 (1973).

"The Source of Swami Akhilananda's Remarkable Influence", *Indian Philosophical Quarterly*, Vol. 2, No. 1 (1974), 71-75.

"The Wedding of the World's Civilizations", *Main Currents in Modern Thought-Retrospective Issue*, Vol. 32, Nos. 2-5 (1975), 158-162.

"Avoiding the Corruption of Today's Communication," *Communication*, Vol. 2, (1975), 63-67.

"Can Interpersonal Neurophysiological Relations be Rigorously Defined Mathematically and Assessed Experimentally Within a Systems Approach as a Human Factor in Psychology and Psychiatry and in Legal Science and its due processed Political Practices?" *If Life. then One Among at Least Four*, Vol. 1, No. 1 (1975), 4-8.

"Methods and Grounds of Religious Knowledge", *Zygon*, Vol. 12, No. 4 (1977), 273-288.

"The First Principles of Verified Theoretical Mathematical Physics" (1980) Unpublished paper.

"Contemporary Einsteinian Epistemology and Neoplatonic Christianity." The expansion of a paper read before the *International Society for Research in Neoplatonic Studies* (1979) Unpublished paper.

BOOKS: CONTRIBUTED TO BY NORTHROP

Philosophical Essays for Alfred North Whitehead (Longmans, Green and Company, 1936). 1-40. "The Mathematical Background and Content of Greek Philosophy."

The Nature of Religious Experience: Essays in Honor of Douglas Clyde Macintosh, (1937), pp 183-200. "The New Scientific and Metaphysical Basis for Epistemological Theory."

The Heritage of Kant. Whitney and Bowers (ed.). Princeton University Press, 1939. "Natural Science and the Critical Philosophy of Kant."

Louis Wirth (ed.), *Eleven Twenty Six: A Decade of Social Research.* (University of Chicago Press, 1940). "Generalization in Social Science." Reprinted as chapter xiv in LSH.

The Philosophy of Alfred North Whitehead. Library of Living Philosophers, Vol. 3 (Evanston: Northwestern University, 1941). "Whitehead's Philosophy of Science."

Bryson, Lyman, and others (ed.). *Approaches to World Peace* (New York: Harper and Bros., 1944). "Philosophy and World Peace."

Charles Moore (ed.). *Philosophy: East and West,* Princeton University Press, 1944. "Complementary Emphases of Eastern Intuitive and Western Scientific Philosophy."

Bryson, Lyman, and others (ed.). *Conflicts of Power in Modern Culture.* Seventh Symposium. "Towards a Religion with World Transferring Power." Harper & Bros. New York, 1947.

Anshen, Ruth Nanda (ed.). *Our Emergent Civilization.* Science of Culture Series, Vol. IV, Harper, 1947, 65-74. "Toward a Removal of the Ideological Causes of World Conflict."

Wigner, Eugene P. (ed.). *Physical Science and Human Values,* Princeton University Press, 1947, 159-162.

Remarks ("A Critique of P.W. Bridgeman's paper on Operational Definitions at the Nuclear session at the Princeton University Conference Proceedings.")

College Reading and Religion. Being Reports of a Survey of College Reading Materials, The Edw. W. Hazen Found & the Comm. on Religion and Education of the Amer. Council on Education. Yale University Press, 1948, 324-345. "Biological Sciences."

Galdston, Iago. *Social Medicine: Its Derivations and Objectives.* Commonwealth Press, 199-216, 1949. "The World Scene."

Windolph, F. Lyman (ed.). *Man's Destiny in Eternity.* Beacon Press, 1949. "The Idea of God as Affected by Modern Knowledge" (Carvin Lectures), 221-234.

Goethe--UNESCO'S Homage. Berichthaus, Zurich, Switzerland, 1949. "Goethe and the Creative Factors in Contemporary Culture," 83-98.

Autour de ia Nouvelle Declaration Universelle des Droits de i'Homme, Sagittaire, 1949, 150-153. "Vers une Declaration des Droits pour les Nations Unies."

Human Rights. Edited by UNESCO. London: Allan Wingate, 1949, 182-185. "Towards a Bill of Rights for the United Nations."

Maquet, Jacques J. and Nauwelaerts, E. (Editeur). *Sociologie de la Connaissance.* 2, Place Cardinal Mercier, Louvain, Belgium. "Preface," 9-17.

Sorokin, P.A. (ed.). *Explorations in Altruistic Love and Behavior.* Boston: Beacon Press, 1950, 194-202. "Scientific and Philosophical Foundations for Altruism."

Sorokin,P.A. (ed.). *Forms and Techniques of Altruistic Love and Behavior.* Boston: Beacon Press, 1954, "Philosophical Anthropology and World Law." 357-363.

Persons, Stow (ed.). *Evolutionary Thought in America.* Yale University Press, 1950, 44-85. "Evolution in Its Relation to the Philosophy of Nature and the Philosophy of Culture."

Inge, The Very Rev. W.R. et al. (eds.). *Radhakrishnan, Comparative Studies in Philosophy Presented in Honour of His Sixtieth Birthday.* London: George Allen and Unwin, Ltd., 1951, 362-378. "The Relation Between Eastern and Western Philosophy."

Schilpp, P.A. (ed.). *Albert Einstein: Philosopher-Scientist.* Library of Living Philosophers, 387-408. "Einstein's Conception of Science."

Maquet, Jacques J. *The Sociology of Knowledge. Its Structures and Its Relation to the Philosophy of Knowledge. A Critical Analysis of the Systems of Karl Mannheim and Pitirim A. Sorokin.* Boston: The Beacon Press, 1951, xi-xix. "Preface."

"The Problem of Integrating Knowledge and the Method for its Solution," *The Nature of Concepts, Their Inter-Relation and Role in Social Structure.* Proceedings of the Stillwater Conference (June, 1950), 25-42.

"Ethics and the Integration of Natural Knowledge," *The Nature of Concepts.* 116-139.

Voss, Carl Hermann (ed.). *The Universal God: The Eternal Quest in which all men are Brothers- An Interfaith Anthology of Man's Search for God.* Cleveland & New York: World Publishing Co., 1953. 131-133. "Remarks"

Structure, Method and Meaning: Essays in Honor of Henry M. Sheffer; Henle, Paul, et al. eds. New York: Liberal Arts Press, 1951, 99-114. "The Importance of Deductively Formulated Theory in Ethics and Social and Legal Science."

Freedom and Reason. Studies in Philosophy and Jewish Culture in Memory of Morris Raphael Cohen. Conference on Jewish Relations, Jewish Social Studies, Publications No. 4. New York, 1951, 269-273. "The Absolute and the Non-Absolute in Scientific Knowledge in Its Bearing on Toleration."

Moore, Charles A. (ed.). *Essays in East-West Philosophy.* An attempt at World Philosophical Synthesis. Honolulu: University of Hawaii Press, 1951, 151-160. "Methodology and Epistemology, Oriental and Occidental."

Moore, Charles A. (ed.). *Essays in East-West Philosophy,* 1951, 371-382. "The Theory of Types and the Verification of Ethical Theories."

Anshen, Ruth Nanda (ed.). *Moral Principles of Action. Man's Ethical Imperative.* New York: Harper & Brothers, 1952, 122-139. "Criterion of Universal Ethical and Legal Norms."

Kroeber, A.L. Chairman. *Anthropology Today, An Encyclopedic Inventory.* Chicago: University of Chicago Press, 1953, 668-681.

Seventy-Five. A Study of a Generation in Transition. New Haven: Yale Daily News, 1953, 127-128, 199. "The Student and Culture."

Powdermaker, Hortense (ed.). *Mass Communications Seminar.* New York: Werner-Gren Found. for Anthrop. Res., Inc., 1953, 39-50 inc., 50-54 inc. "Images of America Among Peoples Outside of the United States, as Presented Through Mass Communications."

1954 Yearbook of Education. London: Evans Brothers, Ltd., 1954, 79-89. "Moral and Ethical Implications of Technological Development, Part One: A Western View."

Colloquium on Islamic Culture in Its Relation to the Contemporary World. Princeton University Press, 1954, 108-110. "Summary of Addresses Given."

Radhakrishnan, S., Ewing, A. C. and Schilpp, P.A. etc. (eds.). *A. R. Wadia. Essays in Philosophy Presented in His Honour.* Madras: G. S. Press, 1954. "Linguistic Symbols and Legal Norms."

Bryson, Lyman, Finkelstein, Louis, Hoagland, Hudson, Maclver, R.M. (eds.). *Symbols and Society.* 14th Symposium of the Conf. on Science, Philosophy and Religion. New York: Harper & Bros., 1955, 55-64, 64-78 passim. "Linguistic Symbols and Legal Norms."

Actes du IVᵉ Congres Internationaldes Sciences Anthropologigues et Ethnologigues, Vienne 1952, Adolf Holzhausens, Vienna, Vol. II, 1955, 10-13. "The Unity and Dynamics of a Culture."

Thomas, William L., Jr. (ed.). *Man's Role in Changing the face of the Earth.* University of Chicago Press, 1956, 1052-1067. "Man's Relation to the Earth in Its Bearing on His Aesthetic, Ethical, and Legal Values."

Hook, Sidney (ed.). *American Philosophers at Work. the Philosophic Scene in the United States.* New York: Criterion Books, 1956, 440-455. "Ethical Relativism in the Light of Recent Legal Science."

Modern Education and Human Values. Pitcairn-Crabb Foundation Lecture Series, Vol. VI. University of Pittsburgh Press, 1957, 69-104. "The Union of the Sciences and the Humanities."

Principes d'Education. Toumliline I. Morocco, 1957, 149-160. "The Meeting of the Civilizations."

Hook, Sidney (ed.). *Determinism and Freedom in the Age of Modern Science.* New York: New York University Press, 1958, 188-199. "Causation, Determinism, and the 'Good'" Comments on First N.Y.U. Institute of Philosophy, February 9 and 10, 1957.

Heisenberg, Werner. *Physics and Philosophy, The Revolution in Modern Science.* New York: Harper & Bros., 1958, 1-26. "Introduction."

Walter, Erich A. (ed.). *Religion and the State University,* Ann Arbor: The University of Michigan Press, 1958, 269-281. "Students from Other Lands."

Galdston, Iago (ed.). *Medicine and Anthropology.* Lectures to the Laity, No. XXI. International Universities Press, Inc., New York, 1959, 78-107. "Cultural Mentalities and Medical Science."

Wyman, Mary A. *The Lure for Feelings in the Creative Process.* New York: Philosophical Library, 1960, p. vii. "Foreword."

The South-East Asian Round Table. A Symposium on Tradional Cultures and Technological Progress in South-East Asia, published by the South-East Asia Treaty Organization, SEATO Headquarter, Bangkok, Thailand, undated, 24-36: 38-41 passim. "The Nature of Modern Technology."

Sherburne, Donald W. *A Whiteheadian Aesthetic. Some Implications of Whitehead's Metaphysical Speculation.* New Haven: Yale University Press, 1961, xiii-xxix. "Foreword."

Lieb, Irwin C. (ed.). *Experience. Existence. and the Good.* Essays in Honor of Paul Weiss. Southern Illinois University Press, 1961,, 158-168. "Is the Word *Reality* Meaningful?"

Rosenau, James N. (ed.). *International Politics and Foreign Policy.* A Reader in Research and Theory. New York: The Free Press of Glencoe, Inc., 1961, 313-315. (Reprinted from *The Taming of the Nations.*) The Normative Inner Order of Societies.

The Challenge of the '60's. Palo Alto Unified School District, Palo Alto, Calif., 1961, 115-123. (Rec'd. April, 1962.) "The Challenge of the World Today."

Moore, Charles A. (ed.). *Philosophy and Culture-East and West.* East-West Philosophy in Practical Perspective. Honolulu: University of Hawaii Press (1962) 521-532. "Comparative Philosophy and Science in Light of Comparative Law."

Moore, Charles A. (ed.). *Philosophy and Culture-East and West.* pp 770-779. "Comparative Philosophy and World Law."

Baumrin, Bernard (ed.). *Philosophy of Science. The Delaware Seminar.* Vol. I, New York: Interscience Publishers, a division of John Wiley & Co., (1963) 3-19. "The Relation between the Natural and the Normative Sciences."

Galdston, Iago (ed.). *Man's Image in Medicine and Anthropology.* New York: International Universities Press (1963)   477-501. "The Neurophysiological Meaning of Culture."

Our Race with Catastrophe, Conference for Fullbright Scholars, June 24-27, 1962 Yale University Press (1964) pp 6-7. "The Scholar's Role in the Present Crisis."

Metraux, Guy S. and Crouzet, Francois (ed.). *Religions and the Promise of the Twentieth Century.* New York: Mentor Book New American Library (1965) "The World's Religions at Mid-Century: An Introductory Essay."

Rouner, Leroy S. (ed.). *Philosophy, Religion and the Coming World Civilization: Essays in Honor of William Ernest Hocking.* the Hague: Martinus-Nijhoff, (1966)   320-329. "The Interplay of Physics, Politics and Religion in Today's World."

Hollins, E.J. (ed.). *Peace is Possible: A Reader for Laymen.* New York: Grossman, (1966)   190-198. "The Wedding of the World's Civilizations."

Singh, Ram Jee (ed.). *World Perspectives in Philosophy. Religion and Culture: Essays presented to Professor Dhirendra Mohan Datta.* Patna, India: Bharati Bhaevan Publisher (1968)   255-278.   "The Philosophical Roots and Validity of Tagore's Genius."

Raju, P.T. and Castell, Alburey (eds.). *East-West Studies on the Problem of the Self.* The Hague: Martinus Nijhoff (1968) 1-12. "Towards a More Comprehensive Concept of the Person."

Smith, John E. (ed.). *Contemporary American Philosophy: Second Series.* London: George Allen and Unwin New York: Humanities Press (1970) Chapter 5. "The Relation Between Naturalistic Scientific Knowledge and Humanistic Intrinsic Values in Western Culture."

Lewis, Benjamin F. (ed.). *The Moral and Religious Predicament of Modern Man.* Brooklyn: Pageant-Poseidon Ltd. (1972) "The Present World-Wide Religious Reformation."

Morris, Richard Knowles and Fox, Michael W. (eds.). *On the Fifth Day: Animal Rights and Human Ethics,* Washington D.C.: Acropolis Books LTD (1978) Chapter 10. "Naturalistic Realism and Animate Compassion."

BOOK REVIEWS BY NORTHROP

Haldane, J. S. *The Sciences and Philosophy;* Whitehead, A. N. *Process and Reality.* "A New Philosophy," *Sat. Rev. of Literature* (January 4, 1930).

O'Hara, John. *Academy for Souls.* "A Super-Scientist from Mars," *Sat. Rev. of Literature* (May 30, 1931).

Dingle, Herbert. *Science and Human Experience,* "Contemporary Physics," *Sat. Rev. of Literature,* (June 4, 1932).

Planck, Max. *The Universe in the Light of Modern Physics. Journal of Philosophy* (May 26, 1932).

Joad, C.E.M. *Philosophical Aspects of Contemporary Science.* "Science and Scientists," *Sat. Rev. of Literature* (September 9, 1933).

Whitehead, A.N. *Adventures in Ideas.* "Adventurous Philosophy" *Sat. Rev. of Literature* (June 3, 1933).

Tomson, Sir J. Arthur and Infeld, Leopold. *The World in Modern Science.* "Science for the Layman," *Sat. Rev. of Literature* (September 8, 1934).

Eddington, Sir A. *New Pathways in Science,* "Frontiers of Modern Science," *Sat. Rev. of Literature* (May 18, 1935).

Schrödinger, Erwin. *Science and Human Temperament. American Mathematical Soc. Bull.,* XLII (1936).

Robin, Leon. *Greek Thought and the Origins of the Scientific Spirit* "Greek Thought." *Sat. Rev. of Literature* (March 8, 1930).

Jeans, Sir James. *The Mysterious Universe.* "Physics and Platonism" *Sat. Rev. of Literature* (December 27, 1930).

More, Louis Trenchard. *Issac Newton* "Newton and the Modern Age" *Sat. Rev. of Literature.* (February 2, 1935).

Rukeyser, Muriel. *Willard Gibbs: American Genius.* "A Poet Discovers the Mathematical Physicist," *Mathematical Soc. Bull.,* XLII (December 19, 1942).

Carr, E. H. *The Soviet Impact on the Western World.* "Review of E. H. Carr's The Soviet Impact on the Western World," *Yale Law Journal,* Vol. 57, No. 3 (January, 1948), 497-504.

Nussbaum, Arthur. *A Concise History of the Law of Nations. Columbia Law Review* Vol. 48, No. 4 (1948).

Human Law and the Laws of Nature in China and the West, January, 1952. Needham, Joseph. "Review of Human Law and the Laws of Nature in China and the West," *Philosophy East and West,* Vol. VII, No. 1 (April, 1952), 81-84.

Barrett, Edward F. (ed.). *Natural Law Institute Proceedings,* Vol. 5. "Review of Natural Law etc.," *Northwestern University L. R.,* Vol. 48, No. 3 (July-August), 396-400 inc., 1953.

Asia and Western Dominance. Panikkar, K. M., "Review of etc." *Far East,* Vol. XIV, No. 2 (February, 1955), 261-266.

Dialogues of Alfred North Whitehead: as recorded by Lucien Price. "Conversations with a Great Philosopher," *The New York Book Review* (May 9, 1954), p.3.

Strauss, Leo. *Natural Right and History;* Wild, John, *Plato's Modern Enemies and the Theory of Natural Law.* "Review of etc.," *Yale Law Journal,* Vol. 63, No. 8 (June, 1954), 1209-1213.

War, Communism and World Religion. Braden, Charles S. "Review of War, etc.," *Religion in Life,* Vol. XIII, No. 2 (Spring, 1954), 297-299.

Lawson, F. H. *A Common Lawyer Looks at the Civil Law,* "A Common Lawyer, etc.," *Michigan Law Review,* Vol. 54, No. 7 (May, 1956), 1029-1039.

Petrazycki, Leon. *Law and Morality.* "Petrazycki's Psychological Jurisprudence: Its Originality and Importance," *Univ. of Penn. Law Rev.,* Vol. 104, No. 5 (March, 1956), 651-662.

Hoebel, E. Adamson. *The Law of Primitive Man, A Study in Comparative Legal Dynamics.* Vol. 16, (1956) 455-464.

Indian Students on an American Campus. Lambert, Richard D., and Bressler, Marvin (Minn: Univ. of Minnesota Press, 1956). Lambert, Richard D. and Bressler, Marvin. "Review," *Journal of Higher Education,* Vol. 28, No. 4 (April, 1957), 231-232.

De Jouvenel, Bertrand. *Sovereignty: An Inquiry into the Political Good.* Trans. J. F. Huntington (Chicago: The University of Chicago Press, 1957), "The Paradox of Political and Legal Obligation," *Yale Law Journal,* Vol. 67, No. 7 (June, 1958), 1300-1316.

The Tao of Science. Siu, R.G.H. "Review," *Science,* Vol. 127, No. 3312 (June 20, 1958), 1438-1439.

Kelsen, Hans. *What is Justice?* Berkeley: University of California Press, 1957. Kelsen, Hans, "The Importance of Kelsen's Legal Positivism," *Virginia Law Review,* Vol. 44, No. 5 (June, 1958), 815-819.

"The Relation between the Natural and the Normative Sciences" Vol. 1, *Delaware Seminar in the Philosophy of Science,* Bernard Baumrin, ed., New York: Interscience Publishers, 3-19, 1961-1962.

"Toward A General Theory of the Arts" *The Journal of Value Inquiry,* Fall 1967 .

"The Relation Between Naturalistic Scientific Knowledge and Humanistic Intrinsic Values in Western Culture" *Contemporary American Philosophy: Second Series.* J. E. Smith, ed., London: Allen and Unwin, 1970.

"The Relationally Analytic and the Impressionistically Concrete Components of Western Music" *Journal of Research in Music Education,* vol. 19, #4 (1971)

INDEX

Abyssinia, 75
Adams, 97
aesthetics, 164
analysis argument, 22
Anaxagoras, 162
Anaximander, 162
Archytas, 162
Aristotle, 4, 7, 8, 9, 11, 20, 24, 29, 37, 61, 65, 86, 102, 106, 146, 152, 162
Augustine, 44, 60, 86
Austin, 127
Australia, 91
Austrian economics, 41, 43, 50, 59
Bach, 136
Bacon, 32, 96, 105
Bali, 79
Beethoven, 136
Bentham, 90, 127
Bergmann, 17
Berkeley, 39, 42, 57, 132, 153
Bhagavadgita, 77, 78, 106
Bigelow, 119, 121
blank tablet, 169
Brahman, 78
Brown v. Board, 103, 140
Buddhism, 77, 79
Buddhists, 153
Burma, 79
Canada, 91
capitalism, 82
Catholicism, 58, 94
Ceylon, 79
Charvakian materialism, 134
China, 79
Cogito, 169
Cohen, 32
Collins, 158

communism, 58, 79, 81, 82, 91, 97, 108
concept by intuition, 35, 42, 48, 49, 58, 65, 96, 118, 133, 134, 136, 159, 166
Concept by Perception, 40
concept by postulation, 35, 48, 58, 59, 65, 91, 97, 118, 134, 136, 144, 149, 159, 166, 171
concepts by imagination, 36, 40
Concepts by Intellection, 40, 82, 166
concepts by intuition, 37, 46, 57, 59, 79, 134, 155, 156
concepts by postulation, 36, 47, 48, 57, 80, 82, 118, 133, 135, 138, 146, 147, 155, 156
Confucianism, 79
consciousness, 21, 22
Constitution of the United States, 97
counterpoint, 134, 135
Dalton, 26
Dasein, 169
Declaration of Independence, 97, 105, 138
democracy, 83
Democritian, 9
Democritos, 162
Democritus, 13, 44, 70
Descartes, 32, 49, 68, 153
Dewey, 32
Dialectical and Historical Materialism, 87
different factor, 57
differentiated aesthetic continuum, 38, 40, 170
Differentiations, 41

drone, 134
efficient cause, 7
Ego, 169
Ehrlich, 74, 94, 117
Einstein, 3, 10, 13, 28, 29,
37, 42, 44, 47, 57, 102, 118,
134, 147, 158
emergent quality, 16
Emerson, 97
Empedocles, 4, 6
empiricism, 65
Engels, 108
epistemic correlate, 46
epistemic correlation, 45, 65,
67, 154, 166
epistemology, 26, 164
ethics, 164
Euclid, 33, 60, 70
Eudoxos, 162
Euler, 164
evolution, 11
fallacy of division, 16
Feuerbach, 82, 88, 90
Fichte, 85
Field Concepts by Inspection,
41
final cause, 61
first-order, 110
form, 7, 8, 29
Foundations of Leninism, 87
Franklin, 97
functional theory, 6, 10
Galilei, 26, 28, 63
Galileo, 17, 19, 63
Gandhi, 76, 77
Gibbs, 58, 86
God, 25, 80, 143, 146, 147,
149, 152, 153, 154, 156,
157, 158, 159
Greeks, 80

Hammurabi, 101
harmony, 134, 135
Hegel, 18, 81, 88, 90, 153
Heisenberg, 147
Hilbert, 33
Hinduism, 78, 79
Hindus, 78
Hippocrates, 4
Hiroshima, 75, 76
Hitler, 109, 128
Hobbes, 19, 63, 137
Hu Shih, 105
Hubble, 13
Hume, 28, 39, 52, 81, 88,
102
hypothetical deductive
scientific methodology, 6
Id, 169
Immortale Dei, 62
India, 76, 78, 79, 91, 92, 93,
95, 97
Indo-China, 79
Iraq, 94, 95
Islam, 79, 80, 91, 94, 97
Japan, 75, 79
Jefferson, 96, 97, 138
Jefferson principle, 91
Jeffersonian principle, 138
Jesus, 80, 82, 92
Jevons, 88, 127
John, 144
Johnson, 18
Judaism, 92
just war, 93
Kant, 19, 37, 44, 85, 106,
108, 164
Kluckhohn, 115, 119
Korea, 75, 78, 79, 93, 95
Korovin, 87
Kuhn, 32

Kuwait, 94
Lao-tze, 105
Lavoisier, 20
Laws of Manu, 78
League of Nations, 75
legal positivism, 100, 109
Leibniz, 153
Lenin, 81, 87, 90
Leonardo, 71
Limit, 146, 149, 151
living law, 74, 79, 83, 94, 95, 104, 109, 113, 116
Locke, 49, 64, 68, 81, 88, 90, 96, 105, 153
Logical Concepts by Intuition, 40
logical realism, 61, 147
logos, 92, 144, 147
logos , 135
Luther, 81
macroscopic atom, 4, 5, 11, 12, 13, 25, 29, 164
macroscopic atomic theory, 3
macroscopic theory, 11
Manchuria, 75
Marx, 41, 51, 81, 85, 87, 88, 90, 108, 137, 153
materialism, 82
mathematical theory, 6, 10
Matter, 7, 8, 29
Maxwell, 86
McCulloch, 116, 119, 120, 123
mechanical causation, 4
Mein Kampf, 128
melody, 134
Merleau-Ponty, 36
Metaphysics, 164
Mexico, 58
mind-body problem, 48

Mises, 90
Mohammed, 80
Moses, 80
Muslims, 78
Mussolini, 75
mysticism, 154
naive realism, 60, 61, 82, 131,156
naive realistic, 123, 139
natural law, 102, 104, 105, 106, 109, 110
naturalistic jurisprudence, 100
nature of appearance, 63
Navaho Indians, 119
Nehru, 76, 79, 93, 95
New Delhi, 78
New Testament, 80, 82
New Zealand, 91
Newton, 26, 28, 42, 52, 57, 58, 63, 64, 86, 96, 105, 117, 121, 147
Nirvana, 153
non-cognitivists, 100
non-Euclidean geometry, 60
Nó, 120
ntuitive ethical jurisprudence, 100
Old Testament, 91
omnipotence, 148
omniscience, 147, 148
Pakistan, 78
panpsychism, 15
Parmenides, 13, 14, 15, 162, 166
Pax Romana, 92
Pearl Harbor, 76
Philo, 144
philosophical anthropology, 119

philosophy of science, 164
physical theory, 4, 9
physics, 10
Pitts, 116, 119, 120, 123
Plato, 4, 9, 37, 44, 46, 63, 65, 86, 152, 162, 166
Plotinus, 46
politics, 164
Pope Leo XIII, 62
Positive law, 74, 94, 104, 109, 112, 117
Positivism, 41
pragmatic legal realism, 100
Principia Mathematica, 171
principle of being, 4, 6
principle of identity, 4, 6
principle of mechanical causation, 6
principles of becoming, 6
Protestantism, 58, 62
Pythagoras, 4, 9, 70
quantum mechanics, 147
Quran, 80
Radin, 115
rationalism, 65
Reichenbach, 44
remainder argument, 22
rhythm, 134
Ricardo, 82
Rizzuto, 158
Robbins, 50
Roman Catholicism, 60
Rosenblueth, 119, 121
Russian Communism, 80
Saddam Hussain, 94
same factor, 57
Santayana, 37
science, 11
scientific realism, 61
second-order facts, 110

serial order, 150
Sikhs, 78
Smith, 41, 51, 82
sociological jurisprudence, 100, 109, 110, 161
Sorokin, 117
Soviet Union, 84, 93
Spain, 92
St. Thomas, 60, 61, 62, 86, 102, 105, 108,146
Stalin, 84, 87, 109
Stoic, 106, 144
Stoics, 92, 162
Superego, 169
symbolic logic, 140
Tao, 58
Taoism, 79, 94
techne, 135
teleology, 6
Thailand, 79
Theaetetus, 70
theology, 11, 152
thermodynamics, 10, 102
Tibet, 79
undifferentiated aesthetic continuum, 39, 41, 78, 80, 112, 143, 146, 154, 157, 171
uniquely known argument, 23
United Nations, 75, 76, 79, 93-96
United States, 79, 93, 97
Vaiseshika dualism, 134
Van Gogh, 58
veto, 93, 94
Webb, 84
Webbs, 85
Whitehead, 15, 19, 37, 42, 45,162
Wiener, 119, 121

windowless monad, 169
Wittgenstein, 15, 155

PROBLEMS IN CONTEMPORARY PHILOSOPHY

1. Petra von Morstein, **On Understanding Works of Art: An Essay in Philosophical Aesthetics**

2. David Basinger and Randall Basinger, **Philosophy and Miracle: The Contemporary Debate**

3. Francisco Peccorini Letona, **Selfhood as Thinking Thought in the Work of Gabriel Marcel: A New Interpretation**

4. Corbin Fowler, **The Logic of U.S. Nuclear Weapons Policy: A Philosophical Analysis**

5. Marcus P. Ford (ed.), **A Process Theory of Medicine: Interdisciplinary Essays**

6. Lars Aagaard-Mogensen (ed.), **The Idea of the Museum: Philosophical, Artistic, and Political Questions**

7. Kerry S. Walters, **The Sane Society in Modern Utopianism**

8. Steven William Laycock, **Foundations for a Phenomenological Theology**

9. John R. Jacobson and Robert Lloyd Mitchell (eds.), **Existence of God: Essays from** *The Basic Issues Forum*

10. Richard J. Connell, **The Empirical Intelligence - The Human Empirical Mode: Philosophy As Originating in Experience**

11. Sander H. Lee (ed.), **Inquiries into Values: The Inaugural Session of the International Society for Value Inquiry**

12. Tobias Chapman, **In Defense of Mystical Ideas: Support for Mystical Beliefs from a Purely Theoretical Viewpoint**

13. Donald Stewart (ed.), **Entities and Individuation: Studies in Ontology and Language in Honour of Neil Wilson**

14. Peter Preuss, **Reincarnation: A Philosophical and Practical Analysis**

15. Tibor R. Machan, **The Moral Case for the Free Market Economy: A Philosophical Argument**

16. George Frederick Schueler, **The Idea of a Reason for Acting: A Philosophical Argument**

17a. William and Harriet Brundage Lovitt, **Modern Technology in the Heideggerian Perspective, Volume I**

17b. William and Harriet Brundage Lovitt, **Modern Technology in the Heideggerian Perspective, Volume II**

18. William Cooney (ed.), **Contributions of Gabriel Marcel to Philosophy: A Collection of Essays**

19. Mari Sorri and Jerry Gill, **A Post-Modern Epistemology: Language, Truth, and Body**

20. Adolf Portmann, **Essays in Philosophical Zoology By Adolf Portmann:** *The Living Form and The Seeing Eye*, Richard B. Carter (trans.)

21. George Englebretson, **Essays on the Philosophy of Fred Sommers: In**

Logical Terms

22. Kevin Doran, **What is a Person: The Concept and the Implications for Ethics**

23. Ronald Roblin (ed.), **The Aesthetics of the Critical Theorists: Studies on Benjamin, Adorno, Marcuse, and Habermas**

24. William Lane Craig and Mark S. McLeod (eds.), **The Logic of Rational Theism: Exploratory Essays**

25. Barrie A. Wilson, **Hermeneutical Studies: Dilthey, Sophocles, and Plato**

26. John D. Jones, **Poverty and the Human Condition: A Philosophical Inquiry**

27. Fred Seddon, **An Introduction to the Philosophical Works of F.S.C. Northrop**

28. Henry Benedict Tam, **A Philosophical Study of the Criteria for Responsibility Ascriptions: Responsibility and Personal Interaction.**

29. Loretta Dornisch, **Faith and Philosophy in the Writings of Paul Ricoeur.**

30. Charles Goossens, **Toward a Theory of Relativity of Truth in Morality and Religion.**

31. Gerald Rochelle (ed.), **Time and Duration: A Philosophical Study by S. V. Keeling**

32. A. P. Martinich and Michael J. White, **Certainty and Surface in Epistemology and Philosophical Method: Essays in Honor of Avrum Stroll**

33. Albert B. Randall, **The Mystery of Hope in the Philosophy of Gabriel Marcel, 1888-1973: Hope and *Homo Viator***